Inventing Los Alamos

INVENTING LOS ALAMOS

The Growth of an Atomic Community

JON HUNNER

UNIVERSITY OF OKLAHOMA PRESS : NORMAN

Also by Jon Hunner
(*coauthor*) *Las Cruces* (Chicago, 2003)
(*coauthor*) *Santa Fe: A Historical Walking Guide* (Chicago, 2004)

This book is published with the generous assistance of the McCasland Foundation, Duncan, Oklahoma.

Library of Congress Cataloging-in-Publication Data

Hunner, Jon.
    Inventing Los Alamos : the growth of an atomic community / Jon Hunner.
    p. cm.
    Includes bibliographical references and index.
    ISBN 0-8061-3634-0 (alk. paper)
    1. Los Alamos (N.M.)—History—20th century. 2. Los Alamos (N.M.)—
Social life and customs—20th century. 3. Los Alamos (N.M.)—Social con-
ditions—20th century. 4. Family—New Mexico—Los Alamos—History—
20th century. 5. Community life—New Mexico—Los Alamos—History—
20th century. 6. Nuclear weapons—Social aspects—New Mexico—Los
Alamos—History—20th century. 7. Nuclear weapons—Social aspects—
United States—History—20th century. 8. Cold War—Social aspects—New
Mexico—Los Alamos. 9. Cold War—Social aspects—United State. I. Title.
    F804.L6H86 2004
    978.9'58053—dc22

                                                              2004046086

The paper in this book meets the guidelines for permanence and durability of
the Committee on Production Guidelines for Book Longevity of the Council
on Library Resources, Inc. ∞

1 2 3 4 5 6 7 8 9 10

Contents

ILLUSTRATIONS

PHOTOGRAPHS

MAPS

ACKNOWLEDGMENTS

Many people have assisted me with *Inventing Los Alamos*. First, I would like to thank those I interviewed concerning their experiences growing up at Los Alamos. Their stories formed the foundation of *Inventing Los Alamos*. Carlos Vásquez with the Oral History Program and Rose Diaz with the General Library at the University of New Mexico helped me in listening to and recording their voices. The faculty and graduate students (especially Abbe Karmen and Tom Gentry) of the History Department at UNM also greatly assisted me as I explored the social history of Los Alamos and the cultural history of the Atomic Age. The dedicated historians at UNM and later my equally gifted colleagues in the History Department at New Mexico State University have guided the creation of *Inventing Los Alamos* in numerous ways. At UNM, Richard Etulain, Ferenc Szasz, Virginia Scharff, and David Holtby all helped with the early drafts of this book. Walter Ganz, Polly Rose, and Steve Pate critically read the final drafts. Jay Fultz, copyeditor for the University of Oklahoma Press, carefully went over the final draft and provided invaluable input. All of them helped correct my mistakes both simple and serious. The mistakes that remain are solely mine.

As I researched and wrote *Inventing Los Alamos*, many libraries and archives provided the grist for my historical mill. At the Los Alamos Historical Museum Archives, Hedy Dunn, Theresa Strottman, Rebecca Collingsworth, and Theresa Connaughton provided able assistance. Roger Meade at the Los Alamos National Laboratory Archives allowed access to his extensive holdings, as did Richard Ray and Virginia Salazar at the National Atomic Museum in Albuquerque.

Tom Ribe at the Los Alamos Environmental Reading Room aided me in tracking down some of the recent publications from the laboratory concerning environmental issues. Nancy Brown at the Center for Southwest Research at the UNM General Library in Albuquerque hauled numerous boxes out of their Special Collections. At the New Mexico Archives and Records Center in Santa Fe, Paul Saavedra assisted in combing through the state's records, and Ingrid Vollnhofer, the Southwest Librarian at the New Mexico State Library in Santa Fe, also provided cheerful service whenever I arrived, often unannounced. Claudia Thompson of the American Heritage Center at the University of Wyoming also assisted me with finding the atomic holdings in their collection.

The presidential libraries of Dwight D. Eisenhower and Harry S. Truman hold essential material on the first years of the atomic age. Jim Leyerzapf at the Eisenhower Library in Abilene, Kansas, and Randy Sowell at the Truman Library in Independence, Missouri, suggested where to look and quickly processed my requests for items in their holdings. The staff at National Archives II in College Park, especially in the text reference room and with the photographic collection, were always friendly and professional. The archivists at the Manuscript Division of the Library of Congress, Washington, D.C., also greatly aided my research. *Inventing Los Alamos* was vastly improved by this essential research at the National Archives and the Library of Congress, made possible by a faculty research grant from the College of Arts and Sciences at New Mexico State University. Finally, toward the end of the preparations of the manuscript, I received a Senior Fulbright Fellowship in Sweden. While there, I had the luxury to think about Los Alamos in new ways. At the University of Oklahoma Press, Charles Rankin took on this manuscript. For that, I am forever grateful. Also at the Press, Marian Stewart, Candice Holcombe, and DiAnne Huff helped with the concluding stages of production and marketing. Thanks, too, to Bill Nelson for the fine maps.

Finally, this history of the community at Los Alamos would not have happened without the support of my own family. My mother, Anna Jane Fair, and my father, Paul Hunner, veterans of both World

ACKNOWLEDGMENTS

War II and the Cold War, introduced me to the Atomic West as a young boy. Since my father administered nuclear weapons for the Air Force, we lived on bases dedicated to the new duties of managing these weapons. Mary Ellen, my wife, encouraged me by listening to my half-formed ideas and, after reading various drafts, offered valuable comments and suggestions. And my son, Harley, who patiently waited for me to finish a thought or a paragraph before we could play catch or more recently, go for a driving lesson, continues to remind me of the responsibilities of the present generation to the future.

Inventing Los Alamos

INTRODUCTION

Although Los Alamos's military contribution to the defeat of Japan and then to the arms race that followed has been acknowledged many times, the complete story of Los Alamos must include (and often does not) its hesitant evolution after the war into a permanent outpost on the frontlines of the Cold War. From its location in north-central New Mexico, Los Alamos even today holds the distinction as the nation's premier center for nuclear energy and weapons research and development. Since 1943, when the United States Army constructed an instant city at Los Alamos to house the top-secret Manhattan Project, scientists, technicians, and their support staffs have conducted experiments at the site to release the binding energy of the atom. As a consequence of the Manhattan Project, the men and women at Los Alamos created the first nuclear bombs and, after the war, developed ever more powerful weapons. *Inventing Los Alamos* narrates the incredible growth of the town, first as a wartime army post and then as a permanent fixture in the nation's nuclear firmament. To do so, *Inventing Los Alamos* not only focuses on the scientific and technical accomplishments of the laboratory but also on the establishment of a town that confronted many of the social and cultural issues of the Atomic Age before the rest of the country. Out of the chaos of the wartime post, Los Alamos invented itself as a modern model community, an atomic utopia for postwar America.

The story of Los Alamos, of the men and women who worked there and of the families who lived there, has attained a mythical status in the United States. Thrown together on a remote plateau in the West, the scientists ventured beyond the known frontiers of science in creating

3

a totally new weapon that ended the war. Of course, this story has been told many times, but the retellings usually focus on the scientific achievements of the project and are mainly confined to World War II. Other aspects of the story, such as the social history of the community and the growth of the town in the decade after World War II, deserve closer scrutiny.[1] To be sure, the laboratory at Los Alamos did concoct a new weapon and usher in a new age, but it also invented a new community. The town housed people from all walks of life as well as highly trained scientific and technical personnel. Los Alamos grew in population from two hundred to more than twelve thousand between 1943 and 1957. The people of Los Alamos built a laboratory that developed a wide variety of nuclear weapons. They also created a thriving community in which they lived and raised their families and, thus, developed a culture for the Atomic Age.

During the early Cold War, the American public rarely penetrated the veil of secrecy that, like the barbed wire fences, guarded Los Alamos. Most Americans felt confident that the anonymous workers in the laboratory were patriotic Cold Warriors protecting America's national security. Some worried about shadow figures that diabolically held the world's fate in their hands. Behind the security fences, scientists and technicians did create awesome weapons capable of Cliocide (the death of Clio, the muse of history). At the same time, however, the community developed into a model town, with excellent schools, civic-minded citizens, and a pace-setting consumer culture. Just as the winning of World War II cannot be told without including the home front, the history of Los Alamos both during and after the war cannot be recounted solely by reciting the scientific successes of its laboratory. Cold War realities concerning secrecy, civil defense, and the manufacturing of radioactive elements affected not just the scientists at Los Alamos but impacted the evolution of the town and the families at the site. These issues, driven by wartime and then Cold War urgencies, made paradoxical claims on the people of Los Alamos and laid a foundation for the rest of the nation's accomodation to the atomic age. *Inventing Los Alamos* looks at the men and women who chose to live there, at the children who grew up there, at the families that called Los Alamos home, and at the culture they created. At the same time, it considers what the scientists, technicians, and military personnel *did* there to change history.

It is easy to portray the founders of the Atomic Age as heroes or villains, either as saving Western civilization or as threatening the very existence of the human race. But taking sides on this emotional topic misses the complex nature of the issues and of the community at Los Alamos. Despite the impressive scientific work at Los Alamos (including discoveries that won Nobel Prizes), the majority of the people there (including those Nobel Prize winners) shopped for groceries, cooked meals, argued with their spouses and children, and carried on as normally as possible in that unique community.

Three interesting paradoxes surface when looking at the community of Los Alamos. First, it was an exclusive place that developed weapons capable of colossal destruction at the same time that it evolved into a model community with all the amenities of postwar America. Second, with the residential part of the town sealed off by fences and guards, residents considered it a safe place while at the same time the lab produced and dumped in nearby canyons some of the most toxic elements known to man. Third, with the breadwinner's job hidden by secrecy, spouses and children often knew little about what was done at work. The surprise here is that families did not submit to the enforced silence, but rather found other ways to express themselves, from poking fun at army rules to challenging governmental policy. *Inventing Los Alamos* explores these and other aspects of the social history of Los Alamos.

Several interlocking groups of people impacted the community at Los Alamos. The town existed almost entirely for the core community of scientists and technicians working in the top-secret laboratory who experimented at first on nuclear weapons and then increasingly on high-speed computers, lasers, nuclear medicine, and other spin-offs of high-energy physics. Because of national security, secrecy veiled their work. The secrecy meant that the men and women working on sensitive projects often confided in their co-workers more than their own spouses. A community of families surrounded this core scientific community at the laboratory. The residential area of Los Alamos, like an oyster surrounding a pearl, supplied support for the staff at the laboratory to engage in their research. The residential community included stores, theaters, churches, and schools—many of the services required for a town of families. Between the outer fence surrounding the entire community at Los Alamos and the inner fence guarding just the laboratory, the residential area was the first place in the United States that families encountered the challenges of the Atomic Age and invented identities to respond to that challenge.

Beyond the fences at Los Alamos, two other forces contributed to the town's growth. First, the towns, villages, and pueblos of northern New Mexico supported Los Alamos with workers who built and maintained the town's facilities, drove the trucks and buses, assisted with experiments, and operated the power plants. For many native New Mexicans, employment at Los Alamos provided a cash income in one of the poorest regions of the nation. Conversely, northern New Mexico impacted Los Alamos since Los Alamosans soaked up the ancient history and appropriated the diverse cultures of the region. This cultural switching is a time-honored tradition in northern New Mexico. After contact with the Spanish settlers in the sixteenth century, American Indians taught the Europeans how to live in the challenging environment. Upon the opening of the Santa Fe Trail in 1821, Hispanics and American Indians similarly tutored the newly arrived Anglo Americans. And in the 1940s and 1950s, many of these native New Mexicans instructed the residents at Los Alamos in the mysteries and delights of living in northern New Mexico. A borrowing or switching of cultures often occurs on the frontier between societies. At the birthplace of the bomb, on the frontier of a new age, such cultural switching assisted residents in negotiating the dangerous shoals of nuclear energy.

Another force that affected Los Alamos was neither local nor regional. Since Los Alamos was a federal reserve, controlled and funded by the federal government, events and policies emanating from the nation's capital often affected it more than the laws passed by the New Mexico state legislature in nearby Santa Fe. Although Los Alamos lay in northern New Mexico, it was more connected to Washington, D.C. These four spheres—the scientific, the residential, the regional, and the federal—all influenced the growth of Los Alamos. Needless to say, with such a conglomerate revolving around the activities on the Hill (a nickname for Los Alamos), the development of the site was a complicated and fragmented liaison of sometimes conflicting interests.

In addition to the people residing there, process and place also mold a community. Examining a physical location without exploring its history, or studying its history without surveying its place, misses the impact that each has on the growth of the community. No history of a community can escape the dual influences of place and process. Thus, Los Alamos is both place and process, both a high desert platcau in the West and the sum of events that occurring there that harnessed the power of the atom for military purposes. The people of Los Alamos lived in the West, on the frontiers of nuclear science and of a new age.

From the beginning, secrecy surrounded Los Alamos. Secrecy accomplished two important purposes in the field of atoms: first, it prevented some of the nation's enemies (but not the Soviet Union) from acquiring the secrets for building an atomic weapon. Second, secrecy provided a shield protecting nuclear enterprises from the scrutiny of the American public. Thus, although the secrecy generated by the Manhattan Project and later the Atomic Energy Commission safeguarded the nation's nuclear discoveries, it also prevented the country's nuclear matters from receiving an open hearing and, perhaps more importantly in a democracy built on a system of checks and balances, it circumvented congressional and public oversight.

Communities like Los Alamos also resonate with the myths and dreams of their times. When the Pilgrims landed in New England in 1620, they sought to create a utopia, a City on the Hill, as a shining example to guide humans in their earthly travails. Since then, utopian dreams have fueled many new communities in the country, including those established in the westward expansion. Many people at Los Alamos adopted the images and myths of the Old West. Thus, the Atomic City was additionally steeped in these cultures and traditions.

A promise of utopia has infused many western communities, witness the Mormons who built their Mecca at Salt Lake City and the African-American exodusters who constructed new communities at Nicodemus, Kansas, and Blackdom, New Mexico. The possibility of creating a community from scratch, based on rationality and modern scientific principles, excited many immigrants to Los Alamos. Due to the consuming urgency of the bomb project and wartime shortages, the initial attempt to create a utopian community at Los Alamos failed, but the town received a second chance. During the postwar era, it self-consciously reinvented itself as a model community of the future, an Atomic City on the Hill for all to see.

As the foundation of any community, families adapt and adjust to the dynamic demands of life. *Inventing Los Alamos* attempts to investigate families within the context of their place in the atomic community at Los Alamos and in the nuclear firmament of Cold War America. In the early 1940s, families provided stability and hope for the war-torn world. In the late 1940s and 1950s, the family circle offered refuge for a shell-shocked and fearful world. To learn how families adjusted at Los Alamos, *Inventing Los Alamos* explores how the community grew and created its own identity as well. As family historian Frederick le Play observed, families are not found within a set of walls but in attitudes of the mind, in culture, and in ideas.[2]

Because families are so integral to culture, because one's identity depends upon one's own family, and because there is no precise model of the ideal family, recent studies challenge the historian to look for new ways to investigate and narrate this basic component of society.[3] In addition to the traditional historical sources of community histories, *Inventing Los Alamos* also utilizes oral histories of people who were youngsters or adults on the Hill, memoirs of residents (written mainly by Los Alamos women), as well as articles in regional newspapers and national magazines.

Using these sources to study families at Los Alamos, *Inventing Los Alamos* investigates the attitudes and cultures of those who lived in the shadow of the bomb. The events and conditions at Los Alamos, during and after the war, greatly influenced the living strategies of families there. These strategies entailed adapting to the secrecy, living on a guarded federal reservation, worrying about the consequences of the bomb, and, after the war, basking in the attention and media focus of a jubilant nation. Families cannot be studied apart from their community any more than communities can be examined apart from their region and country. Los Alamos, isolated by distance and fences from the rest of the world, nonetheless held an exalted position in the nation's postwar consciousness. In the 1950s, the town of Los Alamos symbolized a community blessed by the benefits of nuclear energy but shadowed by the powerful weapons of atomic destruction perfected in its lab. *Inventing Los Alamos* examines the interplay between family and secrecy, local community and federal laboratory, and atomic hope and nuclear fear.

The people of Los Alamos also influenced the country's response to the Atomic Age. The crack and roar of the first atomic explosion heralded the beginning of a new age, one that could end with a nuclear Armageddon. The impact of atomic weapons on the military, on foreign relations, even on the economy is more obvious than the way the country adapted culturally to this new age. *Inventing Los Alamos* will probe the development of an atomic culture and the role Los Alamos played in its creation.

In order to address these issues of family life, community identity, and cultural creation at Los Alamos, *Inventing Los Alamos* explores the growth of the town from 1943 to 1957. The first chapter, "Rendezvous at Site Y," describes the transformation of Los Alamos from a quiet plateau where Hispanic farmers homesteaded and Anglo boys attended an elite boarding school into a bustling army post vital to the war effort. It also covers the first frenzied year of the town as families settled in for the duration of the war. Grocery stores appeared, schools were built, and residential areas took form to accommodate the crush of personnel.

Chapter Two, "Fishing in the Desert with Fat Man," follows the townspeople's activities as work at the laboratory reached a feverish pitch. Social gatherings like square-dances, parties, clubs, church meetings, and sporting events helped the residents deal with the tension of their top-secret wartime work. The overcrowding of the town and the conflicts between the civilians and the army threatened to derail the progress at the laboratory. With the atomic explosions over Japan in August 1945, Los Alamos burst onto the world's stage, and some Hill residents discovered the true purpose of their town at the same time that the rest of the country read about it in the newspapers. Despite their pride in ending the war, and the jubiliation, many residents of Los Alamos held mixed emotions about their creation.

Chapter Three, "Postwar Los Alamos," investigates the first year of postwar development in the town. It begins with a survey of the atomic destruction of Japan as seen through the eyes of the Los Alamos personnel who studied Hiroshima and Nagasaki in September 1945. The chapter then returns to Los Alamos as wartime activity ceased in the fall of that year and the fate of the town lay in the hands of federal policymakers. From the autumn of 1945 to the summer of 1946, debate raged nationally over who would control atomic energy and, thus, Los Alamos. Atomic scientists, some from Los Alamos, played key roles in deciding the future of the bombastic new kid on the block. Chapter Three also explores Los Alamos's participation in Operation Crossroads, the testing of two nuclear weapons in the South Pacific in the summer of 1946.

Chapter Four, "Los Alamos Transformed," examines the transfer of Los Alamos from the U.S. Army to the Atomic Energy Commission (AEC) in 1947 and the town's rebirth as it consolidated its status at the apex of the nation's nuclear weapons research program. Along with the administrative change from the army to the AEC, Los Alamos also transformed itself from an jerry-built army post into a modern community. Building houses and a modern shopping center and improving the schools, all paid for by massive appropriations from the federal government, made Los Alamos a model postwar community, an atomic utopia on a hill.

Chapter Five, "A Cold War Community Up in Arms," focuses on the push to create a hydrogen bomb in the early fifties, which caused a new influx of workers and their families to come to the Hill. It looks at the strife within the laboratory as some of the same men and women who created the atomic bombs at Los Alamos protested against the hydrogen bomb. This chapter also explores the country's response to the Soviet Union detonating its own atomic weapon in 1949. As federal policymakers sought for ways to make the bomb acceptable to Americans, they used the town of Los Alamos to experiment with community civil defense strategies. Chapter Five ends with the security revocation of Robert Oppenheimer in 1954, and the effect it had on the residents at Los Alamos.

Chapter Six, "Toward Normalizing Los Alamos," continues to examine the evolution of Los Alamos into a modern suburban community and ends with the removal of the fences around the residential parts of the town. In 1957, Los Alamos opened up its gates and allowed the public to enter without security passes. Thus ended the initial period when this gated community ushered in a new era.

Chapter Seven, "Atomic City on a Hill," reviews the development of the town and its impact on the rest of the country as well as some of the lab's recent research and development projects. This last chapter also listens to those people who grew up on the Hill and to what they say is the legacy of Los Alamos.

Clearly then, Los Alamos is a complex community. Born to fight totalitarianism and protect democracy, it created weapons that defeated the Japanese but also transformed the world we live in. Atomic energy, nuclear medicine, computers, and lasers all received early attention at the laboratory. Through its work, the lab changed the nature of scientific research in the United States as nuclear physicists received more financial and legislative aid from the federal authorities than any research group prior to that time. The town revolutionized the power of the federal government, and the community's secrecy shielded a large bureaucracy from public view and from congressional oversight. In conducting its atomic experiments, Los Alamos also altered the environment by dispersing invisible toxins into its neighborhood. And finally, the community of Los Alamos, invented during the war, reinvented itself as a model town. It emerged as a vision of America hewn from the Atomic Age and a place for families to adapt to the challenges of the Cold War.

CHAPTER 1

RENDEZVOUS AT SITE Y

THE INSTANT CITY

*"God alone knows there was never another place
like this on the face of the earth."*
CHAPLAIN MATTHEW IMRIE,
QUOTED BY ELEANOR JETTE,
INSIDE BOX 1663

General Leslie R. Groves arrived late at Jemez Springs, New Mexico, on November 16, 1942—but one waits for a general, especially in wartime. J. Robert Oppenheimer, Colonel John H. Dudley, and Colonel Edwin McMillan had reached the town earlier to survey the site for a top-secret weapons' laboratory. The selection criteria required the location to be isolated, but with access to a railhead; to be set in a natural bowl for easy security monitoring; and to contain preexisting buildings for quick occupancy, with the capacity to accommodate more structures. Although Jemez Springs was isolated, the steep volcanic cliffs rising from the narrow river valley proved too rugged even for horseback patrols and the closest railhead lay thirty miles away. As Oppenheimer, Dudley, and McMillan argued about the suitability of the place, Groves arrived and muttered: "This will never do." Oppenheimer, who thought the location too gloomy, had spent summers in northern New Mexico and knew the region well. He suggested an alternative site, an exclusive boys' school on the other side of the mountain range.[1]

To get there that afternoon, the convoy of military men and the physicist traversed forty miles of mountainous dirt roads through one of the most isolated areas in the nation. Setting out, the cars skirted the southern slopes of what was once a monumental volcano. This volcano erupted one million years ago, throwing debris as far as Kansas and burying the nearby land under hundreds of feet of hot ash that fused to form the light-colored layer of rock called Bandelier Tuff. After the explosion, the volcano collapsed on itself, forming the Valle Grande, a vast caldera surrounded by eleven-thousand-foot peaks.[2]

Ascending to the Valle Grande, the small convoy bumped over rolling hills, through aspen groves and ponderosa pine stands. A 1940 Works Progress Administration guidebook cautioned against traveling this track, State Road 4, in bad weather. Even in 1942, this route accommodated horsedrawn wagons and sheep herds more often than U.S. Army staff cars. Twenty-three miles from Jemez Springs, the cars labored up a steep grade and burst onto the Valle Grande. Twelve miles across and enclosing 176 square miles, the basin is the largest measured crater on earth.[3]

The convoy traversed the southern slopes of the Valle Grande and then, once out of the crater, it descended the steep eastern slope of the Jemez Mountains to the Pajarito (Little Bird) Plateau. At 7,500 feet above sea level, the plateau is like a hand with its wrist anchored to the Jemez Mountains in the west and its fingers reaching east toward the Rio Grande. Intermittent streams had scored steep canyons between the fingers and made travel problematic between the high desert plateau tops. Less than twenty inches of annual precipitation nourish the mixture of ponderosa pine, scrub oak, piñon pine, and shaggy-barked juniper. Oppenheimer hoped the region's rugged beauty, its majestic pines and expansive vistas, would help attract the necessary scientists to this isolated outpost for the war's duration.

Over the centuries, American Indian, Hispanic, and Anglo settlers and entrepreneurs have farmed, ranched, and cut timber on the Pajarito

Plateau. In 1746, the Spanish crown bequeathed a land grant to a family of Hispanic settlers that gave them ownership of this section of the eastern slope of the Jemez Mountains. In 1851, Antonio Sanchez, an heir to the original grantee, sold it to Ramon Vigil for a yoke of oxen, thirty-six ewes, one ram, and twenty dollars. From 1851 on, the Vigil Grant changed hands as other Hispanic families and then Anglo ranchers and lumbermen tried to live on and make a profit from the plateau.

The names used to identify the places on the Pajarito Plateau reflect its long and complex history of human habitation. Multilingual place names layer the region like the geological stratum of the volcanic landscape. American Indians called the nearest pueblo to Los Alamos "Po-Woh-Ge-Oweenge," which in the Tewa language means "Where the Water Cuts Down Through." Near this pueblo, the Rio Grande tumbles into a narrow valley where dark volcanic cliffs tower hundreds of feet overhead. After contact with Europeans in the late sixteenth century, the American Indian names were replaced by Spanish appellations and Po-Woh-Ge-Oweenge became "San Ildefonso." Once English-speaking settlers came in, many Spanish and American Indian names were replaced by English ones. Thus, names for mountains, pueblos, and groups of people differed, depending on who was talking. This switching of place names is common on the border where people meet and exchange cultures.[4]

To better describe this cultural exchange, we need to turn to linguistics. A person who changes within a sentence from speaking his or her dominant language to another language "code-switches." People code-switch for several reasons: to show off sophistication, to express something their native language cannot precisely communicate. In border regions where people live at the juncture of several cultures, linguistic code-switching is common.

At Los Alamos, on the border between American Indian, Nuevo Mexicano, and European cultures, and on the border between the scientifically known and the unknown, cultural code-switching occurred. It is part of the yeasty concoction of the border, where people who are entering an unknown region borrow from other peoples to help them make the journey and survive in a strange land.

Into this polyglot landscape, General Groves's army convoy in 1942 brought two new ways of communication. First, it brought the language of nuclear physics, one that few in the world outside of this elite field understood. Second, this new wave of immigrants brought a silencing of language, since General Groves and the army would impose a veil of military secrecy over the whole community. The names of things would switch once again as top-secret code names replaced the previously applied appellations to common and uncommon places, objects, and people. The American Indian languages of the pueblos and the European languages of Spanish and English now contended with the terminology of abstract mathematics and higher physics on the Pajarito Plateau, all under an umbrella of secrecy, codes, and mandated silence.[5]

In addition to contributing to the custom of bringing new languages into the landscape of New Mexico, the army also carried on a long-standing tradition in the West. Even as a brand-new territory of the United States in the 1850s, New Mexico enjoyed generous federal subsidies. The cost of stationing the army in New Mexico in the early 1850s was astronomical, totaling more than three million dollars a year. At a time when the cost of a day's ration for a soldier on the Atlantic seaboard was twelve and a half cents and, in Texas, nineteen cents, it cost forty-two cents a day to feed a soldier in New Mexico. Since New Mexico's admittance as a territory in 1850, federal spending had helped the region's economy. Groves and Oppenheimer were merely the point men for a new wave of military and industrial influence and expenditure in the region.[6]

Oppenheimer's destination that afternoon was the Los Alamos Ranch School. Naming the site "Los Alamos" after the Spanish name for the cottonwoods at the site, entrepreneur Ashley Pond founded an exclusive sportsmen's ranch there in 1914. After failing at operating the sports club, Pond dreamed up another use for his portion of the plateau—a boys' preparatory school. Ashley Pond, inspired by Teddy Roosevelt's experience of recapturing his health by roughing it in the West, had established the school to help harden the boys. They wore shorts year around and slept in an unheated, screened porch, even during the winter.[7]

Scions from the industrial families of the East and Midwest enrolled, and graduates of the Los Alamos Ranch School later became the presidents of American Motors, Quaker Oats, and Sears and Roebuck. Other students included Antonio Taylor (President Lyndon Johnson's brother-in-law), Bill Veeck (future owner of baseball's Chicago White Sox and Oakland Athletics), authors Gore Vidal and William S. Burroughs (who complained he was always cold there), and Whitney Ashbridge, future army colonel who would return to serve as a commanding officer of the Manhattan Project at Los Alamos.[8]

To house the students, teachers, staff, ranch hands, their families, and livestock, the Los Alamos Ranch School erected fifty-four buildings. At the center of the complex rose the Big House, a three-story building that was a combination dormitory, instruction hall, and dining room. Several hundred feet to the southwest, separated by bean fields, sat the two-story Fuller Lodge, designed by nationally known Santa Fe architect John Gaw Meem, which used more than seven hundred ponderosa pine logs for its walls and roof supports. A pond, created by and named for the school's founder, Ashley Pond, lay just south of Fuller Lodge. Some people referred to it as Ashley Pond Pond. In the early days, it provided water and ice for the school and in the winter was used for ice skating. The headmaster's and instructors' cottages were situated due north of Fuller Lodge with various barns, shops, sheds, and corrals scattered around the plateau.[9]

Harbingers of war mobilization, the military officers and the physicist arrived at the Los Alamos Ranch School late in the afternoon of November 16, 1942. Snow fell lightly as they looked over the site. Upon initial inspection, the school did not fit the selection criteria. Water was scarce and electrical capacity limited, the railhead lay forty miles away, and roads to the site were not merely inadequate but downright dangerous. On the other hand, with sheer cliffs dropping off from the plateau on three sides, maintaining security at the site would be easy. The established buildings of the Ranch School provided a foundation for houses and laboratory buildings. Most of the plateau belonged to the federal government, divided between the United States Forest Service, the National Park Service, and the Bureau of Indian

Affairs. Groves found that attractive. The only private land was owned by the homesteaders scattered throughout the canyons and plateau tops and by the Los Alamos Ranch School.

Perhaps most importantly, Oppenheimer wanted this site. In the spring of 1942 he had thought Berkeley, California, was a good candidate for the laboratory location, but by that fall he had changed his mind. Oppenheimer had always wanted to combine two of the main loves of his life, physics and New Mexico, and here was such an opportunity. As the convoy drove off to Santa Fe for dinner and further discussion about the suitability of the site, Groves left for Albuquerque.[10]

When Colonel Dudley caught up with Groves later that evening, he reported the dinner conversation in which Oppenheimer had insisted on choosing the Ranch School. Dudley noted that since they were behind schedule in selecting a place, the site criteria could be adapted to include Los Alamos. He said: "Let's pick Los Alamos and get on with our other work."[11] Groves agreed. Acquisition procedures started the next day. At stake on the Pajarito Plateau were 45,000 acres of federally owned land and 9,000 acres held privately. With authority from the War Department, condemnation proceedings began for what would become the Los Alamos Demolition Range. The only person to protest successfully the loss of the plateau was the Ranch School's headmaster, A. J. Connell, and he won only a small victory. Secretary of War Henry Stimson sent Connell a letter on December 7, 1942, condemning the site. The army wanted the school closed immediately and budgeted only $275,000 for purchasing it. Connell claimed it was worth $500,000. A court eventually awarded the school $335,000, with $7,884 owed in interest. In the meantime, the school had until mid-January to complete its academic year. Even before the school closed, the Army Corps of Engineers awarded a contract to M. M. Sundt Construction Company to transform the site into an army post. With contract in hand, the bulldozers moved in.[12]

The army created this top-secret post to pursue scientific research originally conducted in Europe. In the 1930s, European scientists like

Enrico Fermi, Niels Bohr, Lise Meitner, Otto Hahn, and Fritz Strassmann had conducted experiments in nuclear physics. Their work proved that an uranium atom could be split into two smaller atoms, with a release of an enormous amount of energy. Lacking an adequate physics word to describe the phenomena, Meitner code-switched a term from biology and called this process *fission*, a scientific name for the splitting of organisms.[13] In fact, *nuclear* and *atomic*, which denoted the center or nucleus of an atom, were also borrowed from biology. Thus, the very names of *nuclear physics* and *atomic science* are derived from biology.

As Europe moved toward war, fission research advanced in the laboratories of the future belligerents. For the Allies, research was greatly aided by the arrival of more than one hundred émigré physicists fleeing the totalitarian regimes of Germany and Italy. One of these refugee physicists, the Hungarian Leo Szilard, backed by fellow countrymen Eugene Wigner and Edward Teller, persuaded Albert Einstein to send a letter to President Franklin Roosevelt late in 1939. The letter urged the American government to support uranium research for military purposes, and Roosevelt responded by creating the Advisory Committee on Uranium.[14]

During the early phases of this research, scientific laboratories throughout the United States participated. In the summer of 1942, as research expanded and the production needs for manufacturing weapons-grade uranium and plutonium surfaced, better coordination between the various facilities and scientists became paramount. As a result, Roosevelt ordered the Army Corps of Engineers to oversee the construction and maintenance of a central laboratory and the huge plants needed to produce usable quantities of nuclear material. The Corps turned to Colonel James Marshall, who established the headquarters for a new engineering district in New York City. Known as the Manhattan Engineering District (MED), or simply the Manhattan Project, the new enterprise constructed a massive industrial complex at several sites around the country to refine nuclear material, operated research facilities like Los Alamos to create this new weapon, and coordinated all the aspects of research, development, and production.

Marshall's cautious and deliberate approach in selecting the sites for the project's various plants and labs frustrated Secretary of War Stimson and Dr. Vannevar Bush, head of the Office of Scientific Research and Development.

To speed up the process, Colonel Leslie Groves replaced Marshall in September. Groves had just finished overseeing the construction of the Pentagon and was well suited to command the far-flung operations of the Manhattan Project. At first, he resisted the assignment because he wanted to go overseas. Quickly, though, Groves's attitude changed, and even before his appointment became official (with an accompanying promotion to general), he addressed one of the major obstacles that had hobbled Marshall. Beset by wartime shortages, Marshall had been unable to get the highest priority, AAA, for the project. Knowing that ample supplies of everything from precious metals to truck tires were essential, Groves wrote a letter to himself granting AAA priority, walked it over to Donald M. Nelson, chairman of the War Productions Board, and had Nelson sign it. AAA priority meant the MED had virtual carte blanche in acquisitions, travel, and appropriations in a country wracked by war shortages and rationing.[15]

An efficient and decisive administrator, Groves became a vital force in the race to develop the bomb. As evidenced by his success in building the Pentagon, Groves was an able manager of large projects. He had a "contentious spirit, heavy humor, and sharp tongue [that] sometimes annoyed fellow officers."[16] He also alienated many of the civilians he worked with at Los Alamos. Of course, scientists can be contentious too, especially those trained in the political battles of an academic department, and so Los Alamos at times erupted into heated arguments between the scientific civilians and the army brass.[17]

With the promotion to general, an AAA priority rating, and the procurement of sites progressing, Groves turned to another difficult decision. Who would run the laboratory at Project Y, the code name for Los Alamos? Searching the physics departments of universities throughout the country, he focused on the cluster of nuclear physicists at the University of California at Berkeley. Groves chose J. Robert

Oppenheimer as the civilian director of Project Y, despite some concerns about his left-wing political activities.

Born in New York City on April 22, 1904, Oppenheimer went to Manhattan's Ethical Culture school and then to Harvard. In his third year at Harvard (where he graduated summa cum laude), Oppenheimer took six courses and audited four more. The normal quota was five courses. He later reflected on those early years: "My feelings about myself was [sic] always one of extreme discontent. I had very little sensitiveness to human beings, very little humility before the realities of this world."[18] After Harvard, Oppenheimer went to Cambridge in England and then, in 1927, on to Göttingen University in Germany, where he neglected to enroll. Three weeks after he finally did enroll at Göttingen, Oppenheimer received his Ph.D. He was just twenty-four years old. His Ph.D. thesis was a brilliant paper on quantum mechanics. Back in the United States in 1929, he received a dual appointment at the University of California at Berkeley and at the California Institute of Technology in Pasadena as a professor of physics. During the summer breaks from his hectic travels between Pasadena and Berkeley, he vacationed at his cabin in the mountains of northern New Mexico.[19]

Even though Oppenheimer was a theoretical physicist, other fields attracted his interest. At eleven, he joined the New York Mineralogical Society. The next youngest member was in his sixties. Fascinated by the Hindu religion, Oppenheimer taught himself Sanskrit (his eighth language) so he could translate its religious texts. Until 1936, he was apolitical, but then the Great Depression and the Spanish Civil War awakened his social consciousness.

Oppenheimer's involvement with the Communist Party of the United States remains a debated topic. In 1938, Oppenheimer donated money to the Spanish Republicans by way of the Communist Party (CP) and eventually married Katherine (Kitty) Harrison, a party member, whose second husband had died fighting with the Republicans in Spain. Oppenheimer recalled this period: "I woke up to a recognition that politics was a part of life. I became a real left-winger, joined the Teachers Union, had lots of Communist friends. . . . Most of what I believed then now seems complete nonsense, but it was an essential part of becoming

J. Robert Oppenheimer directed the civilians at Los Alamos during the war.
Courtesy of National Archives II, College Park, Md.

a whole man. If it hadn't been for this late but indispensable education,
I couldn't have done the job at Los Alamos at all."[20]

Although Oppenheimer claimed that he had grown disenchanted
with the Soviet Union before he began working on the atomic bomb,

21

he in fact continued giving money to and meeting with Communists in San Francisco's Bay Area. In October 1941, Oppenheimer gave $100 to Steve Nelson, who was one of the top Communist organizers in the Bay Area, for striking farm workers. He had started working on the bomb project the same month. As late as April 1942, Oppenheimer was giving "Pops" Folkoff, who collected dues for the Communist Party, $150 monthly.[21] Another CP member whom Oppenheimer had close ties to was Haakon Chevalier, a French literature professor at Berkeley. He had met Chevalier at a rally to support the communists who were fighting the fascists in the Spanish Civil War. Their friendship grew, and together they founded a branch of the American Federation of Teachers at Berkeley. With Chevalier's help in 1940, Oppie, as he was called, helped write, print, and distribute *Report to Our Colleagues*, which advocated the party line by calling for the United States to stay out of the war. He signed it "College Faculties Committee, Communist Party of California."[22] Oppenheimer and Chevalier also held political discussion groups at their houses. Oppenheimer later dismissed these groups as innocent and naive, but Chevalier called them "a closed unit of the Communist Party" composed of professionals who did not openly hold party memberships.[23] Because of these activities, which attracted the attention of the FBI, Oppenheimer had difficulty in gaining a security clearance for the Manhattan Project. He served as the director of the laboratory for months with a temporary clearance until Groves finally demanded and obtained a permanent security clearance for him in July 1943.[24]

As Oppenheimer began researching and participating in the early conferences on the atomic bomb, he dropped most of his political activities so that he could focus on the scientific, technical, and administrative challenges. These totally engaged him. Oppenheimer later recalled: "Almost everyone realized that this was a great undertaking . . . the culmination of three centuries of physics."[25] Directed by Oppenheimer (who previously had not even led a physics department at a university), the laboratory at Los Alamos grew to two thousand people and included eminent physicists. Dodging the enormous difficulties he encountered, Oppenheimer modestly explained his success there: "In a way, Los Alamos was a kind of confluence of my highbrow past, my physics, my students, my horses, my ranch, and my slight knowledge of physics."[26]

From its origins, opposing forces tugged at the broadcloth fabric of Los Alamos. Originally, Groves wanted all personnel, including the scientists, to join the regular army, and he did not want families at the post. At first, Oppenheimer agreed with Groves that all scientists should be army personnel; however, the militarization of the laboratory personnel sparked controversy among several scientists. Physicists I. I. Rabi and Robert Bacher strongly opposed the induction of scientists into the military. Even though Oppenheimer had already ordered his military uniform, he reconsidered after hearing from Rabi, Bacher, and others. Bacher later explained: "Rabi and I took an extremely dim view of this and we talked to him [Oppenheimer] in no uncertain terms about it. We pointed out that lieutenant colonels [the rank Oppenheimer had accepted] didn't have anything to say, and that if he tried to establish a scientific laboratory [with] a hierarchy that was composed of military people, that it just plain wouldn't work."[27] Rabi and Bacher also convinced Oppenheimer that the free flow of information between the scientists, vital for their research, would be hindered by military discipline. So convinced, Oppenheimer persuaded Groves not to draft or enlist the scientists. With Oppenheimer and other personnel hailing from Berkeley, Groves chose the University of California as the official operator of the laboratories at Los Alamos.

As added stimulus for recruiting talent, Oppenheimer won permission for families to accompany the scientists, even though Groves feared the problems that would arise with civilians living at the site. As it turned out, tension existed between the civilian families and the military for the duration of the war.

In 1944, Groves convened a meeting of all the army officers stationed at the site with this statement: "At great expense we have gathered on this mesa the largest collection of crackpots ever seen."[28] He then asked the officers to take good care of the crackpots. Later, Groves attributed the discord to "the fact that the two dominant sectors of the group were composed of people of almost directly opposite backgrounds: scientists with little experience outside the academic field; and uniformed members of the armed services . . . who were only interested in bringing the war to a quick and successful end."[29] At times, each group disagreed with the other on how best to complete the mission of the top-secret laboratory at Los Alamos.

For a town that didn't exist, Los Alamos attracted a lot of people. Take, for example, Secundino Sandoval, who arrived as a young boy with his family in 1943. Sandoval's father had been working as a ranch foreman in Arizona. A call from a relative already on the Hill told the Sandovals of the voracious demand for all types of workers at the site. As Sandoval recalled: "We loaded up the truck and instead of the 'Okies,' it was the 'Arizonians,' moving to Los Alamos—a sort of reverse Steinbeck."[30] Receiving extra gas coupons for the trip, the Sandovals drove northeast for 450 miles through deserts and mountains. At the end of their long drive, they hit a delay at the base of the cliffs leading up to Los Alamos. The Sandovals waited five hours as the Highway Department's work crews dynamited the road ahead and then cleared the rubble. Once at their destination, the Sandovals halted at a gate where armed Military Police (MP) processed each member of the family for security clearances. While they waited, Secundino noticed a fifty-foot-tall guard tower with machine guns on top pointed his way. An army tank also trained its cannon on the entrance. Lines of cars, coming and going, queued up as the MPs searched each car. In Arizona, Sandoval had known an Italian family who was sent away to an internment camp. As an eight-year-old Hispanic, Sandoval feared for his own and his family's safety: "My first impression was that I was going to a concentration camp." First impressions faded, his family stayed there, and Secundino Sandoval grew up on the Hill.[31]

John Manley's family also arrived during the early days of the project. Coming from the Metallurgical Lab at the University of Chicago, scientist Manley entered the town on April 4, 1943, while his pregnant wife, Kathleen, stayed in Chicago to have their baby. On June

26, Kathleen, three-year-old Kay, and new-born Kim arrived by train. Since there was no available housing at the site, they took up temporary residence at nearby Bandelier National Monument, where a guest lodge and tents accommodated the Manleys with their young children.[32]

Bill Hudgins heard of Los Alamos by chance. As an engineering student at the University of New Mexico in Albuquerque in 1943, he overheard a conversation about jobs at a project in the northern part of the state and the address where to apply—109 East Palace Avenue in Santa Fe. He sent a letter of inquiry that was answered quickly with an appointment for an interview scheduled for that week. Hudgins went to Santa Fe for the interview and by the next week was offered a job paying $187.50 per month. He left the university immediately and reported, like most new arrivals, to the 109 East Palace address. Engineers were scarce in New Mexico in 1943, and the project was happy to get any it could find.[33]

109 East Palace Avenue, Santa Fe, New Mexico, is a fabled address in the lore of the Manhattan Project. Since the site itself was top secret, surrounded by fences and guards, 109 East Palace served as its gateway and Dorothy McKibbin as its gatekeeper. At the end of many long train, bus, or car journeys, weary travelers stumbled into 109 East Palace "tense with expectations and curiosity" as McKibbin recalled.[34] Some expected a posting in Santa Fe itself. Instead, McKibbin, a congenial woman in her early forties, greeted them, soothed the bewildered, and without divulging too much information issued temporary passes and precise directions for the final thirty-five-mile leg of the trip. Oppenheimer had recruited McKibbin to manage the Manhattan Project office in Santa Fe, which she considered "the entrance to one of the most significant undertakings of the war or indeed, of the 20th century."[35] She first came to Santa Fe in the 1920s to recuperate from tuberculosis and returned in 1932 to settle. McKibbin's office provided a safe haven in Santa Fe for newcomers and a rendezvous place for day-trippers from the Hill. Buses shuttling people back and forth from Santa Fe to Los Alamos made 109 East Palace busier than the bus station on the other side of the historic central plaza. As a transhipment point for incoming freight, trucks from 109 East Palace

delivered baggage, supplies, and even special orders of flowers, hot rolls and pumpernickel, and baby cribs to Los Alamos.[36]

One of the many who passed through 109 East Palace was Richard Feynman, future Nobel Laureate in physics. Feynman came by train in 1943 as a graduate student (close to attaining his Ph.D. in physics from Princeton) to work at the site. Since Princeton was then a small community and many of its physicists were headed for the project in New Mexico, he was warned not to buy his train ticket at the local station in order to obscure the popular destination. Figuring that he could go ahead and buy a ticket locally since everyone else would go to neighboring stations, Feynman purchased his at the Princeton office. The man at the ticket window exclaimed, "Oh, so all this stuff is yours!" For weeks, crates of instruments had been leaving Princeton for New Mexico with nobody accompanying them.[37]

Carson and Kathleen Mark also came by train. Carson arrived first in the summer of 1945, followed by Kathleen and their four children. The train ride began in Montreal, with a transfer at Chicago. When Kathleen marshaled her children through Chicago's Union Station, a soldier emerged out of the crowd with orders to help them make the transfer. He played with the older children at a park while Kathleen nursed the baby and then put them on the train to Lamy, the closest station to Santa Fe and Project Y.[38]

Immigrants continued to pour into the town throughout the war. European scientists and their families, fleeing from Nazism and Fascism, arrived from distinguished universities in Germany and Italy, by way of England and Denmark. The British Mission arrived in December 1943, composed of preeminent scientists from throughout Europe and Canada, including Otto Frisch, Ernest Titterton, Niels Bohr, and Rudolf Peierls, as well as the deep-cover Soviet spy Klaus Fuchs. From Harvard, Berkeley, the Massachusetts Institute of Technology, the University of Chicago, Princeton, Columbia, and numerous other universities in the United States, America's preeminent scientists also traveled to the site.[39]

Many of the wives who accompanied their husbands also worked in the scientific laboratories and offices in the Tech Area. By September

1943, twenty women held scientific posts, fifty toiled as lab technicians, fifteen were nurses, seventy filed and did secretarial duties, and
twenty-five taught in the school. As Charlotte Serber recalled: "In the
early days of the Project, most of the women who worked in the Area
were wives of young physicists and chemists. . . . The force of social
pressure and the obvious need for all hands, trained or untrained,
brought most of them rapidly onto the payroll." Serber worked as the
laboratory's librarian, ordering and distributing scientific manuals
and reports, some classified as top secret. Not all women bowed to
the pressure to join the efforts in the Tech Area though. Eleanor Jette,
a trained mathematician, was recruited but refused, later recalling her
indignation: "I was sure that the wives, who should be home taking
care of the children, were intimidated or encouraged to work because
the penny-pinching Washington administration didn't want to build
housing. I theorized that properly qualified teachers weren't hired for
the same reason."[40] Physicist John Manley, husband of Kathleen
Manley, suggested another reason for employing women in the Tech
Area: "It was the policy to encourage wives to work, not just to keep
the number of inhabitants as small as possible, but as a preventive
treatment against the dangers of an enforced isolation of which they
did not understand the purpose."[41]

In addition to civilians, military personnel crowded onto the Hill.
Joe Weber had received MP training at Fort Riley, Kansas, and then in
the spring of 1943 boarded a train with two hundred other MPs. They
detrained at Camp Walters near Dallas, where they waited because
their barracks at Los Alamos were unfinished. After a week's delay,
they boarded a train for Lamy, where a bus picked them up, took
them through Santa Fe, and drove them over the rolling hills dotted
with piñon trees. Twenty miles beyond Santa Fe, the buses came to
Otowi Crossing, an old railroad bridge over the Rio Grande. Because
their buses exceeded the bridge's weight capacity, the MPs clambered
out and walked across the span. The buses followed, picked up the
GIs on the opposite shore, and began the steep climb up the switchbacks to the top of the Pajarito Plateau. The road had many tight turns
and grades of 12 to 14 percent. Newcomers and grizzled veterans

The original road that climbed up to Los Alamos shows its switchbacks in the center with the newer wartime road curving around the cliff on the right. Courtesy of National Archives II, College Park, Md.

alike felt apprehension as their vehicles clung to the precipitous road scratched into the cliffs just below the townsite. The worst part of the road, the steep switchbacks, remained dirt (and mud) until the New Mexico Highway Department paved it in July 1944, at a cost of $65,500 per mile.[42]

Another group of military personnel assigned to the site came via Albuquerque. To help staff the hospital and offices at Los Alamos, twenty-nine WACs (members of the Women's Army Corps) left Fort Sill, Oklahoma, in late July 1943 for New Mexico. They traveled on an ancient Pullman railcar with worn red velvet seats and pot-bellied stoves at each end of the car. Getting off the train at Albuquerque, they rode by bus to Santa Fe, where they transferred to the back of army trucks for the treacherous final leg of their journey. Another WAC detachment reached Santa Fe, opened a sealed envelope to find a phone number that, when called, summoned a station wagon to take them up the Hill. Once at the site, security personnel interviewed and fingerprinted the WACs and then read them the National Espionage

Act. Finally, the WACs signed an oath of loyalty. All military personnel received such treatment and, eventually, everyone above the age of six obtained individual security passes into the site. The security officers stressed the importance of the secrecy of the post, forbidding anyone to discuss the nature of their work. In the security briefing to the WACs, the security officer mentioned only the name of the site, "Los Alamos," to demand that it not be repeated. Instead, the place was called "Site Y," "Project Y," or just "the Hill."[43]

Military personnel composed one of the largest contingents at Site Y. Four major units resided at the post: the Provisional Engineering Division (PED), the Special Engineering Division (SED), the Military Police, and the Women's Army Corps. As military personnel, the men and women did whatever was necessary to keep the post running. The PED provided maintenance and repairs to the buildings and the equipment in the laboratory and the town. Their duties also included cutting firewood in the winter. The SED, a special unit created just for the Manhattan Project, included many scientific and engineering graduate students who had entered the military. They assisted the physicists and engineers in the Tech Area. The MPs handled security for the site and not only patrolled the fences and checked passes but also monitored mail, listened in on phone calls, and canvassed the Tech Area after-hours to see if sensitive papers were left lying around. The WACs assisted the doctors in the hospital, operated the telephone switchboard, worked in the Post Exchange and the Motor Pool, and provided secretarial expertise for the military officers stationed at the post. The post's commanding officer reported to General Groves, the head of the Manhattan Project. Some officers, like Captain William (Deak) Parsons, were fortunate enough to be accompanied by their families, although Groves frowned on military dependents coming to the already overcrowded community.[44]

Not everyone traveled long distances to get to Site Y. In 1891, Bencés Gonzáles's father had homesteaded Anchor Ranch on the Pajarito Plateau, and two years later Bencés was born. He spent most his childhood summers helping his family farm on the homestead and then served in the army as an infantryman during World War I. After that war, Bencés became an employee of the new Los Alamos Ranch School, where he drove cattle, managed the school store, and cooked for the boys. When the army condemned his family's homestead in 1942, Bencés stayed, eventually managing the vegetables and milk at the post commissary. Since he knew the surrounding countryside well, he suggested sites for picnicking and camping to new arrivals and later was a crucial mediator in resolving several sticky disputes at the site.[45]

Popovi Da also had deep roots in the area. A son of the world-famous potter María Martínez and painter Juan Martínez, Popovi was born nearby at the Pueblo of San Ildefonso. He worked at Site Y until he was drafted in 1944, and then went to Oak Ridge, another top-secret site of the Manhattan Project in Tennessee. He returned to New Mexico when he was assigned to Site Y as a member of the SED, where he worked on the particle accelerator.[46]

Aside from the large military presence and the scientific teams, a sizable number of civilians helped the army in running the town and the Tech Area. Once word spread that abundant jobs existed in northern New Mexico, people flooded to the site like water from a burst *acequía* spreading over a thirsty field. Of course, with the overcrowding on the Hill, preference for these service jobs went to workers who did not have to live there. From the nearby towns of Española, Chimayó, Santa Cruz, San Ildefonso, Santa Clara, and San Felipe, native New Mexicans commuted to Site Y and worked as drivers, carpenters, janitors, maids, furnace stokers, plumbers, and day laborers. Most of the local labor force was Hispanic and American Indian, and when added to the emigré scientists' families, the melange reminded some at the site of a foreign city, or a mini–United Nations. By August 1945, the site's population of five to six thousand included between two and three thousand scientific and military personnel and more than two thousand adult civilians. Children on the Hill added another one thousand people.[47]

All of these people, military and civilian, adults and children, invented an instant city at Site Y. With laboratory personnel and their families arriving at Los Alamos, a community grew. Out of the tense activities of the laboratory and the feverish pace of living in the town, schools and churches grew and social gatherings flourished. The Army Corps of Engineers bulldozed the plateau tops and canyons and changed the landscape just as the languages of nuclear physics and secrecy transformed Los Alamos residents. Residents learned to adapt to the wartime conditions, the urgency and isolation, and families accommodated the commands of the army and the demands of the lab.

Los Alamos was a temporary army post, run by the Army Corps of Engineers "for the duration." As a temporary site spurred on by the urgency of the war, most of Site Y's buildings lacked not just comfort but durability. The initial contract for transforming the boys' school into a top-secret post fell to the M. M. Sundt Construction Company with the firm of W. C. Kruger as the architectural engineers. Sundt, one of the largest construction companies in New Mexico at the time, arrived at the site on December 1, 1942, only weeks after Groves approved its selection. The Army Corps of Engineers requested that Sundt build a small military post. In planning for the post, the army confronted confusing estimates of how many people would live on the Hill. In the spring of 1942, Oppenheimer offered Ernest Lawrence his amazing appraisal that the people needed for the project should number "a total of three experienced men and perhaps an equal number of younger ones."[48] This estimate quickly escalated to a projected staff of fifty scientists with fifty assistants. Groves tripled Oppenheimer's figure to three hundred, and this estimate provided the basis for Sundt's initial work. The first contract called for an expenditure of $300,000. By December 20, Sundt broke ground for the first building, and by the end of the year, work on thirteen buildings in the laboratory complex (or Tech Area, as it was called) had begun, with the completion date set for March 15, 1943. The Army Corps of Engineers promised Sundt the blueprints by January 20 for what they were already erecting. Often, Sundt had to work on a "fast track" that saw the foundation poured while the superstructure was still being designed. Modifications to the original plan expanded Sundt's contract to $1,258,064 in mid-January, and the completion date was extended to May 15. By the end of April,

31

with 96 percent of the original job completed and scientific personnel moving in, the Sundt company began to leave the Hill. Soon, however, Groves ordered "Expansion A," and Sundt embarked on a new round of construction. Many more expansions followed.[49]

By late April 1943, Groves saw that the site needed more buildings, power plants, residences, and auxiliary structures. Modifications were tacked onto the original blueprints like urgent notes on a bulletin board. When Sundt officially completed Modification # 70 on November 30, 1943, the construction costs had topped $7 million. The secrecy, urgency, isolation, and tension surrounding the work strained the resources of the company, and many at Sundt felt relieved to move back to Albuquerque after a year on the Hill.[50]

Under Sundt's chaotic construction, an instant city emerged on the Hill. Adding to the original fifty-four structures from the boys' school, Sundt erected the major buildings of the Tech Area, as well as a boiler-house, the main water tower, and 334 apartment units. The company constructed the best residences at the site during the war; they included amenities that later units lacked, like varnished hardwood floors and fireplaces. Many families coveted the Sundt efficiency, two- and three-bedroom apartments.[51]

The typical two-story Sundt apartment buildings held four families. Each family had two or three small bedrooms and a tiny bathroom with a tin-lined shower. Each kitchen, surprisingly large for wartime construction, had two sinks, numerous cupboards, and a unwieldy huge black coal stove, nicknamed "Black Beauty." As deluxe models of wartime housing, the Sundts attracted competition almost as fierce as that for the houses on Bathtub Row, which were the boys' school residences of the headmaster and other faculty members located just north of Fuller Lodge. With the only bathtubs on the Hill, these single-family houses were the envy of everyone. Babysitters quickly appeared for a chance to soak in a tub after the children had gone to bed.[52]

After Bathtub Row and the Sundt apartments (which lay west of Bathtub Row), the quality of residences on the Hill declined. When the Sundt Construction Company exhaustedly left the site toward the end of the 1943, several new contractors arrived. Morgan and Sons

Looking south to the Tech Area, which housed the top secret Manhattan Project. On the right is the security fence that surrounded the Tech Area. The buildings in the center housed offices as well as laboratories for experiments and processing plutonium. Courtesy of Los Alamos Historical Museum Photo Archives.

appeared in January 1944 with fifty-six prefabricated houses that they installed north of the Sundts. This residential area became known as "Morganville." The Robert E. McKee Company of El Paso also brought up prefab residences and that part of town was dubbed "McKeeville." More prefabs, called "Hanford Houses," were trucked down from Washington state to help relieve the lack of housing. Additionally, Quonset huts, Pacific hutments, and expandible trailers housed the growing population at the site.[53]

While families scrambled for houses, unmarried people, including most of the military personnel, and couples without children crowded into dormitories. With the residential area posed like a crescent moon over the north of the Tech Area, dorms were crammed into whatever spaces could accommodate them. Like the first group of family residences built, the early dorms were the best. In those, every two rooms shared a bathroom. Later dorms had a community bathroom on each floor that serviced sixteen rooms, and one dorm built for sixty men actually housed ninety. Durability of the dorms also declined. At one dorm dance, an army officer praised the sturdiness of all of the buildings at the site. A WAC, to prove her point, gave him a shove. The officer hit the wall and fell right through. With the rapid expansion of Site Y, quick construction prevailed, sometimes resulting in shoddy work.[54]

Because of the tight security, fences surrounded even the residential areas of the rapidly expanding Site Y. Perched atop a high plateau between the Pueblo and Los Alamos Canyons, the town was encircled by a chain-link fence topped with barbed wire. Another high fence enclosed the forest-green buildings of the Tech Area, where the secret work of the site occurred. For those who lacked the proper pass, the Tech Area was as far away as their distant hometowns. Outlying technical sites dotted the Pajarito Plateau, but they were also off-limits to those without proper security clearances. Thus, those who did not work in the Tech Area were caught between two fences, locked out of the primary activity of the site and allowed only occasionally to leave the town for the world outside.[55]

Initially, trips off the Hill were restricted to an area within a radius of one hundred miles, encompassed by Albuquerque, Cuba, Las Vegas, Santa Fe, and Lamy. Later, such restrictions were lifted by Oppenheimer when he stated: "There will be no limitations, in time or in geography, imposed by security on travel of project personnel within the limits of continental United States." Personal travel away from Site Y did require submitting a written statement prior to departure to the Intelligence Office and, upon return, a statement of the visited destinations.[56]

But the majority of families at Site Y lived encircled by fences. On a finger of land running east from the foothills of the Jemez Mountains, the fences enclosed a top of a plateau four miles long and less than a mile wide. Two gates permitted access to the town. The main entrance, East Gate, straddled the road from Santa Fe at the east end of the plateau. At the southwestern boundary of the site, tucked up against the steep flank of the Jemez Mountains, the West Gate allowed

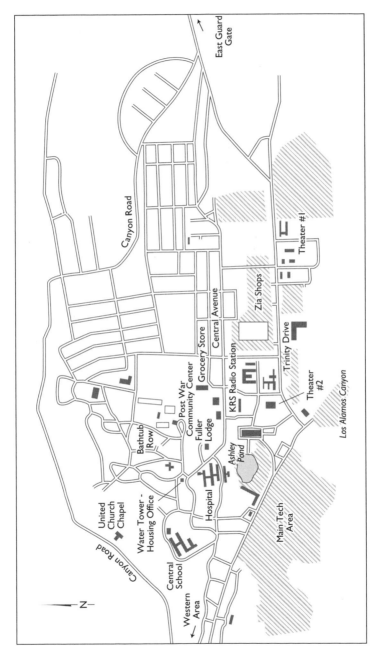

Los Alamos in the 1940s. Based on a guide map, courtesy of Los Alamos Historical Museum Archives.

those living in the temporary quarters at Bandelier National Monument easier passage to the town and the laboratory.

With housing at a premium for this instant city, the Housing Office was the first destination for the flood of new arrivals. After being assigned a residence based on family size and employment position at the lab, newcomers searched the confusing array of streets and buildings for their new home. The saga of the Brode family illustrates what awaited many upon arrival. When the Brodes pulled up in front of their new abode, a throng of neighbors, mainly children and women, welcomed them. Stepping into their Sundt quadroplex, they were surprised to find that the women of neighborhood had left vases of flowers, made the beds, and deposited their rationed milk in the refrigerator. These neighbors offered help in finding the commissary, the school, and other essential facilities and showed the newcomers how most of the key community buildings clustered around Ashley Pond, the locus of the town. North of the pond was the Ranch School's Fuller Lodge, to the northwest lay Central School, and to the east sat the commissary. The Tech Area began on the south shore of Ashley Pond and spread east and west along the southern half of the plateau.[57]

Arriving at Site Y shocked many people, especially women who would have to raise their families there. Eleanor Jette found the place as raw as a new scar, and her son liked it even less. Many women despaired at their first view of the site, since they were unprepared for the primitive conditions and rampant growth. Genia Peierls bemoaned: "What a shame to spoil the landscape with these army huts."[58] Kathleen Mark remembered it as "slummy looking."[59] But not all disliked what they saw. Coming from war-torn England, Peggy Titterton was thrilled. Her new house was warm and comfortable, and food was plentiful. When she complimented Groves, he was so delighted that he gave her the run of a food warehouse. For many, the natural beauty of the Hill at times compensated for the hastily built, ramshackle site. Whatever one's reaction, most were at Site Y for the duration of the war.[60]

These immigrants to Los Alamos followed in the footsteps of many previous travelers. Indeed, millions of people have heeded the call to

Guards at the East Gate stopped traffic both entering and leaving Site Y.
Courtesy of Los Alamos Historical Museum Photo Archives.

"Go West." For some, the journey to Site Y was no different, and cultural code-switching to the nineteenth century westward movement proved helpful in adapting to the difficult situation. Ruth Marshak, who accompanied her physicist husband to Los Alamos from Canada and then taught third grade and worked at the Housing Office during the war, was one of them: "I felt akin to the pioneer women accompanying their husbands across the uncharted plains westward, alert to danger, resigned to the fact they journeyed, for weal or for woe, into the unknown."[61] Like their pioneer predecessors, Site Y women picked up their families and belongings and journeyed to an unknown destination, sometimes with little discussion or debate. The aura of going west, into the unknown and secret world of Site Y, struck a resonant chord with some of these modern-day pioneers and helped them grapple with the journey as they identified with their Old West forerunners.

For pioneers at Los Alamos, going west involved more than a spatial journey, for it included adaptation to new cultures and evoked the frontier myths of rugged individualism, unlimited opportunity, and freedom. These powerful myths combined with the preexisting American Indian traditions and Spanish heritage to form the cultural landscape of the West. Despite the frontier myths of wide-open spaces and pristine landscapes, no cultural vacuum existed in the West. Each culture had borrowed from the one before to survive in an alien land. The pioneers of a new frontier at Los Alamos invented their community, inspired by some of those myths but also grounded in the experiences of those who had lived there for centuries.[62]

Even General Groves acknowledged how the frontier myth motivated him. On the last page of his autobiography, he talks of his early experiences in the West. As a boy, he lived on army posts established during the Indian Wars in the nineteenth century. He recalled: "Here I came to know many of the old soldiers and scouts who had devoted their active lives to winning the West. . . . I grew somewhat dismayed, wondering what was left for me to do now that the West was won. . . . Yet those of us who saw the dawn of the Atomic Age that early morning at Alamagordo will never hold such doubts again. We know now that when man is willing to make the effort, he is capable of accomplishing virtually anything."[63] The powerful pull of the frontier myth and the accompanying images from the winning of the West were a foundation for many of the people who came to Los Alamos to work on the atomic bomb.

From its opening in the spring of 1943, Site Y exploded in population from several hundred residents to almost six thousand people by war's end. The majority of its residents were in their twenties and thirties. Young wives and husbands lived together, as they did not at military bases. Consequently, a critical mass occurred at the maternity ward of the post hospital. Equipped more for radiological or industrial accidents than pregnancy and pediatrics, the hospital staff sought help. In a June 1944 letter to Groves, medical director Dr. Stafford Warren asked for more maternity assistance, noting: "Approximately one-fifth of the married women are now in some stage of pregnancy (the birth rate over the nation elsewhere is decreasing)."[64] Eighty babies were born that first year, and ten newborns arrived every month thereafter. In his account of the Manhattan Project, Groves recalled: "One of the doctors told me later that the number and spacing of babies born to scientific personnel surpassed all existing medical records."[65] One of the rumors about Site Y that circulated in Santa Fe, that it was a camp for pregnant WACs, might be explained by the number of expectant women from the Hill who visited Santa Fe.[66]

At one point, Groves protested to Oppenheimer about the birthrate. The baby boom strained the post's hospital and put additional demands on an already overburdened housing situation. Asked to influence his colleagues, Oppenheimer declined, saying, "This hardly seems to be the responsibility of a scientific director."[67] In response, a limerick swept the town:

> The General's in a stew
> He trusted you and you
> He thought you'd be scientific
> Instead you're just prolific
> And what is he to do?[68]

Surrounded by the babble of babies, men and women undertook the serious duty of harnessing atomic energy for military purposes.

Soon after the scientists and technicians arrived at the site in April 1943, Robert Serber, a protégé of Oppenheimer from Berkeley, gave a series of five lectures to indoctrinate the staff. These lectures became the *Los Alamos Primer*, a twenty-four-page pamphlet packed with diagrams, formulas, and graphs given to new arrivals. The *Primer* stated: "The object of the project is to produce a practical military weapon in the form of a bomb in which the energy is released by a fast neutron chain reaction in one or more of the materials known to show nuclear fission."[69] During the first lecture, after Serber used "bomb" several times, Oppenheimer asked that a different word be chosen to prevent the workmen who were swarming over the site from hearing any secret information. Thereafter, "the Gadget" became the common code name for the bomb.[70] By switching the name of the bomb to a euphemism, scientists were also more likely to postpone considering the consequences of their creation. Instead of inventing an Armageddon bomb, they were working on a gadget or a gizmo.

Using complicated formulas and graphs, Serber illustrated the physics necessary to create an atomic explosion and described the materials to be used in the project: "The materials in question are U=25, U=28 and element 94/239 =49. . . ."[71] In this scientific shorthand, U=25 is 235Uranium (^{235}U), U=28 is 238Uranium (^{238}U), and 94/239=49 is 239Plutonium (^{239}Pu). To prevent security leaks, ^{235}U (the enriched weapon-grade uranium) was called "25," and ^{239}Pu (also weapons-grade material) was called "49." The key problem was how to create a chain reaction with these materials—that is, how to create a condition where bombarded atoms split, released neutrons, and hit and split other atoms. When this critical mass achieved a chain reaction, an atomic explosion occurred, releasing an enormous amount of energy. Originally, Meitner and Frisch had code-switched from biology and called this process "fission," but no one knew how to pronounce the word. In the early days at Los Alamos, *fission* was a noun and *to fish* was the verb form. Thus, *fission* was pronounced like "fishin'."[72]

After calculating the amounts of nuclear material needed to "fish," the *Los Alamos Primer* concluded with speculation on various ways to detonate weapons-grade uranium and plutonium. Two general methods were considered: first, shooting two smaller masses of fissionable (or active) material at each other to achieve a chain reaction, which became known as the Gun Assembly and was later nicknamed Little Boy. The second method surrounded the active material with conventional high explosives and, by "imploding" the device, compressed the material until a critical mass was achieved. This became known as the Implosion Method and was nicknamed Fat Man. Through this series of lectures published in the *Los Alamos Primer*, the basic problems were defined, and the course of the research laid out for the next two years at the Tech Area. This research, which Oppenheimer called "technologically sweet" because it was seductively challenging, attracted scientists to Los Alamos. Whether either of these methods of detonation, Little Boy or Fat Man, would be successful was yet unknown, so both methods were aggressively pursued.[73]

To protect the vital information produced at Los Alamos, Groves insisted on strict military security. The secrecy of the project created code names for places, things, and even people. The code name for the laboratory in New Mexico was Site Y; for the facilities in Tennessee, Y-12, X-10, and K-25 (which might have been grid-map coordinates for the various facilities at Oak Ridge); for the whole project, the Manhattan Engineering District. People with easily recognizable names (at least to nuclear physicists) such as Niels Bohr and Enrico Fermi became Nicholas Baker and Eugene Farmer, respectively. Laura Fermi, not aware of her husband's code name, almost missed her ride at the Lamy train station because she did not respond to the WAC calling out for a Mrs. Farmer. Oppenheimer became James Oberhelm and Edward Teller, Ed Tilden. A certain playfulness also surfaced with the choice of some code names. *Physicist* and *chemist* were replaced by *fizzler* and *stinker*. Secrecy even extended to official state documents. Eric Jette's New Mexico driver's license held little personal information. Instead it read: "Name– '44' Resident Address– 'Special List B'; Signature– 'Not Required'."[74] Most drivers' licenses listed Box 1663 for the home address of the driver.

Since Los Alamos did not publicly exist, mail was sent to P.O. Box 1663 in Santa Fe. Not only did Box 1663 receive letters and packages, it also became a code name for the site itself. People born at Los Alamos during the war have on their birth certificates "Box 1663" as the place of birth. With secrecy strictly enforced, even love letters made romantic reference to the post office box. One soldier wrote his beloved: "Oh, how I wish you were with me in Box 1663."[75]

By renaming people and places, Groves partially accomplished his goal of secrecy. Codes prevented the uninitiated from discovering who worked on what, a reasonable response to wartime conditions.

41

From the beginning, security considerations determined site selection and design, so the more isolated the site, the better. Once staff arrived at the site, communication both to and from the outside was channeled through censors. Los Alamos held the distinction as the only community in the United States where all letters and phone conversations were monitored during World War II.[76]

Residents reacted to the codes and secrecy in various ways. The cultural historian Peter Bacon Hales observes that the Manhattan Project subjected public and private speech to governmental authority. The result was "the generation of a new language common to all, but controlled by the authorities."[77] In Hales's view, Manhattan Project participants, faced with secrecy and authoritarian power, retreated to silence as the only option available: "And so silence became both the final act of resistance and the ultimate act of compliance in the topographies of power that formed the cultural geography of the Manhattan Project."[78] To be sure, secrecy permeated the landscape of Site Y. Laura Fermi later recalled: "Once inside the gates, they [the men] are in a world of their own which cannot be shared by their wives or children, for most of their work is still secret. A scientist in Los Alamos differs from a suburban husband in that he is never asked by his wife: 'What did you do at the office today?'"[79] At home after work, Eleanor Jette left her husband Eric alone as he quietly counted the nail holes in the living room ceiling. How many spouses were kept in the dark by the silence? Many wives knew of the project's purpose, sometimes from being told outright by their husbands, sometimes from reading passages in physics books purposefully left open to chapters on nuclear matters, and sometimes by talking to other women. The degree of secrecy depended upon each couple.[80]

Phyllis Fisher confirmed the secret about Site Y through her unborn child. She related a conversation with her husband, Leon, about naming their child: "At dinner one evening, I asked in a bantering tone, 'Well, how about Uranium Fish. . . ?' I never finished 'Fisher' because a red-faced, furious Leon was roaring at me, demanding that I *never* use that word again. 'What's wrong?' I asked, startled. 'I only said Ur—,' and, blam, his hand was over my mouth. 'Stop that!' he shouted,

'You never know when someone is right near this paper house! Someone might hear you. *Never* say that! You've got to listen to me!'" That night, Phyllis pored over a physics textbook and discovered that "uranium fission" theoretically could produce an enormous explosion.[81]

Strict security did indeed mandate silence, but many residents rebelled against the demand from the top. They reacted not by revealing the secrets at the site, but with humor, anger, and frenzied off-duty social activities. Some took security and the enforced silence as a personal challenge, a position best illustrated by Richard Feynman, who waged war with the censors. Feynman's wife, Arline, dying from tuberculosis in an Albuquerque hospital, sent him coded letters as brain teasers. Censorship regulations forbade letters in code or any language besides English, French, or German. Despite army regulations, Feynman sent a reply back to her in code and included the key to the code for the benefit of the censors, who called him into their office. Feynman made many trips to that office to argue, and his battle with the hapless censors provided comic relief for the tense community. Feynman, a valued nuclear physicist, also contested the silence and secrecy of Site Y. In time, he became an expert on what could get past the censors and won bets with fellow workers by writing letters that phrased forbidden subjects in ways the censors had to allow. His triumphs against the censors and the army provided a relief for others on the Hill who vicariously coped with the silence, the secrecy, and the oppression of wartime regulations.[82]

The secrecy also affected the children at Site Y. For example, Claire Ulam Weiner's parents, Stanislaw and Françoise Ulam, gave parties when Claire was a young girl on the Hill. During these affairs, men huddled in corners talking about secret matters. At the time, Weiner thought all fathers did that.[83] Even the most powerless residents on the Hill, the children, responded to secrecy in ways other than silence. When five-year-old Ellen Wilder Reid arrived on the plateau in 1945, her family lived in a tent at Bandelier National Monument because of the scarce housing at Los Alamos. One day while throwing rocks at the stream, Ellen's brother smashed her thumb. Her father, Edward Wilder, tried to rush her to the post hospital by way of the West Gate. MPs stopped them since Ellen did not have a security pass, and an argument ensued between Wilder and the MPs until an officer granted permission by phone to allow Ellen and her father to proceed to the hospital. During the wait for clearance, Ellen learned that she could not enter because something very secret was going on at the post. Once inside the gate, she searched for that secret but saw only ugly buildings; however, at the hospital, she saw ducks swimming on nearby Ashley Pond. Ellen counted the ducks: "There were eleven ducks. That was a lot for me to count, but I figured that was it. I knew the secret! There was nothing else that anyone would care about there, obviously." When her family moved up to the Hill, she was still angry about the delay in getting to the hospital. So she stood next to the exterior perimeter fence to tell the secret to enemy agents that lurked in the woods beyond. Disappointed that no one came, she persuaded her brother to crawl through a culvert to spread the news about the top-secret ducks. He got stuck, the neighbors responded to his howls, and young Ellen feared that she would never get a security clearance.[84]

Ellen offers another example of the impact of the site on children. Having heard that the lab was developing powerful new bombs, she was unimpressed because she had known about bombs all her young life. Ellen also had heard that if a lizard ran through a fire, it would turn into a dragon or a dinosaur. Even at five years old, she knew a dragon would be a truly unique secret weapon. She herded lizards toward their campfire at Bandelier and finally succeeded in forcing one to scamper across the hot coals. Ellen grew so terrified that she ran to the park ranger and demanded that he bring his gun to shoot the dragon that would appear. The above stories of a sly expectant mother, a humorously subversive wordman, and an imaginative child illustrate that, even when secrecy mutes people, they can react in unconventional ways against the silence.[85]

The secrecy enveloping nuclear energy was an originating condition that clashed with democratic principles. Granted, security and codes prevail in wartime for obvious reasons, and previous wars had suspended traditional constitutional rights; however, the secrecy of the Manhattan Project outlasted World War II and was intended to curb nuclear weapons proliferation. As we will see later, wartime secrecy became Cold War policy. Enforced silence, which muted individuals and families at Los Alamos, also deafened the national debate over nuclear weapons. Later in life, Oppenheimer warned of the threat to democracy by a culture of secrecy when he said that history might have been changed "if we had acted wisely" and rid ourselves of "the delusions of the effect of secrecy."[86] His view was that secrecy did not prevent the Soviet Union from obtaining nuclear weapons but, rather aggravated the arms race and worsened the Cold War. At the core of the Manhattan Project's success lay a vacuum of secrecy, in opposition to a democratic government that is accountable to its citizens. Thus, the Manhattan Project illustrates both a success of the American government as well as a threat to American democracy. Secrecy is hard, if not impossible, to enforce in humans, who speak even before they walk. Even when the mind is willing, the spirit, whether childlike or calculating, creates mythical dragons and top-secret ducks, Uranium Fisher, and atomic spies to subvert the enforced silence.

Despite the contrary reactions by the residents against the secrecy, many felt an abiding sense of safety and camaraderie in the town because of the security policies. Surrounded by fences, guarded by MPs, and with residence restricted to those who held security passes, inhabitants lived in a secure oasis, and felt safe in a war-torn world. The enforced security also cemented friendships as people faced hardships together. As Jane Wilson, who taught English at Los Alamos High School, wrote: "It was a Barnum and Bailey world. We citizens loved it. Our hardships were pretty petty. We were animated by a drive to finish a vast and awful task. Compensation for security, the water shortage, and all the rest of our ordeals lay with the people who shared them with us. They were the great, the near-great, the have-to-be-great. They were our friends and neighbors. Their personalities made Los Alamos the wonderful experience it was."[87] Living at Los Alamos during the war combined secrecy with security, conflict with safety, and frivolity with deep contemplation.

To summarize, after the nuclear pioneers arrived at the site in 1943 and settled in for the duration, residents began to develop a community. They faced profound challenges, including wartime shortages, secrecy, isolation, and journeying into the unknown. These inaugural conditions shaped the instant city and the families who lived there. Partly due to the conflict between the army and the civilians, partly due to the intense work in the Tech Area, tension settled over the town, and the urgent drive to contribute to the war effort made Site Y a unique community. Los Alamos's mission, to create an atomic bomb, strained the Tech Area, the town, and the people who worked and lived there. Their success was not preordained, and the community they invented while inventing the bomb created a double legacy—that of a new weapon and of a new way of living.

CHAPTER 2

FISHING IN THE DESERT WITH FAT MAN

CIVIC TENSION, ATOMIC EXPLOSION

"So much depends on chance, even in science."
OTTO FRISCH, *WHAT LITTLE I REMEMBER*

A vibrant community grew around the Tech Area, surrounded by war and secrecy. Women, men, and children developed friendships and created social and civic organizations. The process of living together under trying circumstances, compressed between fences, feverishly working on a top-secret, high-priority project to end the war created this unique community. Sometimes, health problems, water and electrical shortages, poor roads, and harsh weather hampered life on the Hill. Additionally, the initial plans called for the community to hold three hundred people, but eventually almost six thousand lived there. Under all these strains, Site Y could easily have failed to fulfill its mission. Why it did not can be attributed to how the army and the civilians responded to the challenges and secrecy they faced. And to the manner in which the residents of Los Alamos invented a community and an identity amid the confusion and chaos.

Part of the tension at Los Alamos arose from the conflict between the army and civilians at the site. A "Mental Hygiene Survey" of Site Y in August 1944 revealed deep discontent among some of the residents. The report noted: "For the non-athletic, the introvert, the older people, the confirmed city-dweller, and a large part of the enlisted personnel, residence on the area produces unhappiness and dissatisfaction."[1] For the military men and women, "the greatest single problem is the discrepancy between civilian and military life, so that minor points become unduly exaggerated. Both the officer-group and the enlisted personnel have complaints that they feel discrimination in matters of finances, quarters, privilege and freedom."[2] Some soldiers resented guarding the young scientists who had not joined the army to fight overseas.

Army regulations, obeyed to the letter by the army personnel, were at times a springboard for civilian protests. At one point, the survey claimed: "The feeling prevails that the civilians are pampered lest they leave the project while the army group have no such similar opportunity."[3] Even during wartime, civilians enjoyed many allowances and freedoms on the Hill; however, they had their own complaints. On one occasion, Mici Teller (wife of Edward Teller, who helped invent the hydrogen bomb), saw a bulldozer knocking down the ponderosa pine trees near her apartment. She approached the GI operating the machine to protest. He said he had his orders to remove all the trees on that part of the plateau. Teller gathered her neighbors, who circled their chairs around a threatened pine tree, and forced the army to leave some trees standing. Over the next few years, women on the Hill confronted the military and, at times, reversed or altered army policies that hindered the development of a family-oriented town.[4]

To help defuse conflicts between the scientists and the military administrators, a town council began meeting in August 1943. Composed of men from various offices and laboratories, it had little real authority. As Ruth Marshak recalled: "Since it could only make recommendations to the military administration, it was scarcely a potent force. However, it was a necessary outlet for steam when things became too impossible."[5] In effect, the town council served merely as advisors to the military since all decisions by them still had to be approved by the post's commanding officer.

At first, the six representatives were limited to four-month terms because residents knew little about each other and were reluctant to elect unknown people for longer periods. By December 1943, bylaws and election laws were drawn up, and the council chose Richard Feynman as chairman. He delighted in proving his arguments mathematically to bewildered army officials. Laura Fermi considered the town council's role as "teaching the Army democratic manners." The main goal of the advisory town council was to sustain morale and prevent delays to the steady progress of the Tech Area. In small ways, the council did help alleviate strife through council-sponsored projects such as the community radio station, a public library, and, allied with the Parent-Teacher Association, neighborhood playgrounds.[6]

More importantly, the Monday night town council meetings at Fuller Lodge provided both an outlet for civilians as they publically vented their frustrations and a forum where change could happen. Health concerns, inadequate housing, prices and quality of commissary food, better food at the mess halls, male visitors to women's dormitories in the evenings, and other issues provoked heated exchanges between military representatives and civilians. One of the most contentious items concerned the commissary. Run by the army, the post commissary sold the food for Site Y. Even though General Groves balked at spending money to improve the post, he insisted on an abundance of food to keep up morale. The post commanding officer, Colonel Whitney Ashbridge, tried to oblige, and enlarged the commissary ten times during the war. Nonetheless, problems surfaced. Wilted but high-priced vegetables raised the ire of many commissary patrons. The post quartermaster at Los Alamos procured the perishables from Texas and blamed the railroads and lack of refrigerated cars for the poor quality of the produce. Acrimonious debate erupted in the council meetings concerning the poor produce until Bencés Gonzáles, who had grown up on the plateau and ran the vegetable and milk sections of the commissary, suggested that better produce could be obtained locally. The town council endorsed his proposal, Ashbridge approved it, and fresh vegetables from New Mexican farms appeared.[7]

Colonel Ashbridge, overworked by the rapid expansion of Los Alamos, suffered a heart attack soon after the fight over the produce, and left the post. When Colonel Gerald Tyler arrived on the Hill in November 1944 as the new commanding officer, Groves cautioned him not to allow "living conditions, family problems, or anything else" to interfere with making the Gadget. Groves warned Tyler that "the scientists detest the uniform" and would make his life "a hell on earth."[8] Tyler, who had just overseen the construction of the Alaskan Highway, tried to defuse civilian anger by distracting the town council with statistics about wartime conditions elsewhere and promised to give the council prior notice of any impending changes at the post.

After housing and commissary concerns, schools attracted the most attention from families at Site Y. From the beginning, civilian residents and military administrators insisted on good schools. Realizing that appeals to patriotism might not reconcile parents to a mediocre school system, officials attempted to create an attractive, even superior educational institution. Groves objected, citing the costs, but his concerns were ignored. Where Groves planned a two-story temporary building, Central School was a one-story facility of more durable construction. One wing of the school held four elementary classrooms, and the other wing held four more classrooms for the middle and high school students. Los Alamos resident and community chronicler Bernice Brode claimed that it "was the only super-building on the mesa. . . . The school was modern and exceedingly well built to last 100 years."[9] As punishment for building the school contrary to his orders, Groves relieved the Army Corps area engineer, Major Sheperd, from his post. That Los Alamos had such an extravagant building was partly due to Captain William (Deak) Parsons, school board president and associate director of the lab. "I insisted on an up-to-date plant," he explained to Eleanor Jette. "Both our girls are in this school." Dr. Walter W. Cook, brought in from Minnesota to design the school system, said, "We certainly got all possible help and cooperation from Captain Parsons. . . . He was a life saver." But the building exceeded Groves's resolution to keep things inexpensive. On a tour of the finished

Central School lay just north of Ashley Pond and the Tech Area. Accommodating all grades at first, it quickly grew overcrowded and was replaced by other elementary, junior, and senior high schools after the war. Courtesy of Los Alamos National Laboratory Archives.

school, he threatened: "I'll hold you personally responsible for this, Parsons." As a navy officer, Parsons was not overly worried about the intimidation coming from the army general and continued to serve in key positions at the site.[10]

Despite Groves's grousing, Oppenheimer knew that a superior school would help recruit scientific staff. Town residents viewed the school as a unique opportunity to create an exceptional facility for gifted children—a "super school with super children of super parents, all adding up to a super education."[11] For Bernice Brode and many other people on the Hill, inventing this super school "was a chance of a lifetime to put our own ideas on education into practice."[12] Due to the abundance of advanced degrees at the laboratory, school officials assumed experts could be found to teach anything. However, this educational utopia failed to materialize.

Several difficulties surfaced quickly. At first, few schoolchildren lived at Site Y since the majority of the project's residents were under thirty. In the fall of 1943, when Central School opened, no official census was taken, but less than one hundred students attended elementary school while approximately forty went to high school. Over the next two years, a massive influx of new families swelled the school's population. From an attendance of less than 140 in 1943, enrollment exploded to over 350 students at Central School by the end of the 1945–1946 school year. A second difficulty emerged because the scientists at the lab had little time to teach at the school as they were caught in the whirlwind at the Tech Area. Not until after the war would members of the lab contribute their scientific talents to the school.[13]

A school is only as good as its teachers. Because of security considerations and housing shortages, the town at first tried to recruit teachers from the people already on the Hill. Wives of the scientific staff also holding advanced degrees included Alice Smith, Betty Inglis, Bernice Brode, Ruth Marshak, and Jane Wilson. They taught during the war, even though they had little formal training for running a classroom. Dorothy Hillhouse was teaching in Santa Fe when she was recruited by Oppenheimer himself. She was hired along with her husband, George, who became head of the meat department at the commissary. In 1943, nine instructors taught at Central School. By the end of 1946, the staff had grown to eighteen grade school teachers and thirteen high school teachers. The average weekly salary for teachers was $72.57. Despite the high expectations for the school, the shortage of good teachers prevented a superior school from developing during the war. The "Mental Hygiene Survey" called the school system adequate, even though some of the teachers were not qualified. However, students benefitted from individualized instruction, and the nursery school ranked better than demonstration Nursery Schools in several universities."[14] Creating a superior educational system continued to fuel family concerns on the Hill.

In addition to struggling to secure qualified teachers, the school tried to provide adequate meeting spaces for its students during the first year. Construction contractor Sundt did not finish the Central School building until the end of September in 1943, so school started late. Missed days were made up with Saturday sessions that fall. The scramble to staff the classrooms resulted in a lot of shuffling of the students. Joan Mark Neary initially attended Mrs. Hillhouse's second-grade class, but after two weeks transferred to Mrs. Shell, who taught in her own living room. In third grade, Joan again had Mrs. Shell as her teacher, this time in a formal classroom at Central School. Bill Jette bounced around even more that first year. He had five different teachers at seven different intervals. The high point for some in the elementary school occurred in 1944–45 when the famous Puebloan potter María Martínez held a demonstration of her art for the students. She hardly spoke as she demonstrated how to make pots by coiling the clay into bowls. Then the children made their own pots, which María took down to the Pueblo of San Ildefonso for firing. Eventually, Popovi Da, her son, brought the finished pots back to the children. Terell Tucker, a student in the school, recalled that visit and thought he learned more from watching María work than from a good deal of his subsequent schooling.[15]

Health concerns afflicted the schoolchildren. An outbreak of lice among the first graders forced boys and girls to get closely cropped haircuts. Bernice Brode later recalled: "My boys looked queer—crew cuts in those days were associated only with prisoners of war." When Mrs. Long, the high school chemistry teacher, died from polio, the school closed temporarily.[16]

The elementary school's difficulties were minor compared to those at the high school. At first, truancy ran rampant among the older students, aided by the army's policy of letting teenagers check out jeeps from the motor pool. After one group of teens pushed a jeep over a cliff, the army judiciously halted the policy. The school situation worsened when its first superintendent, Chalmer Stacey, took one look at the community with its mud and fences and left. By the time Margery Crouch assumed the position of high school principal, the high ideals of creating a super school had faded. As Crouch inspected the school on her first day at work, she looked at the beautiful view of the mountains through a cracked window shot out by one of the teens. A strict disciplinarian, she required "Saturday School" for anyone playing hooky. Within weeks, she had restored order.[17]

Changes in school administration caused confusion among the teachers. During the first three years of its existence, the school had four superintendents. At one point, no one held the position. As Ruth Marshak (who taught third grade) observed, a teacher at Los Alamos might "during the spring semester, . . . find herself a conservative instructor of the fundamentals, while in the fall, she might teach under the most avant-garde methods of progressive education."[18] Due to the revolving door at the superintendent's office, teachers had to be flexible.

During the Manhattan Project, the high school's curriculum lacked consistency. Because of the difficulty of hiring outside teachers, some academic areas were ignored. Ironically, with some of the greatest scientific minds only yards away, the physical sciences suffered most from the lack of qualified teachers. Teachers focused on the social sciences or languages because anyone with a scientific background was quickly recruited to work in the Tech Area. Clearly, as a temporary wartime school at a high-priority, top-secret post, Central School fell short of the initial high expectations. Even though it boasted the best Manhattan Project building at Los Alamos, the school, for the first few years, lacked an adequate faculty to fulfill the utopian dreams.

The site's priority, like the school's, centered on the Tech Area, and families struggled to maintain a semblance of normality in the turbulent times. On the one hand, those who worked in the Tech Area put in long hours with steely determination. On the other hand, most of those residents caught between the fences had to accommodate to the hardships of the site without knowing exactly why they should. And hardships abounded. Cramped quarters, electrical outages, water shortages, overcrowding, army regulations, censorship, stress, isolation from the outside world, secrecy, mud, cold, and wind all dampened enthusiasm for the project. Regarding those at Site Y, the "Mental Hygiene Survey" noted: "The morale of the civilian population is spotty as the community is a highly individualistic group and a number who have been city dwellers find the isolation and necessity of living in such close physical contact with neighbors trying. . . . The minority of poorly-adjusted individuals induce undue turbulence and use indispensability and temperament as a useful weapon to force concessions."[19] Some civilians did use their indispensability to force the army to capitulate to some of their demands. For example, the army offered the following benefits: a flower service that delivered fresh-cut flowers to homes on the Hill, a well-stocked commissary that catered to civilians, and house-cleaning and babysitting services available for many Los Alamosans. Although hardships did occur at Site Y, Los Alamos was privileged as the nucleus of the Manhattan Project, and the army deferred to and even pampered its civilian personnel and their families.

Military personnel, subjected to more stringent discipline and living conditions than the civilians, at times chafed at many of their mundane activities, mindful that fighting raged overseas. Although the WACs assisted military officers as secretaries, drove vehicles back and forth from the Hill to Santa Fe, and operated the telephone switchboard, they also babysat, worked as cashiers at the commissary, and marched elementary schoolgirls around the site for physical education. As the "Mental Hygiene Survey" found: "The WAC contingent presents many problems. . . . The difficulties are chiefly natural expectations in any large group of women of different ages, cultural and educational backgrounds and interests who are forced to live in intimate contact in a routine pattern devoid of excitement."[20] The WACs, like the other military personnel at Los Alamos, grumbled at the discrimination against them and at the privileges that the civilians enjoyed.

Residents did complain about the site, but ample opportunities for fun also existed. First, the outdoors beckoned. People hiked, rode, skied, climbed, camped, fished, hunted, and picnicked during off-times and on Sundays. Fishermen and hunters roamed the canyons and plateaus in search of game. Amateur archaeologists explored the nearby cliff dwellings, and neophyte geologists scoured the hillsides for crystals, ores, and unusual rocks. During the winter, the stream running through Los Alamos Canyon became a popular skating rink. To aid skiing, Ukrainian emigré chemist George Kistiakowsky used plastic explosives to clear runs at nearby Sawyer Hill during the winter of 1944–45.[21]

For those between the fences, social activities also offered release. Clubs of all kinds helped newcomers to get acquainted and allowed residents to relax amid the wartime pressures. The biweekly square-dancing club became one of the most popular. Every other Saturday night, Europeans and eastern seaboard novices do-si-doed alongside midwesterners and westerners who had square-danced since childhood. Square-dancing brought together people from throughout the community as George Hillhouse, the commissary's butcher, called out lively routines. Besides dancing squares, the group also performed polkas, waltzes, and schottisches. A welcome addition to the square-dancing club was Willie Higginbotham, who along with his "Stomach Steinway," or accordion, inspired great hilarity at the dances. As Jean Bacher, a contemporary chronicler of Hill activities, observed: "Square-dancing was one of the few activities which cut through social and intellectual barriers."[22] Despite Bacher's claim of egalitarianism, not everyone was welcomed at these dances.

One Saturday night, several families from the trailer camp near the East Gate joined the festivities. In Brode's account, they were "real hillbillies" who would show "what real hillbilly dancing was like—without the sophisticated adulteration." These families arrived with liquor "in glass jugs along with babies, although we allowed neither babies nor liquor." Actually, Brode had mentioned earlier that beer was a standard refreshment at these parties. One of the hillbilly women said to a hostess: "Where y'all been, dearie, where're keepin' yerselves? Ain't seen non o'youse aroun afore. Real fancy folks y'got here."[23] The grandfather of the clan played a song on his fiddle that "had no tune, no rhythm, and it was, of course, impossible to dance to." Any square that these families joined in on "got so hopelessly balled up, we finally had to stop." Regular attendees left in disgust, and "fights broke out among the newcomers." They knocked down a stovepipe, and broke fixtures in the men's rest room. Then they left. As a consequence, access to future dances was limited and uniformed army personnel kept out "any who looked as if they would be disorderly. We felt rather mean and snooty, but our open door policy had gotten us into trouble."[24] Although square-dancing allowed people from different backgrounds to mingle, this episode illustrates that class friction did occur at Los Alamos.

Other entertainment activities enlivened the site. A community theater was organized on the Hill in the autumn of 1943. A name for the new theater presented a problem as security concerns prevented any words that might specifically identify their geographic location. Thus, the innocuous "Little Theater Group" became the name for the troupe. Over the next two years, the Little Theater Group performed seven plays, packing houses with Kaufman and Hart's classic *You Can't Take It with You*, a military farce titled *Right About Face*, and Noel Coward's *Hay Fever*. During their production of *Arsenic and Old Lace*, Oppenheimer surprised the audience when he appeared as the first corpse, followed by corpses played by Nobel Prize-winner Enrico Fermi, theoretical physicist Hans Bethe, and other men prominent in the Tech Area.[25]

Certainly, social activities helped alleviate the isolation and tension in the community. During Christmas 1943, a group of carolers requisitioned an army truck and driver and cruised the streets singing seasonal favorites. KRS, the community radio station, broadcast performances by local musicians and storytellers; however, to avoid sending out a radio signal that could serve as a homing beacon for enemy aircraft, the programs were broadcast over the power lines. Because of chronic electrical shortages, the site eventually hooked into a supplementary supply from Albuquerque that inadvertently carried KRS into Albuquerque homes. Some of Dorothy McKibbin's Albuquerque friends were puzzled. "They can't imagine where the broadcasts come from and why none of the entertainers have last names. Children's stories read by Betty, newscasts compiled by Bob, and Mozart's piano Sonatas played by Otto have them guessing."[26] To adhere to the security regulations, the KRS radio station used only first names over the airwaves.

For many residents at Los Alamos, weekend parties attracted the greatest interest and a wide variety of such entertainment abounded at Site Y. As Eleanor Jette recalls: "The pioneers of the new and frightening era escaped their tasks with hard play whenever opportunity

Otto Frisch played classical music on the air for KRS, the community radio station. Courtesy of Los Alamos Historical Museum Photo Archives.

offered itself, which was every Saturday night and Sunday." On Saturday nights, elegantly attired couples emerged from clapboard huts, walked along muddy streets past rows of hanging laundry to have dinner with world-renowned scientists and their spouses. Sometimes, Otto Frisch or Edward Teller played classical music on a piano after dessert. Elsewhere on the Hill, dormitory residents would clear out all the furniture from their commons room, mimeograph invitations, and with alcohol brought in from Santa Fe, mix a potent punch in bowls borrowed from the Tech Area. As Bernice Brode recalled: "On Saturdays, we raised whoopie. . . . There was [sic] always too many people, too much noise, and too much liquor."[27] Theater # 2 held dances on Saturday nights, when the big band Keynotes or the combo Sad Sacks played until the early hours.

In 1946, Jean Bacher, wife of Robert Bacher (who helped persuade Oppenheimer to remain a civilian), wrote: "Our parties and athletic activities were a healthy escape from the nervous strain of the great

From left to right, Eric Jette, Charles Critchfield, and J. Robert Oppenheimer socializing at a party in the Big House during the war. Courtesy of Los Alamos Historical Museum Photo Archives.

Project in which we were involved. Without this release in alcohol and fresh air we would have gone mad. As it was, we had a very good time."[28] A more tenebrous appraisal came from Elsie McMillan: "We had parties, yes, once in a while, and I've never drunk so much as [I did] there at the few parties because you had to let off steam, you had to let off this feeling eating your soul, oh God, are we doing right?"[29]

Social networks also provided some relief and support. An informal news and rumor "grapevine" informed inhabitants of events inside and outside the fences, and spread the word when trucks delivered coveted commodities like milk to the commissary. Scientists' wives, who sometimes had known each other from prewar academia, rekindled old friendships. Camaraderie in the face of sacrifice forged new friendships or strengthened existing ones, and many of these relationships continued long after friends left the Hill.[30]

In times like these, people turn to religion. At first, Site Y was an exception to that trend. Wartime conditions hindered the Hill's religious organizations. For the first half-year of operation, the site hosted no organized religious services. In the fall of 1943, five women met in a post movie theater to discuss this lack of organized spiritual observances. They requested permission from the post's commanding officer to allow clergy to visit the town, at least. From fall 1943 to summer 1944, military chaplains from Albuquerque and Santa Fe conducted occasional interdenominational services. A permanent minister, Chaplain Matthew Imrie, arrived in August 1944 to provide full-time pastoring for the community. Imrie, an Episcopal priest who had served overseas for almost three years, joined Los Alamos after recovering from a serious wound received in the South Pacific. The "Mental Hygiene Survey" enthusiastically endorsed him, finding him to be "an unusually alert, broad-minded sympathetic man, with good understanding and a keen, healthy sense of responsibility for the community. Because of his harrowing overseas' experience, he is chiefly interested in the military personnel and inclined toward impatience with the complaints of the civilians."[31] Though particularly attuned to GIs, Imrie served all of the Christian faithful on the Hill.

With no permanent religious facility, Imrie held services in unusual places. Theater # 2 hosted most of the Sunday meetings, but Theater # 1 and the Central School also were utilized. When Theater # 2 accommodated dances on Saturday night, the hall reeked of stale beer and cigarettes during the next morning's religious services. The wooden benches also tested the faithful. For some, they got harder the longer the sermon.[32]

Los Alamos also hosted Jewish observances. When a small group began holding meetings in Hebrew on the Hill in September 1944, they had trouble keeping observances, especially dietary practices. Finding appropriate foods at local stores proved impossible, and so friends and family in the East sent supplies like matzo meal and kosher chickens for Seder. Despite the difficulties, the Jewish faithful on the Hill celebrated holidays such as Passover, Hanukkah, and Rosh Hashanah.[33]

Like the contentious town council meetings or the struggle in building the school, the establishment of organized religion at Project Y was a complex dance between the army and the civilians. Although the spirit was willing, the bureaucracy on the Hill was not. The army, worried about the expenses of building additional facilities, reluctantly provided for religious observances. Consequently, women on the Hill led a grassroots effort to organize religious services in spite of the army's opposition. And they were successful. In numerous episodes at Site Y, vocal civilians contested the army's policies, and at times, the army changed its position when so challenged. Granted, many of these community issues seemed unimportant compared to the savage fighting going on overseas. Perhaps the occasional protests by the civilians showed their resistance to the silence or perhaps they merely expressed the tensions and frustrations many felt at Los Alamos.

Whatever was at stake—town meetings or church services or fresher vegetables—the army often relaxed its regulations to quell rebellion among the ranks of the civilians. Far from succumbing to silence, some people on the Hill vocally registered their reaction to the tension at Los Alamos. As Laura Fermi explained, Hill residents were "high-strung because the altitude affected us, because our men worked long hours under unrelenting pressure; high-strung because we were too many of a kind, too close together, too unavoidable even during relaxation hours, and we were all crack pots; high-strung because we felt powerless under strange circumstances, irked by minor annoyances that we blamed on the Army and that drove us to unreasonable and pointless rebellion."[34] Granted, some of the army's difficulties derived from the contentious nature of the influential families at the site; however, many serious problems also arose from the residential areas that housed the working-class families.

For the families of nonscientific service personnel, living at the site presented just as many if not more difficulties than it did for the scientific residents. Many of these families lived on the east side of town in overcrowded trailer and hutment parks, which resembled urban slums. Children played in muddy streets, and community restrooms sometimes served too many families. One camp with eighty-three trailers had only one latrine. Because of inadequate sewage lines, raw

Trailer parks and hutment areas housed many residents. The square building
in the center is a communal bathroom. Courtesy of Los Alamos National
Laboratory Archives.

waste sometimes spilled onto the ground. As a result, Eleanor Jette
was fearful of an epidemic in the trailer camps near the East Gate.
With Chaplain Imrie's help, she brought the army's attention to the
problems of sanitation and overcrowding.[35]

Housing for service personnel remained one of the biggest head-
aches. Since scientific families received the best residences and technical and military families the next best, families of the construction
and maintenance crews often lived in the worst accommodations on
the Hill. Many of the service personnel came from the region and
were Hispanic. At one point, the Housing Office ran out of units to
assign to the scientists and their families. To free up more housing
for the scientists' families, the army considered moving the families
of the Hispanic workers into one-room residences in the trailer and
hutment parks. Jette's contemporary account of the crisis noted: "The
administration says that the Spanish-American laborers in the apartments live with their families in only one or two rooms and don't

understand modern sanitary facilities. [It] say[s] this type of housing is adequate for them."[36] Faced with the official attitude that Hispanics would be content with substandard housing, the politically astute Hispanics, led by Bencés Gonzáles, threatened to write their congressmen. The mere whisper of a congressional investigation about Los Alamos forced the army to alter its plans, and the military joined portable huts together to make two- and three-bedroom dwellings for workers.[37]

Wartime Los Alamos had a definite social structure. "Los Alamos was not a casteless society," Ruth Marshak observed. "Lines were drawn principally, not on wealth, family, or even age, but on the position one's husband held in the Laboratory."[38] One's position at the lab depended on higher education and advanced degrees, which excluded the working class and almost all non-Anglos. Thus, social stratification at Project Y centered on educational status, and because of the elite nature of graduate degrees in science and engineering, also revolved around class and ethnic divisions. With the army assigning housing according to one's position of employment at the lab, residential areas reflected a de facto discrimination. Where one lived told everyone what one did on the Hill. Neighborhood designation became shorthand for whether one worked in a scientific/administrative capacity or in a service position.[39]

Two-tier in class structure, Site Y was also multiethnic. Anglo personnel, European emigré scientists, local Hispanics, and American Indians all contributed to the operation of the town. Men from the neighboring pueblos of San Ildefonso, Santa Clara, San Juan, and Pojoaque worked as carpenters, furnace stokers, and janitors, as well as in other service jobs. Local men, such as Popovi Da, assisted lab scientists like Kenneth Bainbridge (who had disassembled his cyclotron at Harvard and brought it with him to New Mexico). But the majority of American Indian and Hispanic personnel toiled in service positions.[40]

American Indian women also contributed to the Manhattan Project. In May 1943, the post administration established a maid service using women from the neighboring pueblos. The administration hoped this would free up the town's wives and mothers to work in the

Tech Area. Maids also provided temporary assistance for families with new babies. Six days a week, Puebloan women boarded army trucks and buses in the valley and rode up the hill to work. Their workday started at the Maid Service Bureau in a building near the water tower where the day's work assignments were posted. Anita Martínez, wife of Popovi Da, helped recruit and organize the maids. The Puebloan women earned three dollars per day. During the summer, as many as one hundred women worked as domestics, but in the winter and during feast and saints' days, the number dropped dramatically because of inclement weather or commitments to the religious observances at the pueblos. At the end of the workday, many Puebloan women drank Cokes at the post exchange or shopped for groceries at the commissary before taking the buses back to their homes. Friendships emerged between some of the Indian and Anglo women, and the absence of maids on the feast days was often compensated for with invitations to the dances at the pueblos.[41]

Eventually, the Maid Service created a priority system that allocated the sometimes short supply of maids. As a result, full-time working mothers received full-time help. For example, Ethel Froman, the pharmacist at the hospital with two children at home, had the highest priority. Next came women with newborns, who welcomed the full-time help for their first two weeks at home. Part-time working mothers came next on the priority list, and women with large families after that.[42]

For some residents, this was their first contact with American Indians. As Bernice Brode recalled: "Each morning, except Sundays, as we sat at breakfast, one of the sights on the road was groups of Indian women coming slowly down from the Water Tower to our houses. They dressed in Pueblo fashion, short, loose, colorful mantas, tied with a woven belt, high deerskin wrapped boots, or just plain stout walking shoes; gay shawls over the head and shoulders, and wearing enough turquoise jewelry to stock a trading post. All of them, young and old, had a serene dignity, and they were more guests than servants."[43] Perhaps, with their admirable demeanor, they appeared to Brode to be more guests than servants, but the ancestors of these American Indians had roamed the Pajarito Plateau for centuries. They were more permanent residents of the region than even Bencés Gonzáles. In truth, the atomic immigrants to Los Alamos were the guests.

With Puebloans, Hispanics, Europeans, and people from throughout the United States in residence, the town of Los Alamos contained a multifarious mixture of traditional and modern. Without the cooperation of all the people who worked there, the project might have disintegrated into Babelian chaos. Instead, the people at Site Y found a common language through codes and code-switching, which enabled them to combat chaos and work together to end the war. That end came in the summer of 1945.

During the spring of 1945, the pace at Site Y quickened, and the tension mounted. Work for many became more frantic, and many of the staff disappeared into the desert for weeks at a time. With renowned scientists and the military's top brass visiting and with an increased pace of activity in the Tech Area, the grapevine whispered that something big was afoot. Early in the summer, Oppenheimer sent a coded invitation to Arthur Compton, director of the Met Lab in Chicago, where the first nuclear chain reaction occurred. He wrote: "Anytime after the 15th [of July] would be good for our fishing trip. Because we are not certain of the weather, we may be delayed several days. As we do not have enough sleeping bags to go around, we ask you please not to bring anyone with you."[44] Unable to break away from his own work, Compton declined the invitation but added: "Best luck to catch the big one." Atomic anglers headed into the desert to go fishin'.

Two hundreds miles south of Los Alamos lay one of the most inhospitable stretches of desert in the United States. Called the Jornada del Muerto (Journey of the Dead Man) by travelers along the Camino Real in Spanish colonial days, the area was sparsely populated with desert ranchers. During the war, the Jornada was used by bombing crews from the nearby Alamagordo Air Base as they prepared for overseas assignments. Site Y chose the Jornada del Muerto in August 1944 for its test of the Gadget, and the construction of a base camp was completed by December 1944. The physicist Kenneth T. Bainbridge had assumed the job of overseeing all on-site preparations for the test earlier that spring. The actual naming of the site as "Trinity" is shrouded in atomic folklore. Some attribute it to Oppenheimer's reading of John Donne's poem "Hymne to God My God, in My Sicknesse" or to his interest in Hindu religion; others to a nearby turquoise mine; and still others to the nearest railroad siding called "Pope's Landing."[45]

Obviously, as the site of the world's first nuclear explosion, Trinity attracted more than just military attention. Six scientific groups set up experiments to monitor the blast. These groups measured the implosion, energy release, blast damage, general phenomena, radiation, and meteorology. High-speed cameras, invented at Los Alamos specifically for the test, photographed more than eight thousand frames per second. Oscilloscopes, ionization chambers, sulphur threshold detectors, quartz piezoelectric gauges, seismographs, and numerous other gauges and equipment dotted the test site connected by five hundred miles of cables and wires to document all of the effects of the blast. Air-borne measurements from barrage-balloons and observation planes also added to the information about the explosion.[46]

Preparations for monitoring the radiation released from the explosion began in the spring of 1945. Initial discussions centered around the dangers to people in the immediate vicinity, specifically to laboratory personnel. Radiation fallout was not an original worry; however, medical director Stafford Warren, along with physicists Joseph O. Hirschfelder and John L. Magee, insisted that General Groves heed the threat from the fallout cloud. Although planning for the radioactive danger from the fallout took backseat to the military and political timing of the test, Warren, Nolan, and Hempelmann did organize a monitoring team to track the cloud and possibly evacuate any civilians downwind from the blast.[47]

The "Gadget" tested at Trinity was an implosion device of the Fat Man series. Its exterior consisted of bolted metal plates, shaped like a bathysphere, festooned with junction boxes and electrical wires woven around its outside like Medusa's hair. Inside, an intricate assembly of nearly one hundred high-explosive wedges encircled a plutonium core. In order to detonate, the conventional explosives had to fire within milliseconds of each other to compress consistently the plutonium into a critical mass. It took several days to assemble all the components, hoist the Gadget to the top of the one-hundred-foot test tower, and connect all the wires. During the night of July 15, summer thunderstorms swept the Jornada, and nervous men wondered whether a lightning strike would prematurely set off the atomic age. Political pressure to detonate the Gadget was intense from President Harry Truman as he met with Josef Stalin and Winston Churchill at Potsdam, Germany, during this time to chart the end of the war with Japan and map the postwar world.[48]

Whether the Gadget actually would implode remained a contested topic. Some scientists at Trinity organized a gambling pool, placing bets on the magnitude of the bomb if and when it detonated. When Ed McMillan left Los Alamos for Trinity, he told Elsie, his wife: "We ourselves are not absolutely certain what will happen. In spite of calculations, we are going into the unknown. We know there are three possibilities. One, that we all [may] be blown to bits if it is more powerful than we expect. Two, it may be a complete dud. Three, it may, as we hope, be a success, we pray without loss of any life."[49]

Leon Fisher, Phyllis's husband, overheard colleagues speculating on the possibility of an out-of-control chain reaction that would set the atmosphere on fire. He declined an opportunity to attend Trinity and, instead, he took his family on a camping trip the evening of July 15, as far away from the Trinity site as he could go. He spent an anxious night while his wife and son slept peacefully under the stars.[50] His fear was not of radioactive fallout, since prevailing winds ran from west to east. Fisher was afraid that the explosion might be bigger than anticipated and might even ignite the atmosphere.

At Trinity, few slept for very long the night before the test. Three observation shelters—one north, one south, and one west of Ground Zero—held the closest observers at ten thousand yards (almost six miles) away. McDonald's Ranch House, the site's base camp, housed additional personnel ten miles away to the southwest. All over the site, men nervously bided their time. An additional group of scientists, military officers, and VIPs waited at Compañia Hill, twenty miles to the north. Only security and radiological monitoring personnel were

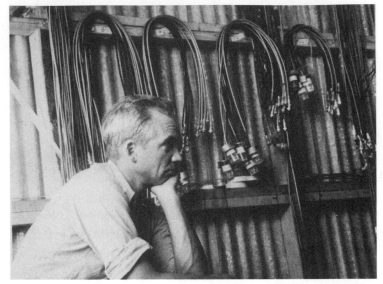

Norris Bradbury oversaw the assembly of Fat Man on top of the tower at Trinity the day before the detonation. Courtesy of Los Alamos Historical Museum Photo Archives.

assigned east of the tower, since they might be in the path of any radioactive fallout cloud.[51]

The test, scheduled for 4 A.M. on July 16, was postponed until 5:30 A.M. because of thunderstorms in the area. The last men to leave the tower departed at 5:05 A.M. The world's first countdown began twenty minutes before the scheduled blast. As the countdown approached zero, a local radio station intruded on the same wave length the site was using. Strains of Tchaikovsky's *Nutcracker Suite* intermixed with the final seconds of countdown.[52]

At 5:29:45 A.M., the Gadget imploded. The flash from the blast lit up the sky and was seen by people in three states. Trinity personnel had been warned not to look at the explosion since they might be blinded by the flash. Nonetheless, the ever inquisitive Richard Feynman covered one eye and looked at the fireball. He was blinded in that eye for several days. After the flash, a shock wave rocked the Jornada. Anyone standing was knocked to the ground, and a seismol-

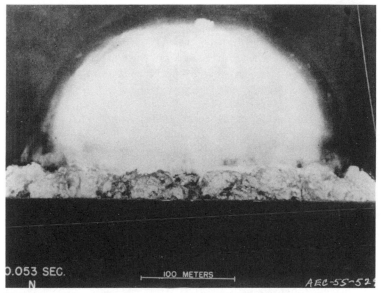

0.053 SEC.

N

100 METERS

AEC-55-52

This view of the world's first atomic bomb explosion at Trinity, July 16, 1945, was photographed .053 seconds after detonation. Courtesy of National Archives II, College Park, Md.

ogist fifty miles away remarked that it felt like an earthquake. Despite the visual violence of the blast, silence reigned for thirty seconds at the observation posts ten thousand yards away. Then, the sound wave brought the crack and roar of the detonation that engulfed the observers and bounced between the mountains surrounding the plain. Eye-witnesses at Compañia Hill heard nothing for ninety seconds as they watched the mushroom cloud rise, and then the thunder shook them. Some observers later recalled that they heard nothing at all because they were so overwhelmed by the sight of the rising cloud.[53]

Many participants of the first atomic explosion have tried to describe the fireball. One of the better attempts came from Joan Hinton, a graduate student in physics from Wisconsin who worked on the nuclear reactor at Los Alamos. She observed the blast from a hill twenty-five miles to the south:

It was like being at the bottom of an ocean of light. We were bathed in it from all directions. The light withdrew into the bomb as if the bomb

69

sucked it up. Then it turned purple and blue and went up and up and up. We were still talking in whispers when the cloud reached the level where it was struck by the rising sunlight so it cleared out the natural clouds. We saw a cloud that was dark and red at the bottom and daylight on the top. Then suddenly the sound reached us. It was very sharp and rumbled and all the mountains were rumbling with it.[54]

William L. Laurence, a special correspondent from the *New York Times* brought in by General Groves to witness the test, wrote this: "Up it went, a great ball of fire about a mile in diameter, changing colors as it kept shooting upward, from deep purple to orange, expanding, growing bigger, rising as it was expanding, an elemental force freed from its bonds after being chained for billions of years."[55]

Reactions of the other eyewitnesses varied. Groves's assistant, Colonel Thomas Farrell, gasped: "Jesus Christ! The long hairs have let it get away from them."[56] Otto Frisch, looking at the developing mushroom cloud, thought of a "red hot elephant balanced on its trunk."[57] Rudolf Peierls had mixed emotions—he was both awed and impressed by the violence of the blast. He was also relieved that the Gadget worked.[58] Perhaps Oppenheimer was the most relieved of everyone. Around 6:30 A.M., he commented: "My faith in the human mind has been somewhat restored."[59] His relief was also tempered by worry. Sometime during that morning, Oppenheimer recalled Hindu scripture from the *Bhagavad Gita*: "I am become Death, the destroyer of worlds."[60] In the Hindu religion, the god Shiva is eternally poised to destroy the Earth but, up to now, has always relented due to a benevolent action by one of his human devotees. Oppenheimer knew thoroughly the science and the physics behind the explosion, but he had to code-switch to Hinduism to fully express what he had unleashed in the desert that morning.

Other observers in addition to Farrell and Oppenheimer had misgivings. James Tuck of the British Mission exclaimed: "What have we done?"[61] Chemist George Kistiakowsky reflected "that at the end of the world—in the last millisecond of the earth's existence—the last men will see what we saw."[62] Test director Kenneth Bainbridge searched out Oppenheimer to congratulate him by stating: "Well, now we're all sons of bitches."[63] Victor Weisskopf summed it up for many at Trinity: "Our first feeling was one of elation, then we realized we were tired, and then we were worried."[64]

At Los Alamos, 180 miles to the north, some of the residents, alerted to the coming climax by their work or by their husbands or just from rumors, stayed up all night on July 15 and waited. On the Hill, Elsie McMillan and Lois Bradbury shared coffee to keep awake in their vigil. At 5:30 A.M. on July 16, a bright flash of light flooded into the baby's south-facing bedroom at the McMillan home, and they knew something had happened. Having heard that the culmination of the project would occur on July 16 in the desert in the south, Dorothy McKibbin drove from Santa Fe to the top of the Sandia Mountains east of Albuquerque in the rain. As she looked south, a full quarter of the sky lit up, and the leaves around her shone like gold. She felt awe at the sight and knew that the world had changed forever. Eric Jette left Eleanor, his wife, with this advice. "You might see something if you stay up all night." From her house, she beheld a sun rise at 5:30 A.M.—in the south.[65]

Another group of residents gathered at the south end of the Pajarito Plateau with a short-wave radio and listened to transmissions from the observation planes. They also saw a sun rise at 5:30 and then quickly set. Square-dance caller George Hillhouse knew something big was about to happen as well. He sent Dorothy and Jean, his daughter, away for safety to Kansas right before the event. After the day the sun rose twice, he sent a postcard to his vacationing wife and child, telling them: "The cat screamed all night the night you left." Jean was perplexed. They did not have a cat. She did not know that this was a coded signal telling her mother that it was safe to return to the Hill.[66]

A momentous event had indeed occurred before dawn on July 16th. Whether the flash meant success or failure, many people who remained on the Hill worried until an Albuquerque radio station broadcast a news bulletin at noon that an ammunition dump had exploded near Alamogordo. This prearranged news release, like the note about Hillhouse's cat, meant that all had gone well. Beginning in the early evening, men from Trinity straggled back into town. Congratulations spread throughout the community as the weary staff returned. Physicist Stanislaw Ulam, who had stayed at Los Alamos, watched the buses and cars arrive back on the Hill. Looking at them, he thought: "You could tell at once they had a strange experience. You could see it on their faces. I saw that something very grave and strong had happened to their whole outlook on the future."[67] The meaning of that experience would become a contested topic for those who worked at Los Alamos as well as for the nuclear future.

Even Peggy Pond Church, who would write about Los Alamos in *The House at Otowi Bridge*, experienced something unusual early in the morning on July 16. After being evicted from the Pajarito Plateau by the Manhattan Project in 1943, Ashley Pond had moved his family to Taos. Before dawn on July 16, 1945, Peggy woke from a disturbing dream with a deep sense of foreboding. In her dream, a strange wind arose that sucked a carpet sweeper from her hands and blew a group of Indians off their horses. Trees were shattered and buildings destroyed by the wind. Pond later wrote: "It was no ordinary wind but a great cosmic power unleashed that men could not deal with and that haunted me with its suggestions of doom."[68] She went outside and looked at the familiar sky of stars. And then she returned to her house, and for the first time since she moved to Taos, she locked her doors.

The explosion at Trinity raised the curtain of secrecy between the fences at Los Alamos. With the success of Trinity and an expected quick end to the war, security eased, and lips loosened. Phyllis Fisher likened it to a dam bursting: "Fever-pitch excitement held sway on our hill, as people went wild with the release of long-suppressed emotions. Suddenly, everyone was talking to everyone."[69] Husbands told wives, friends confided in friends, and if nothing else, euphoria blew away the tension of the site like an afternoon thunderstorm sweeping away the desert heat. The summer thunderstorms in the desert that bring life also bring flash floods and lightning-caused wildfires. Like such a storm, Trinity brought relief but also apprehension about the aftermath.

Between Trinity and Hiroshima three weeks later, moods swung radically on the Hill. Fisher remembered jubilation "mixed with profound concern." In the midst of celebration, anxiety dogged some Hill residents. But the overwhelming emotions were relief with the success of the project and joy at the pending victory over Japan.[70]

The Gadget worked. Although groups of scientists (especially from the Met Lab) petitioned Groves not to use the bomb in combat, the decision was out of the scientists' hands. At the time, the majority of the Manhattan Project's scientists had few qualms about using the device to end the war. Parts of the bombs were already en route to Tinian Island, which lay fifteen hundred miles south of Japan, in preparation for the atomic bombing of the home islands. On July 26, the ill-fated *USS Indianapolis* delivered the nuclear components of Little Boy (the ship was sunk several days later by a Japanese submarine with great loss of life). On July 28 and 29, more parts arrived by air to Tinian. Soon after Trinity, Captain Parsons flew to Tinian and joined more than fifty other men from Los Alamos working on assembling the devices. Another group, the Army Air Corps' 509th Composite Group, had trained since September 1944 to drop the massive atomic bombs.

Discussions on which Japanese cities to target had taken place at Los Alamos and Washington, D.C., since May. General Groves listed the criteria for target selection as cities that were military headquarters or had troop concentrations, were centers of war production, and were sites whose destruction "would most adversely affect the will of the Japanese people to continue the war." Additionally, in order to assess adequately the effects of the bombs, the target cities should have escaped previous bombing raids by the army. Since early spring, General Curtis Le May's Twenty-first Bomber Command had devastated most of Japan's major cities.[71]

Before leaving for the Potsdam conference, President Truman had given final approval of the atomic bombing of Japan. As Deak Parsons later recalled: "All orders necessary for carrying out the atomic missions had arrived in Guam well ahead of the active material."[72] With approval from Truman, Little Boy was loaded onto the *Enola Gay*, a specially modified B-29 Superfortress, late on August 5, 1945. Once the bomb was aboard, Brigadier General T. F. Farrell, Groves's deputy, signed a receipt for a "projectile unit containing [censored] kilograms of enriched tubealloy at an average concentration of [censored]." Immediately below this description, Farrell wrote: "The above materials were carried by Parsons, Tibbets & Co. to Hiroshito as part of 'Doomsday' leaving Tinian. . . ."[73]

The *Enola Gay* took off at 2:45 A.M. on August 6 and flew to Japan. At 8:15:17 A.M. Hiroshima time (9:15 Tinian time), Little Boy cleared *Enola Gay*'s bomb bay doors and fell toward the city. Forty-five seconds later, Little Boy exploded at 1,900 feet above Hiroshima. The *Enola Gay* and two other accompanying B-29s circled the city, taking pictures and observing the cloud, which quickly rose to over 40,000 feet. They lost sight of the mushroom cloud at 10:41 A.M. when they were 363 miles away from Hiroshima. Navy Captain William Parsons, who had headed the Ordnance Division and was an associate director at Los Alamos and who rode on the *Enola Gay* to arm Little Boy after take-off, wrote on Farrell's receipt: "I certify that the above material was expended to the city of Hiroshima, Japan at 0915 6 August."[74]

On August 6, 1945, at 9 A.M. Mountain War Time, a press release from the White House announced the atomic bombing of Hiroshima. Hill residents, electrified by the announcement, gathered around radios and waited for Santa Fe's afternoon daily, the *New Mexican*, to arrive. Its headlines told all: "Los Alamos Secrets Disclosed by Truman; Atomic Bombs Drop on Japan." The stories were compiled from governmental press releases, including the official announcement from President Truman as well as one prepared in Los Alamos. The front page burst with news about the destruction of Hiroshima by a single bomb with the force of twenty thousand tons of TNT. The bomb exploded with the equivalent of "2,000 times the power of the Great Grand-Slammers dropped on Germany," and this "one bomb pack[ed] the wallop of the bomb loads of 2,000 Superforts [B-29 bombers]."[75] Although reconnaissance planes could not immediately see through the dense cloud of dust and smoke that covered Hiroshima, the damage was obvious.

Los Alamos figured prominently in the stories about the nuclear attack on Japan. Hill residents read about the Tech Area and their community, and some found out for the first time the true purpose of their efforts. On the same front pages of the newspapers, sometimes in the same articles that reported the atomic chaos in Japan, Los Alamos was described with population figures, building descriptions, social activities, and profiles of key men at Site Y. This information did not come from inquisitive reporters since Los Alamos remained closed to outsiders. The stories came from the Manhattan Engineering District, prepared ahead of time for news wire distribution. Overnight, Los Alamos lost its secrecy and isolation and burst onto the national and international scene. Through information released by Project Y and printed in the papers around the world, the secrecy partially lifted, and people outside of the fence discovered Los Alamos.[76]

For two years, strange activities emanating from the Hill had mystified Santa Feans. On August 6, a *New Mexican* reporter wrote: "There were lights to be seen miles away; there were days when fires raged and smoked [*sic*] billowed in the mountains and always the mysterious explosions."[77] But local reporters and editors wrote nothing about the site: "The taboo on the mention of Los Alamos was final, complete, and until today [August 6, 1945], irrevocable and not susceptible to any exceptions whatsoever." Now, the *New Mexican* wrote: "A whole social world existed in nowhere in which people were married and babies born nowhere. People died in a vacuum, autos and trucks crashed in a vacuum and the M.P.'s baseball team materialized out of a vacuum, trained in a vacuum and after their games at Fort Marcy Park [in Santa Fe], returned to the vacuum."[78] Like nature, humans abhor a vacuum. On August 6, with the secrecy breached, the demand for news about Los Alamos so overwhelmed the *New Mexican* that its printing press malfunctioned. A plane rushed to Albuquerque for a replacement part, and once the press was repaired, reprints of the first two pages of the August 6 edition were issued to satisfy the public's clamor for news about Hiroshima and Los Alamos. All of the stories of substance about the atomic bomb came from preconstructed press releases supplied by the Manhattan Engineering District.[79]

Residents of Los Alamos gained a perspective about Hiroshima not found in the usual media. Ellen Reid recalled hearing a recording of the approach, release, and detonation of the Hiroshima bomb broadcast over radio station KRS. Since her family had no radio in their home, her father shepherded them into the car where they listened to the plane and men as they flew to Hiroshima, the countdown and release of the bomb, the airplane's noises as it raced away, and the men exclaiming: "There's the cloud. There's the mushroom cloud."[80] Unfortunately, that recording has been lost.

Three days later, a Fat Man bomb fell on Japan. By chance, the primary target, the port city of Kokura, was obscured by ground haze and smoke, so *Bock's Car*, the B-29 carrying the bomb, diverted to Nagasaki. At 11:50 A.M. on August 9, the plutonium implosion device was released. The *Bock's Car's* flight log noted with supreme understatement: "The bomb functioned normally in all respects."[81] The combined punch of the two atomic bombs forced the Japanese government to concede defeat. World War II ended on August 10 when Japan accepted the Allied surrender terms. On September 2, 1945, representatives of the Japanese government and armed forces signed the instrument of capitulation aboard the *USS Missouri*. With the signing of the peace treaty, the islands of Japan opened up to Allied forces. Shortly thereafter, a team from Los Alamos headed to Hiroshima and Nagasaki to study the effects of the nuclear explosions on these communities.

On August 9, 1945, in the same newspaper stories reporting a second atomic bombing of Japan, fuller details about the destruction of Hiroshima surfaced. A 4.1-square-mile area (about 60 percent) of Hiroshima was leveled. Radio Tokyo broadcast that "practically every living thing there was annihilated." In truth, people survived the attack; however, casualties were heavy. Later estimates put the number of dead from the Hiroshima bomb between 70,000 and 80,000, with an equal number of people injured, out of a population of approximately 250,000.[82] The Japanese will to war was broken. On August 10, the United States received a surrender offer from Japan.

Like the celebrations after Trinity, the post-Hiroshima exuberance was tempered by apprehension. Los Alamos had opened Pandora's Box. Granted, the war was over, but an awesome power had been released, and few people had thought through the implications. Laura Fermi, wife of Nobel Prize winner Enrico Fermi, wrote in 1951: "Perhaps because they [the men] could not even mention the word 'atomic' in front of us, perhaps because they were so much absorbed in their tasks that they had little time and desire for general speculation . . . to us wives they appeared politically aloof and unconcerned with the problems that their discoveries might create."[83] Phyllis Fisher later reflected that "we all were simultaneously laughing and crying."[84] Oppenheimer himself expressed his troubled state of mind in a letter on August 26 to a friend, Herbert Smith: "You will believe that this undertaking has not been without misgivings; they are heavy on us today, when the future, which has so many elements of high promise, is yet only a stone's throw from despair."[85] Indeed, sober reflections in the midst of celebrations occurred throughout the country. On August 12, radio newsman Edward R. Murrow commented: "Seldom if ever has a war ended leaving the victors with such a sense of uncertainty and fear, with such a realization that the future is obscure and that survival is not assured."[86]

In spite of misgivings, most Americans celebrated the bombing with an overwhelming joy. Site Y was no different as parties rocked Los Alamos. With the announcement of the atomic bombing of Hiroshima, impromptu celebrations rang out on the Hill. Kim Manley remembered: "We had a parade. All of the kids in the neighborhood got together and marched around the neighborhood, banging pots and pans and spoons on lids and anything that we could find."[87] Phyllis Fisher wrote home to her mother: "By comparison the excitement on the hill today [August 6, 1945] has put that of July 16 far down on the scale of insane rejoicing."[88] Neighbors and colleagues toasted the end

During the end-of-the-war celebration at the Pueblo of San Ildefonso, those watching the square dancing included Willie Higginbotham (playing the accordion) and Popovi Da, sitting in the middle. Courtesy of Los Alamos Historical Museum Photo Archives.

of the war, social invitations flooded in from Santa Fe for the new celebrities, and a hoe-down was planned with San Ildefonso Pueblo. Popovi Da, in conjunction with the square-dancing club, organized a party at a community building on the pueblo. The San Ildefonsans, accompanied by their chanting drummers, first performed a Comanche war dance. Next, the Hill residents danced four squares, practiced especially for the occasion. Before too long, the Indians joined in on the square-dancing. After a short Coke break, the drums started again, and a serpentine dance snaked through the hall, led by the pueblo's governor. The drumbeats quickened, the dance steps changed and became more intricate, and as the dancers whirled faster and faster, one of the Puebloans jumped up on a table, chanting in time to the drumming: "This is the Atomic Age—this is the Atomic Age."[89] Part of this celebration acknowledged the special bond that had developed between the Hill and the Pueblo of San Ildefonso. Another part illustrated the cultural code-switching that both groups did as they danced and chanted with each other.

A magazine article written about Los Alamos after the war likened the wives of Los Alamos to motorists "lost in a thick Pacific Coast fog. All their efforts had to be concentrated on the white line of their family routine and their community duties. Sooner or later the way would clear and they would reach their destination. [After Hiroshima], the fog lifted, the tension cleared and every man, woman, and child shared the release of now-it-can-be-told."[90] Many did tell their stories.

To the outside world, Los Alamos did exist in a vacuum. After August 6, the public craved news about the atomic city, but with access still denied to reporters, many of the first stories written about Los Alamos came from official army sources. The blank canvas of Site Y began acquiring masterful strokes of detail and color, supplied by the army to slake the public's thirst for information about the site and the creation of the atomic bomb. On August 6 and 7, articles appeared revealing the Trinity test, describing the "Men behind the Atom Bomb," and carrying an assurance from Oppenheimer to the laboratory workers that "the instrument will avert future wars."[91] Thus, hours after the announcement by Truman, front pages across the country carried in-depth stories about the atomic towns and their pioneers.

In the history of the twentieth century, few events rival the atomic bombing of Japan in importance. As President Truman noted in his address to Congress in October 1945: "Never in history has society been confronted with a power so full of potential danger and at the same time so full of promise for the future of man and for the peace of the world."[92] The news accounts coming out of the Manhattan Project focused the world's attention of the culmination of centuries of physics experiments, the ending of World War II, and the dawning of a new age.

These first articles, crafted by the Manhattan Project, began inventing the history of the making of the atomic bomb. It is a contested history. Since August 6, 1945, other people have added their own brush strokes to the canvas to question and negotiate the meaning of atomic enterprises, but the initial stories came from the project itself. These army press releases laid the foundation for future understandings about Los Alamos, but the reality of the town, this town where families had lived for over two years, remained hidden from investigative reporters for years to come. Because of its role in creating the atomic bombs, Los Alamos was a symbol for America's nuclear enterprises, a symbol invented and nurtured by the Manhattan Project's authorities. With World War II over, a Cold War emerged, and nuclear weapons played a dominant role in national and international affairs over the next half-century. Los Alamos was a nucleus of this atomic future.

CHAPTER 3

POSTWAR LOS ALAMOS

EXODUS, NEW GROWTH, AND INVISIBLE DANGER

*"This is the first time in the history of this country
and probably of the world where a community has
sprung up full-fledged, with absolutely no restrictions as to the kind of town they can have."*
CAPTAIN C. L. TYLER, MANAGER, SANTA FE OPERATIONS,
AEC. FROM JOE ALEX MORRIS, "CITIES OF AMERICA: LOS
ALAMOS," *SATURDAY EVENING POST*, DECEMBER 11, 1948

The Gadget ended the war. The two bombs had performed perfectly. Now, men and women around the world left their battlefields and went home. With mission completed, residents began a "Great Exodus" as they returned to their prewar occupations. Many on the Hill wondered how long the army post would remain open, but not everyone wanted to close down the laboratory. Indeed, the marriage of the atom and the bomb, consummated at Los Alamos, enjoyed a lengthy honeymoon with America. The offspring from their union arrived quickly and for the rest of the century, like a brash new kid on the block, swayed the nation's affairs in economics, defense, politics, and culture. In the first year of the new age, many social, political, and military aspects of atomic energy had to be sifted and arranged. Progress at times crawled slowly through the first year of the Atomic Age. Some of the first faltering steps occurred at Los Alamos.

Nuclear enterprises became a growth industry of the postwar years. Embraced by politicians, corporate leaders, doctors, diplomats, and military officials, atomic energy necessitated the creation of a new

branch of the military (the Air Force), revolutionized energy production, and offered new techniques for the diagnosis and treatment of
the body's ills. As the nation sorted out the ramifications of atomic
energy, reports from Japan focused on the potential health hazards
from radiation. On the socially constructed canvas of atomic history,
one of the most contentious topics concerns the effects of radiation on
the human body.

Even before a second atomic bomb exploded over Nagasaki, the
nation's newspapers debated the long-term health effects of radiation
from the atomic bomb. On August 8, 1945, the War Department issued
a statement that "denied reports that areas devastated by the atomic
bomb [would] continue for years to react with a death-dealing radioactivity."[1] Responding to an allegation of long-term, residual radioactive
danger made by Dr. Harold Jacobson of Columbia University, Oppenheimer stated: "There is every reason to believe that there was no
appreciable radioactivity on the ground at Hiroshima and what little
was, decayed very rapidly."[2]

The Associated Press relayed news from a Tokyo radio broadcast
that claimed 480,000 people were "killed, injured or made homeless"
by the two atomic bombs. "The number of dead is mounting," the
report continued, "as many of those who received burns cannot survive their wounds because of the uncanny effects the atomic bomb
produces on the human body."[3] The report stated that at Hiroshima
160,000 people were killed or injured with 200,000 homeless and, at
Nagasaki, casualties equaled 120,000. The Japanese at Hiroshima and
Nagasaki died from many causes, including the radioactivity released
at the moment of radiation. The claims that a mysterious radioactive
disease killed people on the ground worried General Groves.

Groves responded with two initiatives. First, he ordered Colonel
Thomas Farrell, who was still on Tinian Island after having helped
assemble the Hiroshima and Nagasaki bombs, to put together a team of
scientists and military personnel to inspect Hiroshima and Nagasaki.
For the same purpose, he called Colonel Stafford Warren, who was
examining the mesas and canyons downwind from Trinity in New
Mexico. As Warren was searching for hot spots (places where radio-

In this earliest known photograph of the Hiroshima explosion, taken at 11 A.M. on August 6, 1945, survivors are shown seeking help 1.4 miles from Ground Zero. Courtesy of National Archives II, College Park, Md.

activity from the Trinity atomic blast fell out of the mushroom cloud), an orderly drove up and told him that Groves wanted him on the phone. Warren sped back to the base camp and called the general, who asked Warren to go to Japan and help with the survey of Hiroshima and Nagasaki. Warren agreed, rushed back to Los Alamos, and assembled a team to accompany him to Japan. The team left the next day. His party reached Hiroshima on September 8 in six transport planes carrying the survey crew along with emergency supplies. The crew took Geiger counter readings at both Hiroshima and Nagasaki. After the initial survey of the two cities, the team returned to Hiroshima for a more thorough examination.[4]

On a second front, General Groves telephoned Lieutenant Colonel Rea at the Oak Ridge Hospital on August 25 to discuss the effects of radiation on humans. Rea explained to Groves that "as far as radiation is concerned, it isn't anything immediate, it's a prolonged thing. I think these people have, they just got a good thermal burn, that's what it is."[5] Reading from a news story, Groves queried Rea: "This is the thing I wanted to ask you about particularly—'an examination of soldiers working on reconstruction projects [in Hiroshima and Nagasaki] one week after the bombing show that their white corpuscles had diminished by half and [they had] a severe deficiency of red corpuscles'."[6] Rea replied, "Those Jap scientists over there aren't so dumb either and they are making a play on this. . . ." He added, "Anybody with burns, the red count goes down after a while, and the white count may go down too, just from an ordinary burn. I can't get too excited about that."[7] A second conversation occurred that same day:

> Rea: Do you have the report from Col. Warren in here on the New Mexico tests?
> Groves: Yes.
> R: Listing of the blisters, of course, they mention here. . . . They say what I told you about the kilometers, this reference might mean second or third degree burns—I think they give it away right there—what they're referring to.
> G: Yes, I think so. When was that report of Warren's written?
> R: On the first test in May.[8]

The test on May 7, 1945, at the Trinity site was the 100-Ton Test, a trial run for the Fat Man detonation. The 100-Ton Test blew up one hundred tons of TNT, with plastic tubes of radioactive material inserted in the stack of explosives to simulate the radioactivity of a full-scale test.[9] Thus, the report that Groves and Rea depended on referred to a test which did not produce a full-scale radioactive event. Armed with the 100-Ton Test report, Groves publicly attacked the reports of radioactive deaths from Japan, labeling them "pure propaganda."[10]

A few days before Groves called Rea at Oak Ridge, an experiment at Los Alamos went seriously awry. On August 21, 1945, Harry K. Daghlian was working alone in an isolated laboratory at S-Site. Daghlian, twenty-four years old, had graduated from Princeton in 1942 where he taught until he joined the Manhattan Project in November 1943. He assisted in experiments that determined the amount of fissile material needed for an atomic explosion. On that August day, he dropped a block of tamper material onto an almost completed critical assembly, releasing a powerful surge of radiation. A burst of neutrons and ions hit Daghlian and exposed him to a lethal dose of radiation, the first radiation accident at Los Alamos. Daghlian died of acute radiation syndrome on September 15, although the local paper simply noted that he died of "burns received in an industrial accident. . . . Details of the accident and the nature of his death were withheld."[11] So at the same time Groves denied that deaths in Japan resulted from radioactivity, a person at Los Alamos had received a burst of radioactivity similar to that given off by an explosion, without the accompanying thermal and shock wave blasts. And Daghlian died from that exposure.

While Groves held press conferences and Daghlian lay dying, Warren and the Manhattan Project Atomic Bomb Investigation Group surveyed the irradiated landscapes of Japan. Donald Collins, a health physicist with the team, recalled that "our mission was to prove that there was no radioactivity from the bomb."[12] They recorded eyewitness accounts of the explosions that became part of their report: *The Effects of the Atomic Bombs on Hiroshima and Nagasaki*, otherwise known as the *Bombing Survey*.

From the eyewitness accounts, the *Bombing Survey* reported that at the moment of detonation tremendous flashes of blue-white light flooded both target areas, followed by intense heat. An immense shock wave from the blast traveling out from the epicenter at an estimated 280 meters per second crashed into homes and buildings, sending glass, roof tiles, and other pieces of material flying. A white cloud quickly ascended into the heavens while, at ground level, a bluish haze and a purple-brown cloud of dust and smoke obscured the neighborhoods.

The scientists in the report explained that four forms of energy— light, heat, pressure, and radiation—were released when the atomic bombs detonated. Traveling at the speed of light, a complete band of rays, from X- and gamma-rays on one side of the spectrum to the radiant heat of infrared rays on the other side doused the immediate area around Ground Zero. Shock waves followed the invisible rays,

Looking across the devastation at Nagasaki. The remains of the city's Medical College are in the foreground. Courtesy of National Archives II, College Park, Md.

radiating outward. Later estimates for Hiroshima noted that "dissipation of energy [was] believed to have been in the ratio of bomb blast (50%), heat (35%), and radiation (15%)."[13]

The *Bombing Survey* noted that the bombs' effects were both immediate as well as delayed. Buildings blown apart by the shock waves sent debris like shrapnel that killed many people outright. Flash heat ignited the wooden structures, causing hundreds of fires to flare up into firestorms. People within 3,500 feet of ground zero had their clothes torched, "though [the clothes] could quickly be beaten out. . . ."[14] Permanent shadows, created by the radiant heat, were etched into the standing walls, outlining the final posture of those unlucky enough to be caught close to ground zero.

A report later compiled by the Peace Memorial Museum at Hiroshima gave this account of the explosion: "At the height of about 570 meters above ground level, [the bomb] exploded with a terrific detonation in a fire-ball 60 meters in diameter. The temperature of this

A train (center) brought aid to Nagasaki. The pole (foreground center) marks the epicenter of the blast. Courtesy of National Archives II, College Park, Md.

fire-ball, often referred to as a 'miniature sun', is estimated at 300,000 [Centigrade], 1/10,000 of a second after the detonation. The terrific explosion sent reddish-blue or dark-brown flames shooting out against the ground at an astonishing velocity, radioactivating some forty percent of the city area."[15]

Many eyewitness accounts have detailed the human suffering at Hiroshima and Nagasaki. These are representative. A young girl asked her father: "Where is Mother?" "She is dead," her father answered. Then she noticed a five-inch nail sticking in her mother's head. She had died instantly.[16] A five-year-old boy remembered: "Near the bridge there were a whole lot of dead people. There were some who were burned black and died, and there were others with huge burns who died with their skins bursting, and some others who died all stuck full of broken glass."[17] Another young boy recalled: "That day after we escaped and came to Hijiyama Bridge, there were lots of naked people who were so badly burned that their whole body was hanging from them like rags."[18] The report from the Peace Memorial Museum gave this detail of "the terrific heat, which, within 4,000 meters from the hypocenter, burnt the exposed skin, which was then ripped by the following blast."[19]

In the aftermath of the atomic explosion, rescue operations were thwarted by the fires, the vastness of the destruction, and the obliteration of Hiroshima's infrastructure. Philip Morrison, who witnessed Trinity and then helped assemble the bombs on Tinian Island, also accompanied Warren to Hiroshima and Nagasaki as a member of the Los Alamos survey team. In December 1945, he testified before the U.S. Senate's Special Committee on Atomic Energy: "Of the 300 registered physicians [in Hiroshima], more than 260 were unable to aid the injured. Of 2,400 nurses, orderlies, and trained first aid workers, more than 1,800 were casualties in a single instant. . . . Not one hospital in the city was left in condition to shelter patients from the rain."[20] As *New Yorker* reporter John Hershey observed: "In general, survivors that day assisted only their relatives or immediate neighbors, for they could not comprehend or tolerate a wider circle of misery. The wounded limped past the screams. . . ."[21] The report from the Memorial Peace Museum added: "In daze and confusion, [the survivors] did not even know what to do to save their own lives. With all means of communication completely paralyzed, rescue parties from neighboring communities were delayed, and with all fire-fighting organs destroyed, the whole city was left to the mercy of raging fires, so that by 2 o'clock in the afternoon, the entire city was enveloped in a vast sea of flames."[22]

Little Boy and Fat Man ushered in a quantum leap in destructive capability. In Hiroshima, Little Boy destroyed 4.7 square miles of the city. In Nagasaki (where rolling hills deflected the bomb's blast), the area of total devastation amounted to 1.8 square miles. All buildings one-half mile from Ground Zero suffered damage and even total destruction, and 99 percent of all buildings within a mile radius from the hypocenter were similarly damaged. The mortality rate per square mile for the central part of Hiroshima was 15,000, and for Nagasaki, 20,000. In comparison, the mortality rate per square mile of the firebomb raids against Tokyo on March 9, 1945, amounted to 5,300. Thus, the atomic bombs greatly multiplied the mortality rate of conventional bombs. In the Tokyo raids, 279 planes dropped 1,667 tons of explosives. At Hiroshima and Nagasaki, two planes delivered one bomb each. Fat Man, the heavier of the two, weighed a mere five tons.[23]

The number of human casualties astonished the investigating team from Los Alamos. At Hiroshima, where Little Boy was dropped, between 70,000 and 80,000 people (30 percent of the residents) died within the first days, and an equal number were injured. The survey team estimated that wounds from flying glass and tiles or from immolation by the firestorm accounted for 50 to 65 percent of the fatalities; flash burns, 20 to 30 percent; and radiation sickness, 15 to 20 percent. The true percentage of the people who might have succumbed from their exposure to radiation is hidden because they died from the more immediate effects of the blast or fires. By November 1945, 130,000 people in Hiroshima had died, and by 1950, an additional 70,000 inhabitants had perished from the effects of the bombing.[24]

In addition to the deadly shock waves and firestorms, these bombs unleashed a new force that the survey team from Los Alamos found especially intriguing. The final energy released by the atomic detonations was radiation. Even before work began at Los Alamos, scientists knew that radiation posed serious health hazards for humans. A wide range of radiation energy was released during a chain reaction. From this, two main sources of radiation threatened human health: first, from the initial radiation of high frequency neutrons, gamma rays, or other unspecified rays released by the explosion; and second, from the residual, lingering radioactivity that was harmful if ingested. The *Bombing Survey* concluded that the major source of radioactive contamination came from the rays released by the initial blasts. These rays altered the body's elements and "in tests of the ground and bones of victims of radiation disease, certain substances—phosphorous, barium, strontium, rare earths—[showed] radioactivity."[25] These rays, primarily gamma- and X-rays, proved lethal in an area radiating out from Ground Zero for 3,000 feet. Within a radius of 7,500 feet of Ground Zero, victims lost their hair, and even two miles from the epicenter, mild effects of radiation exposure surfaced.[26]

For those near Ground Zero who survived the blast, radiation sickness usually manifested itself within two or three days. Autopsies on those casualties showed an almost complete absence of white blood cells, and a deterioration of the bone marrow that produced those cells. Acute inflammation of the mucous membranes of the throat, lungs, stomach, and the intestines also appeared in the autopsies. For those farther away from Ground Zero, radiation sicknesses appeared within the month. Initial symptoms of mild nausea and vomiting subsided and a period of general health ensued. But those people who had received a substantial dose of radiation fell ill again, with loss of appetite, lassitude, and inflammation of the gums, mouth, and pharynx. Fevers rose to 106 degrees, and remained high in those cases that ended in death.[27] Concerning the effect of radiation on the health of bombing victims, the survey concluded: "There is reason to believe that if the effects of blast and fire had been entirely absent from the bombing, the number of deaths among people within a radius of one-half mile from Ground Zero would have been almost as great as the actual figures and the deaths among those within one mile would have been only slightly less. . . . Instead of being killed outright as were most of these victims, they would have survived for a few days or even three or four weeks, only to die eventually of radiation disease."[28] The difference between the short-term and long-term effects of radioactivity seemed minor to the observers from Los Alamos since many people died from the initial exposure to the blasts.

Morrison explained radiation illness in detail when he spoke to the senators in December: "This radiation affects the blood-forming tissues in the bone marrow, and the whole function of the blood is impaired. The blood does not coagulate, but oozes in many spots through the unbroken skin, and internally seeps into the cavities of the body. . . . The white corpuscles which fight infection disappear. Infection prospers and the patient dies, usually 2 or 3 weeks after the exposure."[29] In essence, as atomic historian J. Samuel Walker describes the process, "Radiation causes ionization because of its high level of energy, whether in form of x-rays from machines, or in the form of alpha particles, beta particles, or gamma rays, which are emitted as the atomic nuclei of radiation elements undergo spontaneous disintegration. . . . Gamma rays . . . and x-rays . . . —both energetic forms of light—can penetrate far inside the body from external sources."[30] The fatalities that occurred within the first months after the bombing of Hiroshima and Nagasaki came from the high-energy gamma rays released at the moment of detonation that penetrated victims' bodies and caused irreparable damage to internal organs.

The immediate effect on human health from the penetrating energy released by an atomic explosion was carefully studied in Japan, but the long-term impact of radiation also attracted attention. Alpha and beta particles, too massive or heavy to penetrate even skin, still radiate energy that can alter cells. According to J. Samuel Walker, "If an element that emits alpha or beta particles is breathed or swallowed and lodges in internal organs, . . . it poses a serious biological risk."[31] Such low-level or lingering radiation might cause damage to cells over a long period, which could cause cancer or other health problems. In fact, according to the Research Institute for Nuclear Medicine and Biology at Hiroshima University, exposure to the radiation from the explosion increased the risk of cancer by thirty to forty times the normal average.[32] Although the survey team hailed from Los Alamos, these reports from Japan had little immediate effect on the men, women, and children back home. The *Bombing Survey* took time to research and write and, due to national security concerns, was not publicly released until 1973.

Like the rest of the country, Los Alamos celebrated V-J Day, but even then, jubilation was mixed with uncertainty. After Japan surrendered, Los Alamos changed dramatically. Remaining at the isolated, cramped, clapboard community lost whatever attraction it held for most residents. To complicate matters, Washington wavered in its support for the facility. In October, President Truman warned Congress: "I am informed that many of the people on whom depend the continued successful operation of the plants and the further development of atomic knowledge are getting ready to return to their normal pursuits. In many cases, these people are considering leaving the Project largely because of uncertainty concerning future national policy in this field. Prompt action to establish national policy will go a long way towards keeping a strong organization intact."[33] To complicate matters, the town's unique legal status as a top-secret federal reservation, ignored during the national emergency, emerged as a point of contention between residents, state officials, and federal authorities. In short, the uncertainty of the town's future, the promise of a return to prewar careers and lives, and the harsh winter of 1945–46 led to a "Great Exodus" from Site Y.[34]

Since the army constructed the site as a temporary post, the physical structures lacked durability, and buildings, services, and roads suffered from inadequate planning and shoddy building materials. The weekly *Los Alamos Post Bulletin* constantly implored inhabitants to conserve electricity and water. In a *Bulletin* dated September 14, 1945, the army warned: "For the next several weeks or until the installation of the generating units is completed, there will be a limited amount of electricity for the site. It is mandatory that all unnecessary lights and power be shut off during the daytime and especially between 7 P.M. and 10 P.M."[35] Electrical outages during the evenings made cooking on hot plates more difficult than usual. Water was also in short supply. Daily consumption that autumn equaled 585,000 gallons, but daily supply furnished only 475,000 gallons.[36] The crisis mounted slowly during the autumn of 1945, but many in the community ignored the problems as they celebrated the end of the war.

Parties roared through Site Y. At war's end, children grabbed pots and pans and paraded through the streets. WAC Ensign Cordelia Newkirk received a party invitation written in questionable Latin on an official justice of the peace's summons. It requested her appearance at "the praecipe [injunction] of Majors J.O. Ackerman and Ralph Carlisle Smith in a plea of Imbidens malitia praecognitata melo animo et justa causa [Impeding the foreknown malice by the soul's song and just cause.]" The attorneys for the plaintiff were "Upan, Atom and Boom."[37]

Another party, given by the British Mission, gained the distinction as the best gala of all those honoring the "birth of the Atomic Era" on the Hill. At a packed Fuller Lodge on September 22, the men and women of the British Mission cooked and served dinner, procured enough port wine for toasts to the king, the president, and the grand alliance, and enacted an original play, "Babes in the Woods," lampooning the censorship and security at the post. The play culminated with a recreation of the Trinity explosion, using a flash pot on top of a stepladder as the Gadget's detonation—to the raucous cheers of those assembled.[38]

As another round of celebrations ushered in the Christmas season, the final straw for many residents came not from the army or the federal bureaucracy, but from nature. On December 15, the low temperature in Santa Fe dipped to zero with reports that the severe cold weather would hover over the state for the foreseeable future. As a result, a serious postwar crisis struck Site Y. To save time installing the water system in 1943, pipes had been laid above ground. Weather took its toll on those pipes, which one construction officer called "two strings of holes held together by rust." In the midst of the holiday celebrations, on December 19, the jerry-rigged water system froze, wiping out the entire town's water supply. The lack of water threw party plans into turmoil. Santa Feans had been invited to a progressive party on the Hill, meaning they would hop from one house to another for cocktails and dinner. As reported in the Santa Fe paper:

> The scientists invited a number of Santa Feans for dinner Thursday. . . . Late Wednesday everything was called off because the pipes were frozen. . . . Thursday afternoon about 2 everything . . . was on again . . . and by 3:45, guests were going through the elaborate check-in formalities at the first gate. . . . Each hostess took eight or ten guests for dinner. . . . If your hostess lacked chairs, you picked up the one in which you sat for cocktails and carried it across the street. . . . The person in front of you was probably carrying the roast.[39]

In the aftermath of the grand gala, bodies remained unwashed and party dishes unscrubbed. To alleviate the water shortage, fifteen tanker trucks operated a bucket brigade between the Rio Grande and Los

Alamos, carrying 300,000 gallons a day for both residential and laboratory use.

A serious consequence of the lack of water was that families quit
the frozen town. To accommodate the exodus, furlough tables set up
in one of the cafeterias issued the passes needed to leave the site. As
civilians left Los Alamos, many military personnel also received their
discharge papers and said goodbye to the Hill. Those people who
stayed on the Hill wondered about the future of the community.[40]

Oppenheimer and his family were some of the first people to leave
Site Y. At a tribute before he left, fellow scientists read this testimonial:

> He selected this place. Let us thank him for the fishing, hiking, skiing,
> and for the New Mexico weather. He selected our collaborators. Let us
> thank him for the company we had, for the parties, and for the intellec-
> tual atmosphere. . . . He was our director. Let us thank him for the way
> he directed our work, for the many occasions where he was the elo-
> quent spokesman of our thoughts. It was his acquaintance with every
> single little and big difficulty that helped us so much to overcome
> them. It was his spirit of scientific dignity that made us feel we would
> be in the right place here. We drew much more satisfaction from our
> work than our consciences ought to have allowed us.[41]

So, amid the accolades and celebrations, some of Oppenheimer's colleagues acknowledged that they shared with him a troubled conscience.

The warmth expressed in this tribute repeated itself in many of
Oppenheimer's relationships. Several years later, John Manley, one of
Oppenheimer's closest associates at Los Alamos, wrote him: "It [our
association] has helped me grow in so many ways, in technical and
political understanding but most of all in the important realm of
human relationships. In this latter especially I have a very large debt
to Kitty as well as to yourself."[42]

At a public ceremony honoring him before he departed in October,
Oppenheimer accepted the Army-Navy "E" Award (a certificate of
appreciation from the secretary of war) for Los Alamos. In his farewell
address to the residents of Los Alamos assembled in front of Fuller
Lodge, Oppenheimer predicted: "If atomic bombs are to be added as
new weapons to the arsenals of a warring world . . . then the time will

come when mankind will curse the name of Los Alamos and Hiroshima. The peoples of the world must unite, or they will perish. . . . By our works we are committed to a world united, before this common peril, in law, and in humanity."[43] Oppenheimer left the Hill soon thereafter, but he continued to participate actively in nuclear affairs. He served on committees concerning atomic energy and advised Congress concerning atomic weapons until the government revoked his security clearance in 1954.

On the day that Oppenheimer was honored, Norris Bradbury replaced him as the new director of the laboratory. In his farewell memo, Oppenheimer stated: "As of Wednesday, October 17th, Dr. N. E. Bradbury will assume the direction of the Los Alamos Laboratory. I shall, of course, be available in an advisory capacity to him and to the laboratory."[44] As Oppenheimer's replacement, Bradbury observed: "I feel that the bear which we have caught by the tail is so formidable that there is a strong obligation upon us to find out how to let go or hang on."[45]

Groves also supported Bradbury by stating publicly: "The Los Alamos site must remain active for a considerable period."[46] In his memoir, Groves described the transitory period for Los Alamos right after the war: "It was particularly important to continue the Los Alamos lab so that the nucleus of a staff for future weapon improvement would always be available."[47]

Norris Bradbury's appointment as the interim director of the laboratory also created stability. Born in 1909 in California, Bradbury was a prodigy in physics and chemistry, graduated summa cum laude from Pomona College, and received a Ph.D. from the University of California at Berkeley in 1932. While teaching at Stanford and the Massachusetts Institute of Technology in the 1930s, he quickly acquired a reputation as an expert in atmospheric electricity, the properties of ions, and the conduction of electricity in gases. During the war, Commander Bradbury first went to the navy research center at Dahlgren, Virginia, and then was ordered to New Mexico. He directed the field test of the Gadget at Trinity in July 1945. Fellow navy officer William (Deak) Parsons later recalled: "When a technical crisis arose, we asked

Norris Bradbury replaced Oppenheimer as director of the laboratory in October 1945. Courtesy of National Archives II, College Park, Md.

the navy for Bradbury. . . . And he did such a fine job that when Oppenheimer departed after the war, Bradbury was appointed director."[48] A respected civilian scientist before the war and a trusted navy officer during the war, Bradbury was an ideal person to serve as a bridge between the wartime military base and the postwar laboratory.

Severe difficulties, ranging from personnel departing the plateau en masse to woefully inadequate public utilities, plagued the site. Groves acknowledged that "many things that had been merely troublesome in the past were intolerable in a permanent peacetime community; yet nothing had been done about any of them in the three months after VJ Day."[49] To stem the exodus, Groves set to work. In January 1946, he sent Bradbury a letter committing the army to a permanent scientific community at Los Alamos. On January 21, Bradbury read the letter at a public meeting of the town council, which began to settle some of the concerns of the town's residents.

When Bradbury took the interim directorship for six months before returning to his teaching post at Stanford, many on the Hill thought it was merely to close down the post. Bradbury was not one of them. He wrote to Oppenheimer as he considered accepting the position: "I have always felt that success in the effort of this project would be accompanied by such serious repercussions that the greatest effort would be required to solve the ensuing problems."[50] Bradbury knew "that the laboratory [could] contribute both to basic science and to the peacetime application of nuclear physics without losing sight of its responsibility to the nation for the study of atomic weapons."[51] Attracted by "technologically sweet" scientific research, by ensuring national security, or by well-paying jobs, Bradbury sought to retain not just the scientists but the technicians, machinists, maintenance personnel, and truck drivers on the Hill.[52]

Retaining personnel was Bradbury's first major challenge. In January, he echoed Truman's warning to Congress about the impact of the lack of legislation on the operation at Los Alamos. In a letter to Vice Admiral W. H. P. Blandy, commander of the naval atomic tests slated for that summer, Bradbury stated: "The absence of legislation on the subject of atomic energy is having the direct result that it is impossible for personnel at the Los Alamos Laboratory to predict the character, extent or even general philosophy of research on atomic energy. . . . As a consequence, personnel . . . are rapidly committing themselves to the acceptance of scientific positions in both universities and industry. At the present rate of loss of personnel, the predicted naval tests will be barely possible in early summer, 1946."[53] The uncertainty emanating from the nation's capital was not the only obstacle in retaining personnel.

At war's end, the residents who remained at Los Alamos complained anew about the town's failings. At a coordinating council meeting on October 1, Bradbury commented on the effect of lack of proper housing on the Hill. Without adequate housing, key personnel could not be retained or recruited. To identify the community's needs, a questionnaire was sent to all residents in February 1946. From the answers, a master plan emerged. In March, the army began publishing a newspaper, the *Los Alamos Times*, to boost morale. Results of the questionnaire appeared in the newly launched *Los Alamos Times* in April. The respondents' dream list included a hotel, liquor store, swimming pool, roller rink, and dance hall. For houses, residents requested more privacy, lawns, and landscaping. The government took these suggestions seriously, but ponderously. In 1947, landscaping, paid for by the government, appeared; in 1949, Fuller Lodge received additional wings to better serve as a hotel; and in 1950, an indoor swimming pool was added to the high school.[54]

Years later, Bradbury reflected on the shortcomings of Los Alamos. He mentioned: "It's seldom that a man leaves our employ because he is unhappy with his job. My big worry is that his wife will be unhappy— because she is too far from the supermarkets or the movies, or because her home isn't nice enough, or because she doesn't think the schoolteachers are any good."[55] Now that the war had ended, the lack of the amenities arose as even a bigger problem than during the war. To counter such discontent, Bradbury focused on making Los Alamos a more family-friendly town and more amenable to the renewed postwar culture of domesticity.

Another questionnaire, distributed just to lab personnel, requested preferences on the future composition not of the community but of the laboratory itself. The 287 respondents answered questions concerning who should run the lab, where it should be located, whether they wanted to engage in fundamental research, weapons research, or merely production of atomic bombs, and what their salaries and vacation time should be. Confirming the civilians' antipathy towards the military, 99 percent said the army should not run the lab, and 98 percent wanted the project to be a civilian enterprise, with 64 percent calling

After the war, the original structure of the Boys' Ranch Fuller Lodge, center, had wings added to accommodate the official visitors to the laboratory. Courtesy of National Archives II, College Park, Md.

for a commission appointed by the president or Congress. Surprisingly, respondents did not want much of a university affiliation, either. Only 40 percent desired a university connection with possible academic appointments, and less than 5 percent wanted their salaries to approximate university levels. Perhaps not so surprising, 89 percent wanted salaries to approximate industrial laboratory standards. With regard to what type of research the postwar lab should engage in, 91 percent called for "a relatively large effort on peace-time applications of atomic energy, and fissionable substances."[56]

Concerning the future of the community, only 35 percent of the respondents wanted the nuclear facility to remain at Los Alamos. Asked whether modern housing and improvements to the community would "make Los Alamos into a satisfactory site for the project," 63 percent replied yes, but 26 percent said no. Thus, support for the lab to remain at Los Alamos was only lukewarm. Perhaps the biggest liability was Los Alamos's isolation since 72 percent wanted the lab located near

A 1948 aerial photograph looking north shows the new Western Area (center left) and the rows of wartime dormitories below the new Western Area. The Tech Area and the older residential area are out of view to the right. Courtesy of National Archives II, College Park, Md.

a large city, and only 6 percent did not. On the issue of relocating Los Alamos to a different site, the army did not seriously entertain that option because the government already had much invested there. Instead, the government moved to bring a city to the Hill.[57]

The army did not need a questionnaire to ascertain the most important social improvement needed on the Hill. Housing complaints had swamped Groves, Oppenheimer, and every military post commander throughout the war. As a consequence, the Great Exodus, fueled by inadequate housing, continued into 1946, partly due to the living conditions and partly because many residents never expected to stay beyond the duration of the war. Two hundred families still lived in trailers, 137 families called the primitive wartime hutments home, and much of the rest of the housing was substandard even for wartime conditions. Nonetheless, 245 families signed up for the waiting list to get into these inferior units.[58]

The newly constructed Western Area created an instant suburb at Los Alamos right after the war. Courtesy of National Archives II, College Park, Md.

In May, to staunch the flow off the Hill (which totaled 1,300 terminations in 1946), the laboratory proposed building a new housing division west of the townsite (called the Western Area) on the "dust bowl golf course." As a preview, two models of houses designed by the architectural firm of W. C. Kruger opened for public inspection on July 28, 1946. Some of the women of the Hill criticized the models, citing, among other problems, the lack of kitchen space and basements, the absence of subfloor insulation and rear doors, and the inferior quality of the wood; however, for those families accustomed to the cramped confines of trailers, hutments, and McKeeville apartments, the models appeared almost luxurious. The houses had showers, tubs, closets, storage spaces, carports, and fireplaces. They cost the government approximately $14,000 each. By comparison, Levittown houses built in the same time period cost from $17,500 to $23,500. Certainly, the Western Area housing was better than the inferior housing inherited from the Manhattan Project.[59]

The building boom that hit Los Alamos paralleled that in the rest of the country during the postwar era. The Great Depression and World War II had retarded housing construction for fifteen years, but the demand after the war, fueled by the issuance of federal mortgage guarantees, stimulated an unprecedented boom in home building. In the United States in 1944, only 114,000 new houses were built. Two years later, that number jumped to 937,000, and by 1950 new home construction totaled 1,692,000 units. Many of these new homes were built not in the core cities but on the fringes of metropolitan areas, in the suburbs. After the war, new types of suburbs, like the one at Los Alamos, were influenced by the mass production of war industry housing that revolutionized the construction trade. The leader in this was Levittown on Long Island in New York.[60]

William Levitt had built houses on Long Island since the 1920s. During the war, he received a contract to construct 1,600 units at the navy town of Norfolk, Virginia. Using an assembly-line method where each worker did the same job moving from house to house, Levitt perfected the mass production of homes. In 1946, his company built 2,250 residences on Long Island, and his community continued to expand in the following years. At its peak, Levittown saw thirty new homes completed each day. In all, this development held 17,400 separate houses, and new Levittowns appeared in Philadelphia and New Jersey in the 1950s and 1960s. With communities like Levittown and other suburbs as competition, Los Alamos had to create its own attractive neighborhoods to retain or recruit new personnel. At Los Alamos, the Western Area was a drawing card.[61]

With plans completed and models built, the first postwar housing development launched itself on the Hill. On July 29, the day after the open inspection of the models, the army awarded a contract to build 300 houses in the Western Area to the McKee Company. McKee submitted the low bid of $4,389,846 for 118 two-bedroom dwellings, 112 three-bedroom single homes, and 58 three-bedroom duplex units. Through the rest of 1946 and into 1947, McKee built a total of 350 frame and cinder-block houses. The Los Alamos houses looked like many of the postwar structures constructed in the defense communities

The interior of a new home in the Western Area shows the amenities offered Hill residents. Courtesy of National Archives II, College Park, Md.

of the Southwest. Single-storied houses made of cinder block or wood frame with an attached carport gave rise to an new architectural style—Cold War Moderne. Derived partly from Levittown and partly from military bases, Cold War Moderne changed the housing market in the postwar building boom, especially in defense-related communities and provided comfortable quarters at affordable prices.[62]

In spite of the postwar building boom in the Western Area, housing still remained a hardship for Los Alamos. So, on a part of the plateau northeast of the Western Area, another neighborhood arose when 251 "Denver Steel" units were installed in 1946. Shipped down from Denver, they consisted of prefabricated aluminum walls with steel frames. Another 240 prefabricated homes arrived from the Kansas City office of the United States Engineering District to help alleviate the housing shortage on the Hill. Each of these 24' by 28' units had two bedrooms, a living room, kitchen, and bath. The new accommodations helped diminish the overcrowding in the trailer and hutment neighborhoods.[63]

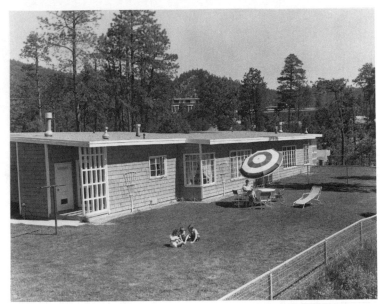

This modern duplex in the Western Area, with grass and lawn furniture, illustrates the move toward postwar normalcy at Los Alamos. Courtesy of Los Alamos National Laboratory Archives.

The Master Plan of 1946 addressed more than just improvements to the residential areas. Recognizing that the lack of shopping facilities frustrated many families on the Hill, architects designed a community center with store spaces, town council chambers, a recreation hall, a bowling alley, and a movie theater. In the fall of 1946, Groves approved a $1,396,000 contract to build this community center on the former site of the Boys' Ranch's Big House. The first phase of the project called for a building with separate quarters for the newspaper, radio, and social services offices. The next stage focused on recreational and service facilities with a theater, bowling alley, recreation center, drug store, market, filling station, and garage. Thus, the postwar urban development of Los Alamos included a planned residential community served by a concentrated assortment of businesses. This concept was popular in the growing suburbs of postwar United States, but why was it such an early priority at Los Alamos?[64]

The Western Area was not a typical postwar suburb, and the town of Los Alamos had none of the conditions that led to flight away from an inner core. The Western Area lay a scant mile from the center of town. For a federally subsidized community, multiple-unit residences like apartment buildings or quadruplexes made more economic sense than the single-family houses in the less densely developed Western Area. Granted, Los Alamos needed new facilities to house its residents, but why would the federal government, in the same year that Levittown began, choose to create a similar community in a region of the country that held no large metropolis and had no precedent for such a development? Partly, Groves and Bradbury knew the town needed to offer modern homes and shopping facilities in order to retain and attract necessary personnel to the laboratory. As the country debated the issues concerning nuclear weapons and energy, the national media turned to the new community of Los Alamos. With the labs off limits, the residential part of the community received national coverage as a model community, indeed, as a town of the future (possibly to counter the stark images from Japan about the city-killing capability of atomic bombs). Thus, the modern postwar community of Los Alamos replaced the top secret laboratories of the Hill in the public mind.

The Western Area created the first suburb in New Mexico. Some residents of the Hill liked to point out that Los Alamos was a suburb without an urb, but with the federal government footing the bill and decisions emanating from the nation's capital rather than from Santa Fe, Los Alamos was more a suburb of Washington, D.C. than a town in northern New Mexico. For New Mexico, Los Alamos was the ur-suburb, the originating suburb in the state. Because Los Alamos lacked the dense urban center that gave rise to suburbs elsewhere, it created suburban living for different reasons. As noted, the Western Area (and subsequent neighboring residential areas) existed mainly for purposes of staff recruitment and retention and for their publicity value in heralding atomic living and culture. Even though the Western Area was a prototypical planned community and looked like a suburb, it lacked some of the geographic justifications and economic motivations for building suburbs.

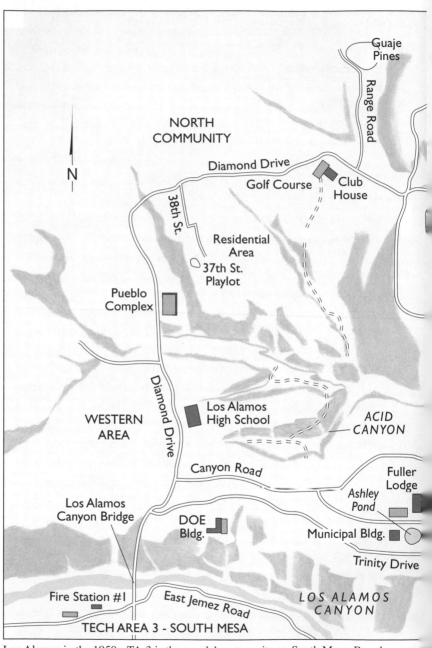

Los Alamos in the 1950s. TA-3 is the new laboratory site on South Mesa. Based on map provided by Los Alamos Historical Museum Archives.

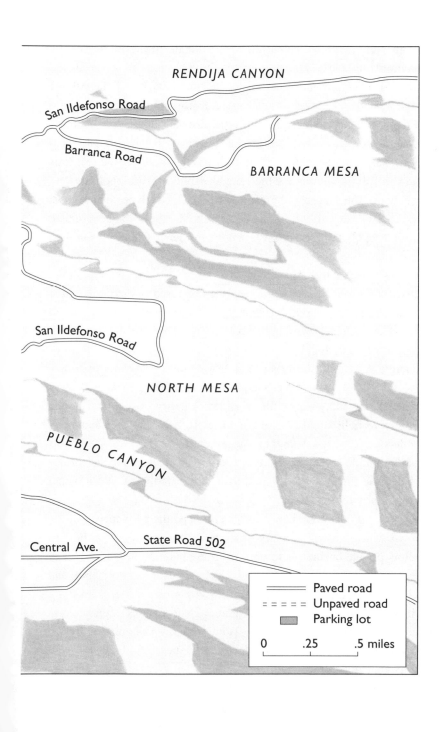

RENDIJA CANYON

San Ildefonso Road

Barranca Road

BARRANCA MESA

San Ildefonso Road

NORTH MESA

PUEBLO CANYON

Central Ave.

State Road 502

———————	Paved road
= = = = =	Unpaved road
▨	Parking lot

0   .25   .5 miles

Inventing suburbs and nuclear weapons at the towns of Los Alamos, Hanford, and Oak Ridge transformed these places. The people in and near these communities accommodated the changes of the Atomic Age by code-switching from a culture of war and military housing to a culture of suburban living. True, the postwar building boom at Los Alamos corrected a serious housing shortage, but it also presented Los Alamos as a symbol for postwar living—both for the residents on the Hill as well as for the general public nervous about nuclear weapons. The suburb in the Western Area helped lab personnel adjust to atomic living. By bringing Levittown to the mesa, the government normalized both housing issues and the residents' feelings about their community.

From behind the fences, a new city on the hill emerged that showcased the promise of nuclear energy as opposed to the peril. In the contested history about the bomb, the postwar public both embraced and feared nuclear weapons. To bolster support for atomic enterprises, officials highlighted other applications of this new form of energy. As atomic historian Paul Boyer notes: "Dreams of a new 'world' of atomic energy just around the corner were a way of dealing with—or avoiding—unsettling realities: America's use of two atomic bombs to obliterate two cities and the prospect that even more terrible atomic weapons might someday devastate the earth."[65] As part of the public relations efforts, national newspapers and magazines touted the town of Los Alamos as it reinvented itself into a model community for a new age.

Although the community center enhanced the permanency of the town with a growing variety of stores, a problem arose on how to allow private businesses to operate on the federal reservation. Many entrepreneurs saw Los Alamos as a golden business opportunity and clamored for the opportunity to open stores or offer services. In 1946, the army solved the quandary by granting concessions to private citizens to operate businesses. The Atomic Energy Commission (AEC) continued the practice afterwards. Usually, successful bidders agreed to pay the government 6 to 10 percent of their gross income. The first concessionaire to arrive on the Hill was Thurman E. "Doc" Gunter, who opened a drugstore toward the end of 1946. His lease called for turning over 10 percent of his gross income to the army for the privilege of serving the captive consumers on the Hill. Over the next two years, a hardware store, a sporting goods store, a shoe repair shop, and an auto supply store moved into the town.[66]

Another movement toward permanency on the Hill involved the town's streets. Throughout the war and into the early postwar period, streets at Los Alamos remained nameless. The water tower served as the community's center, and most directions derived from that prominent structure. At the end of 1946, the *Los Alamos Times* announced a contest to name the streets. Suggestions from residents for christening the roads included California, New Mexico, Manhattan, Einstein, Curie, Eisenhower, Oppenheimer, Groves, Fermi, Atomic Vista, Hiroshima, and Nagasaki. The main thoroughfares won the titles of Central Avenue, Canyon Road, and Trinity Drive. Canyon Road ran along the rim of the canyon, and Trinity Drive honored the first atomic detonation in July 1945. By the end of 1946, almost 250 street signs marked the streets. With its streets now named, Los Alamos had acquired more of the trappings of a normal town.[67]

The issue of greatest interest for Hill residents involved the army's role in the community. Of particular concern for the government was how to operate and maintain the community. Discussions started soon after V-J Day about removing the army's management of the post. Lieutenant Colonel W. A. Stevens, the ranking army engineer at Los Alamos, asked the Robert E. McKee Company whether it would want "to perform the function of operating the town."[68] To handle the job, the McKee Company created the Zia Company and agreed to expand so that it could provide a wide variety of services for the community. In April 1946, Zia took over the divisions of Personnel, Safety, Concessions, Fiscal, Property and Warehouse, Engineering, Maintenance, and Transportation. In addition, Zia ran Fuller Lodge, the hospital, the Youth Center, the library, and the veterinarian hospital. Its work force of fifteen hundred that April did everything from ordering cyclotrons and paying all of the employees at the site to changing light bulbs in the homes on the Hill. For operating the community, the Zia Company received a fixed-fee contract in addition to the expenses incurred in operating the laboratory and community. In 1946, the army estimated that Los Alamos would cost $300,000 a month to operate, with Zia receiving $12,250 for its fixed fee. Thus, the federal government financed Los Alamos, creating a community devoid of private property, and serviced by one company that provided a complete range of services for all the residents without charge. To some residents, Los Alamos ironically resembled a socialistic town more than a capitalistic one.[69]

The sole provider of contracts at Los Alamos greatly benefitted Robert McKee and his companies. In the rush to deliver an operable nuclear weapon before war's end, money had poured into the site. The McKee Company had participated in many of the lucrative contracts that resulted in the hastily-built structures meant to last only for the war's duration. The Zia Company continued the profitable relationship as it bid on the massive construction projects in the postwar years. In his history of the company, Robert McKee noted that at the time Zia took over the operation of the site, "[n]ew Laboratories and technical sites costing approximately $150 million [were] now scheduled because the original ones were built in such extreme haste that many [were] becoming obsolete."[70] Thus, McKee stood to benefit again, as almost all the wartime buildings were eventually demolished, and new structures were erected to replace those built from 1943 to 1945. As the postwar arms race heated up, planners at Los Alamos had to replace the inferior buildings of the war era, which had cost substantial amounts of money, with more sturdy and equally expensive facilities.[71]

As Los Alamos transformed itself from a temporary wartime post to a permanent town, rivalry between the army and the navy helped stabilize the site. On September 17, 1945, the U.S. Navy revealed a plan to tow the captured Japanese battleship *Nagato* out to sea and drop an atomic bomb on it "in an experiment that [could] determine the future form of the world's navies."[72] In October 1945, the navy announced an additional test to explode an atomic bomb underwater to test the vulnerability of its fleet. Even before the navy announced its intention to field test nuclear weapons, an interservice rivalry erupted between the army and the navy on the future of their two branches in a nuclear military. Already facing postwar reductions in forces and budget, the heads of both branches nervously eyed atomic weapons as possibly making their own branch obsolete. The army and the navy also coveted the incredible explosive power that nuclear weapons would bring to future battlefields. Thus, both branches jockeyed for control of the new armaments. In December, they announced a joint test for the next summer. However, the Santa Fe paper was skeptical: "The announcement on the forthcoming tests against warships was cryptic. It said only that plans for the operation involve assembling 'many naval vessels,' extensive use of recording instruments, and the gathering of the necessary personnel." Some of the "necessary personnel" were in Los Alamos trying to figure how to celebrate Christmas without running water.[73]

Operation Crossroads (the code name for the coming tests) reinvigorated the personnel at the laboratory. It gave a purpose and an objective for many at the labs. To carry out the tests of Operation Crossroads, the Joint Chiefs of Staff created Joint Task Force One on January 10, 1946. The order also directed the tests to take place at the Bikini Atoll in the Marshall Islands, two thousand miles southwest of Hawaii. Los Alamos was to oversee the technical aspects of the tests and to supply the atomic weapons. In consultation with the army and navy, the heads of the Manhattan Project decided on three types of tests: Test Able, an air burst over a collection of ships; Test Baker, a shallow water explosion under the ships; and Test Charlie, a deep water burst under another assembly of ships. The laboratory agreed to help plan for the tests, including determining the placement of the ships, the height and depth of the detonations, and the type of bombs used. It was also to write a handbook for the participants in the tests. Most importantly, the Tech Area built the weapons used in the tests. Particularly challenging were the underwater devices, since a nuclear explosion surrounded by water presented unique complications for critical assemblies. As a result of Operation Crossroads, the laboratory had work, at least for the coming year.[74]

As the lab prepared for Operation Crossroads, debate arose within the federal government and at nuclear communities around the country as to who would control the atomic bomb. Two key questions arose. First, should secrecy be breached and nuclear knowledge shared with other countries? Supporters called this the One World Movement.[75] Second, should a military or a civilian agency administer the atom? In September 1945, congressmen from both the House and Senate introduced atomic energy legislation. The resultant May-Johnson bill would have left the control of atomic weapons with the military, and specifically General Groves. A battle erupted between those who favored military and those who favored civilian control of nuclear energy. Not surprisingly, given their animosity toward the army that surfaced during the war, many scientists with the Manhattan Project advocated for civilian control.[76]

As integral players in the development of the atomic bomb, Los Alamos's scientists offered their own influential opinions about the contested history of atomic affairs. They presented an extremely vocal and active opposition to military control of nuclear weapons and, thus, added their own brush strokes to the atomic canvas. On August 30, 1945, the Association of Los Alamos Scientists (ALAS) formed at a meeting in Theater # 2 on the Hill. Approximately five hundred men and women attended the first meeting and decided to create an organization to educate the public about nuclear energy in an effort to influence the growing debate over control of atomic energy. The first president of ALAS was the accordion-playing Willie Higginbotham. In order to gauge public reaction and respond to press reports around the country, ALAS advertised its needs in the *Bulletin*: "Association of L.A. Scientists' clipping bureau is anxious to obtain copies of 5 to 10 representative metro newspapers every day. Would any person who would be willing to donate his papers to the Association within 2 days after receiving them, please call Helmolz, telephone 15?"[77] Women at Site Y pored over these newspapers in Bernice Brode's kitchen and cut out relevant articles. Responding to false information in these articles, the ALAS wrote letters to editors and began sponsoring lectures to educate the public.[78]

Some of the women on the Hill worked tirelessly for ALAS. Women at Site Y had been trapped between the two fences for so long that, once freed from the wartime constraints of secrecy and isolation, they actively participated in the debate about how the atomic baby should be raised. On October 8, 1945, a group of women met to discuss ways to work with ALAS. A women's auxiliary came out of this meeting and, led by Kathleen Manley, assisted ALAS. Besides clipping articles from the nation's newspapers, women took dictation, typed correspondence, and helped ALAS with pending legislation. Women also canvassed the Hill for signatures on the resolutions that the ALAS passed. As part of the auxiliary's efforts, Joan Hinton sent pieces of trinitite, the fused sand from the Trinity Site, to the mayors of large cities. A message attached to the trinitite read: "Do you want this to happen to your city?"[79]

ALAS advocated a unified world entity, a One World government, to oversee nuclear developments. Los Alamos physicist Robert Wilson, a spokesman for ALAS, warned that future bombs one thousand times more powerful than Fat Man and Little Boy made the industrial centers of the United States vulnerable to a surprise attack. He then suggested that the nation had but one choice: "Cooperate with the rest of the world in the future development of atomic power. . . . Use of atomic energy must be controlled by a world authority."[80] As the ALAS moved into action, Oppenheimer, who supported the idea of a One World authority controlling nuclear energy, spoke to them as a group. Just before leaving Los Alamos on November 2, he addressed a meeting and warned: "I think the advent of the atomic bomb and the facts which will get around that they are not too hard to make—that they will be universal if people wish to make them universal, that they will not constitute a real drain on the economy of any strong nation, and that their power of destruction will grow and is already comparably greater than that of any other weapon—I think these things create a new situation."[81] Predicting such an ominous nuclear future, Oppenheimer then suggested four courses of action: regard current proposals as interim solutions; insist that nations participating in any arrangements should have a joint atomic energy commission to pursue constructive applications of atomic energy, like power production and research; arrange for an international exchange of scientists and students to create a fraternity of nuclear scientists; and prohibit the making of any more atomic bombs.[82]

To publicize its position concerning nuclear weapons, ALAS held public meetings in northern New Mexico. It also put out the weekly *Los Alamos Newsletter*, which called for international control of nuclear weapons. The November 20, 1945 edition states: "The central policy of the Association of Los Alamos Scientists is to urge and in every way to sponsor the initiation of international discussion leading to a world authority in which would be vested the control of nuclear energy." The editorial boldly concluded: "We are opposed to any national policy requiring the continuation of security restrictions on nuclear research and technology. . . ."[83] The concerns and strategies of ALAS mirrored the concerns of Albert Einstein, who wrote: "To the village square we must carry the facts of atomic energy. From there must come America's voice."[84] At first, ALAS targeted the village squares of New Mexico to influence America's voice.

To alert the public about the effects of atomic bombs, ALAS published an eyewitness report from the atomic cities of Japan. Dr. Robert Serber, director of physical measurements with the Atomic Bomb Mission in Japan, observed on his return to Los Alamos: "No one that has not actually seen the completeness of the destruction in Hiroshima and Nagasaki can have any idea of what a terrible thing atomic warfare is. . . . In Hiroshima, one walks for miles through a completely abandoned, forgotten, and deserted desert of broken tile and rusty sheet metal—once the residential area. In the center of the city, all that remains are the shells of concrete buildings with completely gutted interiors."[85] Serber concluded: "I hoped that there would be an unanimous insistence [on] the free interchange among all nations of information dealing with atomic power. The alternative seems to me a desperate arms race and one that can only end in terrible catastrophe."[86] Thus, early in the debate over the control of nuclear energy, some Los Alamos scientists advocated international cooperation and at least the partial abolition of the secrecy of the Manhattan Project. To them, the alternative appeared chillingly clear—an unprecedented arms race culminating in a nuclear exchange between belligerents.

On another front, ALAS appealed to the public for support through town meetings. In Santa Fe on November 26, ALAS members spoke to 380 concerned Santa Feans, calling for international control. With fifty "distinguished scientists" from Los Alamos in attendance, speakers told the audience: "All talk about the bomb 'secret' is beside the point since there is no secret. Other nations, including Russia, know the basic principles." They also warned, prophetically, that the lead the United States had would "keep for a few years at best."[87] At the meeting, ALAS called for world control of atomic energy, possibly organized by the United Nations. At one point, Dr. Victor Weisskopf lectured on the development of nuclear energy and emphasized how the international scientific discoveries of Bohr, Fermi, and Meitner, to name a few, led to the Hill's successful creation of an atomic bomb. Addressing the need for ALAS, Weisskopf said: "We realized we faced a tremendous responsibility and we felt we must tell the people. War never did make sense and we believed the atomic bomb should be the means to make it impossible."[88] Weisskopf reflected a growing belief among some nuclear scientists that the atomic bomb made war obsolete.

After speaking, the scientists showed a color movie of Nagasaki to the overflow crowd. Still photographs from Hiroshima also illustrated the effects of the atomic bomb for the Santa Feans. The Santa Fe poet Witter Bynner commented: "Those of us who attended the preliminary meeting . . . where facts were presented in terms laymen could understand and where counsel was given with impressive earnestness, came away clarified and moved."[89] ALAS also sponsored other town meetings around northern New Mexico.

Similar associations of concerned atomic scientists and women's auxiliaries organized throughout the country. At Oak Ridge, Chicago,

Pasadena, Cambridge, New York, and other sites, those who worked on atomic weapons called for an open debate on the future of their offspring, and in particular, advocated for the defeat of the May-Johnson bill. During the first two weeks of October, representatives from the various atomic scientists' associations met in Washington, D.C., to attack the bill. They succeeded in halting the rapid advance of the bill through Congress and created an opening for another bill, introduced by Senator Brien McMahon from Connecticut, on the control of the atom. With input from the associations, McMahon presented a bill in December that addressed many of the misgivings that the atomic community and the nation had about who would govern the atom. These loose associations of scientists and concerned citizens, who spontaneously organized on local levels to bring to the village square the facts of the atom, quickly took the lead in advocating international control and preventing sole control of the atom by the military. They also formed a national umbrella organization, the Federation of Atomic Scientists (FAS), to counter the military's goals and offer alternative viewpoints about nuclear affairs. Los Alamosan Willie Higginbotham became its first president, and he provided a spark when he arrived in Washington in November. His honesty, friendliness, and good nature helped win recalcitrant congressmen over to the FAS position. And FAS's position, spearheaded by Higginbotham, was: "Let's pass something that gets it out of the hands of Groves."[90] As Los Alamos's civilians did during the war, they and others in the nuclear communities organized, resisted the military's plans, and forced the government to change the direction of the nuclear future.

Because of mounting resistance to the military control of atomic energy organized by the atomic scientists, the debate in Congress shifted away from the May-Johnson bill and toward the McMahon bill. After six months of intense debate and partisan sniping, the McMahon bill passed the Senate on June 1, 1946, and the House in mid-July. President Truman signed it into law on August 1. The bill, officially known as The Atomic Energy Act, created the Atomic Energy Commission (AEC) with five civilian commissioners appointed by the president and approved by the Senate. A military applications committee and a military liaison committee were formed to advise the AEC. Thus, civilian control existed, but the military continued to play a major role in production decisions and the overall direction of the atomic program.

The acrimonious relationship between Los Alamos civilians and the army continued even after the Atomic Energy Act passed. The surveys taken in the winter of 1946 showed a deep distrust of the army by many of the scientists on the Hill. Bradbury wrote a long letter to the newly formed AEC in November 1946 that addressed this problem. He said: "We state with reluctance, but with conviction, that we do not believe that a continued army operation of Los Alamos as a research laboratory and attached community will be successful."[91] In administering Los Alamos, the civilian AEC would help to alleviate some of the concerns of the residents.

Despite the resolution of many of the issues surrounding the administration of nuclear energy, a serious problem arose with the creation of the AEC. It had conflicting missions. On the one hand, the AEC was in charge of developing America's nuclear enterprises. On the other hand, it had the regulatory responsibility of safeguarding American families from the toxic and sometimes invisible dangers of the radioactive by-products of the nuclear industry. In a government of checks and balances and the separation of powers, the AEC crossed over the line as it both developed and regulated atomic matters.[92]

The AEC did not always balance its dual roles equally. Writing about Hanford and the government's role in managing the atom, historian S. L. Sanger stated: "The argument must turn on two government determinations: first, that building America's nuclear stockpile, and testing new weapon designs, was more important than an indeterminate threat to the public health represented by radioactive emissions, and, second, that the public could not be consulted about the decision."[93] The atomic historian Paul Boyer expressed his own fears about the impact of atomic matters on democracy: "The compulsions of atomic secrecy . . . would eventually undermine the very structure of democratic government."[94] Another nuclear historian,

Costandina Titus, succinctly summed up AEC's conflict: "From the beginning, the American people learned only what the AEC wanted them to know."[95] The pressure to make progress with atomic energy research and development at times overwhelmed the democratic instincts and constitutional safeguards of the country.

Atomic matters did permeate to the American public through popular culture despite governmental secrecy. In 1946, the film *The Best Years of Our Lives* won seven Oscars for its portrayal of returning veterans. At one point, Hoagy Carmichael consoles Harold Russell, who is having problems adjusting to civilian life. Carmichael says: "Don't worry about it, kid. It'll all work out unless we have another war and then we'll all be blown to bits the first day."[96] From the first years of the Atomic Age, the bomb took its place in popular culture, and the public quickly grasped the dangers of nuclear energy. Popular culture, ALAS, the AEC, and others all contributed their own chapters to the contested history of the atom.

As Congress debated the final forms of the McMahon bill in the summer of 1946, the first peacetime tests of nuclear weapons occurred half-way around the world. After a half-year of planning and preparations, Operation Crossroads culminated in the detonation of two atomic devices at Bikini Atoll. Forty-two thousand personnel assisted with the operation as thousands of instruments monitored the effects of the bombs on a fleet of ships, including captured Japanese and German warships as well as the battleship *Pennsylvania*, once the flagship of the U.S. Navy, and the rugged aircraft carriers *Saratoga* and *Independence*. More than twenty ships were within one thousand yards of the battleship *Nevada*, the target ship, with sixty-seven ships spread out over the entire lagoon. To record the blasts, 328 cameras (some able to take ten thousand frames a second) documented the detonations for future study. As with Trinity and the explosions over Japan, Los Alamos's personnel contributed essential expertise in assembling the nuclear weapons, recording the tests, and analyzing the results.[97]

Tragically, one of those preparations back at Los Alamos went gravely wrong. On May 21, 1946, at the bottom of Pajarito Canyon, eight men gathered in a room as Dr. Louis Slotin experimented with a

Test Baker, in July 1946 at the Bikini Atoll in the Pacific Ocean, threw ten million tons of water into the air and destroyed many of the naval ships seen in the lagoon. Courtesy of National Archives II, College Park, Md.

plutonium assembly. The Canadian-born Slotin, leader of the Critical Assemblies Group, had received his doctorate in physics at the University of Chicago after serving in the Abraham Lincoln Brigade during the Spanish Civil War. At Los Alamos, he had put together subcritical assemblies to determine the amount of plutonium needed to attain a critical mass. On this day, Slotin inserted the plutonium between two hemispheres of berillium that deflected the neutrons back into the nuclear material. Slotin gingerly moved the two hemispheres together, separating the two masses with a screwdriver. As the two hemispheres of berillium came together, the screwdriver slipped, the two hemispheres touched, and a blue flash swept over the room. The assembly, for a split second, went critical. Slotin reacted quickly and with his bare hands knocked the fissioning mass apart. Slotin probably saved the other men in the room, but he received a fatal dose from the prompt burst of gamma rays and neutrons. In fact, the blue glow that flooded the room came from the ionization of the air.[98]

The effects of the accident on those present varied according to their distance from the critical assembly. No one else in the room received the dosage that Slotin did. Dr. Alvin Graves, S. Allan Kline, Dwight Smith Young, Dr. Raemer Schreiber, Theodore Perlman, Patrick J. Cleary, and Marion Edward Cieslicki went to the hospital along with Slotin for observation. Within a week, most of the others left the hospital. By the beginning of June, Schreiber had left for Bikini, replacing Slotin, who had been slated to assist with the Cross-roads tests. Meanwhile, Slotin lay in the hospital at Los Alamos, observed by doctors and radiologists, some flown in from the Man-hattan Project's other sites around the country. He received transfu-sions of whole blood, plasma, and other fluids, primarily glucose and saline, but the radiation had swept through his body. Dr. Louis Hempelmann, radiologist for Site Y, later explained that Slotin suf-fered burns comparable to a "3-D sunburn. . . . As the rays penetrate the body, they burn deep, resulting in injury and destruction of tissues and blood cells."[99]

Louis Slotin died on Memorial Day, nine days after his fatal expo-sure. The *Los Alamos Times* wrote: "Announcement of Dr. Slotin's death came as a shock to the 7,000 scientists, technicians, plant work-ers, and military personnel in this community, who had hoped that medical science might find some means to forestall the ravages of the disease."[100] At the time, health officials code-switched and used "dis-ease" to explain the sickness that came from radiation exposure. The only visible evidence of the accident's lethal nature was the blue flash; otherwise, the exposure of Slotin and the others in the room to massive doses of life-threatening radiation was invisible. This invisi-bility, combined with a long series of trouble-free experiments, had fostered overconfidence at the Tech Area. As a member of the Critical Assemblies Group later recalled: "Those of us who were old hands felt impervious to the invisible danger. . . . I am afraid familiarity breeds contempt of danger."[101] Slotin was a veteran on the Hill, had accompanied the plutonium core to Trinity the previous summer, and knew full well the dangers of working with nuclear materials.

From Slotin's and Daghlian's deaths, from the radium dial workers in New Jersey, and from the surveys of Hiroshima and Nagasaki, doctors knew about the deadly effects of radiation on living tissue. From these sources, they discovered that nuclear energy opened up new pathways of danger for human health, not just because deadly particles released new forms of toxic matter but because these particles penetrated many barriers unhindered. Wooden structures, metal buildings, and the skin of one's body provided little protection against gamma rays and neutrons. The radiations released by a critical assembly penetrated these obstructions like a deadly virus and destroyed internal organs. Writing in 1947, Dr. Stafford Warren explained the sequence of symptoms: "With very large doses personnel may succumb within the first two days. . . . From the second to tenth day extensive rapid disintegration of the intestinal mucosa is indicated by profuse diarrhea containing large amounts of blood. . . . From the second to the sixth week intestinal injury is less extensive . . . and the disintegration of blood forming tissue . . . begins to become prominent. . . . The blood fails to clot and small hemorrhages develop in the skin and throughout the body."[102] Slotin's death illustrated anew the potential invisible danger of nuclear enterprises to the health of the nation's citizens.[103]

Notwithstanding the tragedy of Slotin's death, the preparations for Operation Crossroads continued. To fulfill its duties, the laboratory at Los Alamos assigned 150 of its personnel to the tests. At the time, the Bikini crew equaled one-eighth of the approximately 1,200 scientific and technical personnel at the laboratory. In fact, the demands of the Bikini tests strained the technical divisions on the Hill, with the Ordnance Engineering Division the most overworked because it constructed the new bombs.The laboratory also sent medical teams to Bikini, transferring Drs. James F. Nolan and Louis H. Hempelmann to the Pacific to monitor the effects of radiation on animals and humans. In addition to the military test of the impact of nuclear weapons on ships, Operation Crossroads, like Trinity, promised to provide a wealth of information about atomic explosions. As the fourth and fifth atomic blasts (and the second and third ones where thorough detonation data could be collected), the Able and Baker tests offered nuclear physicists a unique opportunity to record and study an atomic event. Consequently, the laboratory put considerable effort in documenting the tests.[104]

In evaluating the data from Operation Crossroads, the Joint Chiefs of Staff Evaluation Board sent a letter to Oppenheimer about the health hazards of radioactivity. In it, Dr. Karl Compton wrote: "An atomic air burst will carry . . . fission products into the high atmosphere where they will ultimately be spread by air currents throughout the hemisphere. Rain or settling will ultimately bring them to the earth, largely in the inhabited areas of the land. . . . Some of the products will be taken up in plant life and ultimately reach the human system through food in the form of vegetables, milk, etc. Certain of these products—for example, any which are radioactive and of the calcium type—will reach the bone structure with results analogous to radium poisoning."[105] At the highest levels of the AEC and the military, the potential long-term dangers of lingering radiation were verified as a consequence of Operation Crossroads.

On July 1, Test Able exploded a plutonium bomb in the air over the Bikini lagoon and the ships assembled there. On July 25, a second bomb detonated under the lagoon, sending ten million tons of water a mile high before the sea fell back onto the ships arrayed around the target area. At the time, the cloud was called a "cauliflower," not a mushroom. The official history of Operation Crossroads labeled a picture of the atomic water spout: "A Tree Grows in Bikini," referring to a popular movie of 1945, *A Tree Grows in Brooklyn*. A survey of the ships after each shot showed a variety of damages. The blasts bent superstructures, ripped steel plates off of the decks, and sank three vessels outright. President Truman canceled Test Charlie, the third shot, after the successes of the first two.[106]

Although the destruction and radioactivity impressed witnesses, Operation Crossroads also lessened the public's fear of atomic weapons. As atomic historians Richard Hewlett and Oscar Anderson observed: "Before July 1, the world stood in awe of a weapon which could devastate a city and force the surrender of an army of 5,000,000 men. After that date, the bomb was a terrible but finite weapon. To the extent the test dulled men's minds to the dangers that faced the world, the effect was bad. To the extent it supplanted emotionalism with realism, the effect was good."[107] A nation-wide survey conducted by Cornell University in the summer of 1946 also illustrated the public's attitude about the atomic bomb. Approximately six thousand citizens were asked how they felt about the bomb. Tallying results for separate questions, 75 percent wanted the U.S. to keep the secret of making an atomic bomb to itself, and almost 50 percent wanted the U.S. to continue nuclear weapons production. Over 60 percent worried that atomic weapons would fall on the U.S. and a little under 60 percent believed that the U.S. would find an effective defense against the bomb. Half of the survey was conducted before the Bikini tests and half after. Fifty-two percent of the post-Bikini test respondents said that the Bikini bombs did less damage than they thought they would. So the survey suggests that the American public's fear of atomic weapons lessened after the Bikini tests.[108]

Whatever the effects on public attitudes that resulted from the Bikini tests, they insured the continuance of Los Alamos. Improving on the Manhattan Project designs and then creating new generations of nuclear weapons would occupy staff for the foreseeable future. New personnel arrived at Los Alamos to replace those who had left during the previous winter. Working on the vital projects to expand nuclear weapons development, these men and women held different convictions from those who had worked there during the war. Issues of morality and ethics concerning weapons of mass destruction, ignored during the war effort, came to the fore and forced some of the staff to leave during the Great Exodus. Hill veteran Harry Palevsky represented that group. After the war, he confided to his sister that "from the moment he heard of the bombings of the Japanese cities, he had thought they were wrong. And he told her he would never work on weapons again."[109] He did stay in the field of nuclear physics and, like many of similar persuasion, went on to work at Brookhaven National Laboratory, where he helped develop nonmilitary applications of nuclear energy.

Operation Crossroads ended the Great Exodus that had occurred immediately after the war. The personnel and their families who now came to the Hill were different from the liberal scientists that Oppenheimer had recruited. The anthropologist Susan Tiano reflected on her first-hand knowledge growing up on the Hill: "I think what happened is that the enlightened liberals left. . . . And the hardassed conservatives stayed and the only people that would be happy there were the people that shared those belief systems. . . . The selection factor kept increasing the trend toward the conservatives."[110] To be sure, liberal personnel did stay on the Hill, but compared with the Oppenheimer years, staff grew more conservative after V-J Day.

The twelve months from Trinity to Test Baker, from the top secret Site Y to world famous Los Alamos, from the Manhattan Project to the Atomic Energy Commission, witnessed rapid and vast changes on the Hill. Peace replaced war, and families left in an exodus that created gaps in the laboratory's ability to fulfill its mission. New personnel arrived in the winter and spring of 1946 to replace the staff that fled. Permanent housing appeared west of the site and lured residents into staying. As laboratory director Norris Bradbury and General Leslie Groves struggled to keep the installation alive, Los Alamos scientists and their spouses organized to educate their neighbors and to lobby Congress. By adding their voices to the contested history of atomic enterprises, they influenced the national debate concerning the issues of postwar control of nuclear enterprises and helped defeat the May-Johnson bill. It was a heady time for Los Alamos as staff members traveled to the Pacific test site or appeared as witnesses in congressional hearings. During that year, citizens at Los Alamos and beyond felt new anxiety about a force that might protect them from foreign foes–or bring the devastation of war to the nation's cities.

CHAPTER 4

Los Alamos
Transformed

Federal Largesse and
Red Challenge

*"A fever of construction, building and rebuilding,
has always been one of the main features of Los
Alamos."*

LAURA FERMI, "LOS ALAMOS REVISITED"

On January 1, 1947, Los Alamos residents awoke to a new year and a
reinvented town. At the same stroke of midnight that rang out 1946,
the Atomic Energy Commission (AEC) took control of the site.[1] To
commemorate the change, nuclear administrators publicly complimented each other. Praising General Groves, the AEC acknowledged:
"Throughout the difficult months which followed V-J Day, when the
contracting organizations, the scientists, the engineers, and executives
wanted to return to their peacetime pursuits, General Groves has
maintained an effective organization and has planned and carried out
a constructive program for the peacetime utilization of atomic energy."[2]

In his own press release, Groves complimented the men and
women of the Manhattan Project: "Five years ago, the idea of atomic
power was only a dream. You have made that dream a reality. You
have seized upon the most nebulous of ideas and translated them into
actualities. You have built cities where none were known before. . . .
You built the weapon which ended the war and thereby saved count-
less American lives. With regard to peacetime applications, you have
raised the curtain on vistas of a new world."[3] With the transfer of Los

125

Alamos to the AEC, Groves's role in these atomic vistas started to diminish.

To calm the nervous members of the Manhattan Project, the AEC and the War Department jointly announced that the transfer would occur without any interruption of present operations or disruption to facilities. In a press release, Secretary of War Robert P. Patterson looked forward to a "relationship of mutual advantage" between the military and the new AEC. With the army no longer in charge, military personnel would move away, whereas civilian employees, who totaled almost forty-three thousand throughout the entire Manhattan Engineering District, would remain on the job. Under the AEC, America's atomic communities, including Los Alamos, had to adapt to new owners and managers.

With the stability that the AEC brought to America's atomic enterprises, generous federal monies helped Los Alamos become permanent. Ramshackle clapboard buildings had to be replaced by sturdier structures. Pathbreaking research in nuclear physics, nuclear medicine, and computers demanded new experiments in expanded laboratories at the site. The community found itself the subject of numerous articles in national publications heralding it as a modern, pacesetting town on the forefront of the technological frontier. With all the activity and attention, it was a heady time for Los Alamos.

Since the AEC wanted a smooth transition from military to civilian management on the Hill, it had much to do to reinvent the community. Some of the immediate needs included replacing the military police with civilian guards, determining the legal status of Los Alamos and its residents, and removing wartime structures and constructing new buildings. The physical maintenance and servicing of the town site and Tech Area had been transferred to the Zia Company during the previous year, and that arrangement continued under the AEC. To highlight the abilities of the Zia Company, the *Los Alamos Times* published a story about its assumption of winter heating responsibilities. Zia delivered a daily average of twenty to twenty-five thousand gallons of fuel oil, five hundred tons of coal, and four cords of wood to each of almost one thousand servicing points on the Hill. During the frigid

After 1947, the AEC guards seen here replaced the Military Police in checking the security passes of everyone entering Los Alamos. Courtesy of National Archives II, College Park, Md.

winter at the site, fuel oil shipments came in around the clock. At the end of January, Zia assumed further responsibilities as it took over from the army the procurement of additional supplies for the town and became the Hill's property manager.[4]

With the AEC ensuring permanence, Los Alamos added new staff and replaced its wartime facilities with more permanent ones over the next three years. To facilitate this transformation of the Hill, the AEC appointed retired Navy Captain Carroll L. Tyler as manager of the Los Alamos–based Santa Fe Operations Office (SFOO). The SFOO was the local headquarters for the AEC. An AEC press release stated that Tyler "will direct the completion of a construction program which will 'permanentize' and effectively modernize the war built town. . . . More than 1,000 new homes, new schools, new community service and commercial facilities, new streets, new recreational, and new utilities are included in the construction program that will make the isolated town as much like a normal community as possible."[5] Tyler later recalled: "It was necessary to rebuild the town and build the morale of the people up in their own homes. We had to provide them with a community in which they could proudly live and bring up their children. . . . One of the first questions which we are asked when we try to employ a scientist who has children is: How is the housing and how is the school?"[6] As Los Alamos reshaped itself to become more family-friendly, Tyler rode herd over the growth of the community.

Overcrowding, the bane of Los Alamos during the war, continued into the postwar period. In 1947, 7,150 people lived on the Hill; the number rose to 8,200 in 1948 and 8,643 in 1949. This 20 percent population increase in two years illustrates how magnetic Los Alamos was after the AEC took over. In response, the AEC authorized a variety of new construction projects. First, city planners squeezed new residential areas into the original town site and continued to expand on the plateau tops to the west and north. In 1947, 240 prefabricated housing units arrived from Fort Leonard Wood to alleviate the overcrowding, and the Western Area saw more homes built. Six months after the AEC took over, it sent a report to the Hill that detailed all of the current or authorized construction projects. From housing in the Western Area to the Community Center, new construction costs totaled $18,795,121. The next year, 150 more houses were constructed in the Western Area. New apartment buildings also appeared so that Los Alamos acquired 368 total units in 1948 consisting of 276 efficiency apartments in two- and three-story structures east of the Community Center and 92 units near the United Church Chapel north of the center of town. In 1949, the AEC built another sixteen apartment buildings with 280 units. As space became crowded within the original townsite and in the growing Western Area, a new development, the North Community, sprouted on a plateau north of the town. Contracts signed in the summer of 1949 called for 292 three-bedroom quadruplexes, 145 four-bedroom duplexes, and 21 two-bedroom duplexes in the North Community. Residents occupied these houses beginning in 1950. Although massive, this building program satisfied housing demand only for a while. To house the construction crews and their families, a

The stores of the Community Center were connected with covered walkways and shared a common plaza devoid of car traffic, similar to other postwar shopping malls in suburban America. Courtesy of National Archives II, College Park, Md.

new project expanded housing to the nearby area of White Rock. On land five miles southeast of Los Alamos, construction companies installed prefabricated houses for their workers. Planned to accommodate 3,000 people, White Rock opened on July 1, 1949, with 200 trailer spaces, 350 prefabricated houses, and 950 dormitory rooms.[7]

In addition to the new housing construction, a shopping center also contributed to Los Alamos's status as a more typical town. After World War II, new regional malls built on the periphery of cities served the growing suburbs. This boom in shopping center construction was mirrored on a smaller scale at Los Alamos with the Community Center, which Groves had approved in the fall of 1946. Soon after the AEC took over operations, it signed a contract with Robert E. McKee to construct Phase One of the Community Center for $2,178,842. To keep pace with suburbs and shopping centers elsewhere, Los Alamos architects designed a Territorial Revival style

129

one-story shopping mall where stores faced a grassy central plaza divided in two by covered walkways. When the Community Center was finally completed in 1948, it was the first shopping center of its kind in northern New Mexico.[8]

The Community Center, originally conceived in September 1946, finally commenced operations on October 11, 1948, when ten merchants moved into the completed storefronts. A grand opening celebration with special sales, late hours, and a public concert greeted customers. Within a year, the Community Center became "the nerve center of all community activity" and housed approximately seventy stores and businesses. The center replaced the military Post Exchange and Commissary with general merchandise stores, a grocery market, men's and women's clothing establishments, a furniture store, and a movie theater. The concept of the Community Center combined old with new. A two-acre central plaza reminiscent of Hispanic colonial villages was surrounded by an assortment of stores and businesses connected by awnings and walkways.[9]

Former Denver wholesale jeweler Sam Mozer exemplified how businessmen operated at the Community Center. In 1949, Mozer applied for and received a concession to open his store. In exchange for 8 percent of his gross income, Mozer obtained a three-year lease. He was guardedly optimistic: "I have the advantage of being the only jewelry store in Los Alamos. . . . It ought to be a sweet situation. On the other hand, we're less than thirty-five miles from Santa Fe. On Saturdays, always a big shopping day . . . , everybody's going to Santa Fe."[10] Hilltop merchants did prosper, but not surprisingly, doing business at Los Alamos was far from typical.

The AEC paid for the creation of this modern town. Constructing six houses in the North Community cost $10 million. To reach the new development, a bridge of earth-fill that spanned Pueblo Canyon cost $200,000. During the spring of 1948, a new Tech Area south of town was projected at a cost of $70 million. In June 1949 alone, the AEC authorized $16 million in contracts for new construction at Los Alamos. The largest contract went to Haddock Engineers of Oceanside, California, for $5,405,760 to construct 468 houses in the North

Community. Other contracts called for raising twelve laboratory buildings in the South Mesa Tech Area, and in April 1950, the McKee Construction Company submitted the low bid of $2.261 million to build an eighty-bed hospital. A new high school, also built by McKee Construction for $2 million, added to the active pace of construction on the Hill. The first wave of modernization focused on the residential areas and lasted throughout the late 1940s. Thus, by 1949, Los Alamos already represented an $800 million investment. Plans before Congress, even before Russia detonated its own nuclear device that fall, called for a five-year, $100 million replacement, modernization, and expansion program at Los Alamos.[11]

Federal monies flowed uphill to Los Alamos. Indeed, just the amount of money left over from the Manhattan Project was astounding. An October 1948 memo to Truman advisor Clark Clifford from AEC Commissioner David Lilienthal stated there was $798,826,124 remaining from the Manhattan Project account. Of that, $365,464,828 was already pledged for expenditures, but that left $433,361,296 in the Manhattan Project ledger more than a year and a half after the AEC took over control of nuclear matters. From that amount, the National Intelligence Authority received $7 million in September, and the Federal Bureau of Investigation requested over $9.6 million "for character investigations and security violations."[12] With all that money floating around, Los Alamos received its share of funding. By the end of 1948, when the population reached 8,200, the average annual income on the Hill was $3,371. The average American's at the time was $1,500, and citizens of New Mexico averaged even lower. Top scientific personnel at the lab earned $10,000 annually, as compared with up to $12,000 for top government officials there. During that time, lab director Norris Bradbury earned $12,500.[13]

The federal largesse expanded beyond hefty salaries and improved physical facilities. The Health Division of the laboratory received $500,000 for running the hospital and investigating the effects of atomic energy and particularly of radiation on human health. As Dr. Henry Whipple, acting director of the Health Division, observed in

An AEC guard at the East Gate controls access to Los Alamos. By 1952, stylish convertibles replaced older cars as prosperity swept the Hill. Courtesy of National Archives II, College Park, Md.

1948: "The medical possibilities of the Atomic Age are regarded as limitless, with the hope of finding a road toward the ultimate triumph over cancer." As work continued on the military uses of atomic energy, the laboratory also explored nonmilitary applications for it in medicine and technology.[14]

Another change occurred in weapons production that permitted Los Alamos to concentrate on pure research and development. In the fall of 1947, the AEC transferred the duties of assembling atomic weapons to Sandia Base at Albuquerque, New Mexico, seventy-five miles south of Los Alamos. The move enabled Los Alamos Scientific Laboratory (LASL) to focus more on nuclear physics research in general and nuclear weapons development in particular. In 1949, the Sandia Corporation became a subsidiary of Western Electric Corporation and ceased its relationship with the University of California. With the responsibilities for manufacturing the weapons moved to Sandia Laboratories, the nuclear wealth was spread to other regions of New

Mexico, and LASL was free to devote itself to theory, research, and experimentation.

In addition to working on nuclear weapons, Los Alamos pioneered in the field of nuclear reactors. Secret work with atomic reactors at the bottom of Los Alamos Canyon enhanced Los Alamos's ability to conduct experiments in nuclear physics. During the war, Los Alamos constructed the world's third nuclear reactor and the first one to use the enriched uranium isotope ^{235}U. This hollow stainless-steel sphere, one foot in diameter, was code-named the "Water Boiler" Reactor and "Omega West." It first achieved a sustained chain reaction on May 9, 1944. A more powerful version of the Water Boiler Reactor began operating December 1944 and allowed Los Alamos scientists to conduct experiments that few in the world at that time could accomplish. In 1948, LASL started the world's first plutonium-fueled reactor. Physicists named it "Clementine" because of the connection between the code name of plutonium ("49") and the reference to the gold rush forty-niners in the ballad "Clementine." The "fast reactor" was in fact a slow chain reaction that could be controlled and, thus, permitted detailed studies of atomic fission. Clementine aided in the development of reactors that could generate electrical power. Since Clementine was classified top-secret, references to it sometimes took whimsical turns. One scientist sent this telegram to Los Alamos about the fast reactor: "In a cavern, in a canyon, extrapolating must be fine; since you're miners, Forty-niners, tell me how is Clementine?"[15]

During this period, women also operated Clementine. Jane Heydorn was one who did. A veteran of the Manhattan Project, she arrived as a WAC in 1944. By 1949, she had served as a WAC, a phone operator, and then an electronics technician before running the plutonium-fueled reactor. Thrilled to get the opportunity, she later remarked: "I never thought I would ever have a chance to do anything like this. It was a challenge for me to learn how to operate a reactor. I didn't have the background."[16] With few formally trained nuclear technicians, the lab often found capable people within their ranks and, through in-house training, created a cadre of personnel necessary to run the various atomic projects.

At the bottom of canyons, outlying experimental stations also were surrounded by fences. This guard gate controlled access to Omega West, the first nuclear reactor at Los Alamos. Courtesy of National Archives II, College Park, Md.

Dr. Jane Hall also helped run Clementine. She arrived in Los Alamos in 1945 from the Met Lab at the University of Chicago. At LASL, she first worked on atomic weapons. Then Hall served as an alternate group leader in the experimental physics division, where she assisted with the design and construction of Clementine. She also was assistant technical associate director and then assistant director at Los Alamos in the early 1950s. In 1956, she became the secretary of the General Advisory Committee to the AEC.[17]

Attracting and retaining competent personnel remained key to the success of LASL in exploring nuclear energy, from weapons to

The Omega West reactor at the bottom of Los Alamos canyon was the third nuclear reactor in the world. Courtesy of National Archives II, College Park, Md.

medicine to power production. Even as the Great Exodus of 1945–46 decimated the staff, the combination of the latest in nuclear equipment, the beauty of the site, and the glamour of working at the birthplace of a new era helped refill the ranks in the Tech Area. A new wave of more politically conservative staff, attracted by both the opportunity to work in one of the most advanced labs in the world and the patriotic duty to wage the Cold War, were recruited by director Dr. Norris Bradbury. Besides providing stability immediately after the war, Bradbury also assisted the staff in wrestling with the moral dilemmas posed by working on weapons of mass destruction. Bradbury called new employees into his office and discussed the purpose of LASL. In essence, he told the new recruits that "without the slightest shadow of a doubt, we must arm ourselves . . . for a war that we basically know we must not fight until every other diplomatic and political resource is exhausted."[18] Los Alamos was buying time for the politicians to solve the problems of the Cold War. Additionally, he warned the new employees that if nuclear weapons were ever used in anger, Los Alamos would have failed in its mission.[19]

Most personnel resorted to rationalization when discussing their work on nuclear weapons. As Physicist Frederick Reines told a reporter:

> I often ask myself why I'm here trying to figure new ways of killing people. I always arrive at the same conclusion: that making a nation strong means making it powerful for anything it wants to do, peaceful as well as warlike; that the information being uncovered here is fundamental, not only to destructive but also constructive uses of nuclear energy. In the final analysis, I realize we as a nation gain nothing by being weak, much by being strong. . . . The people here are hoping desperately that discoveries incidental to the production of atomic weapons will yield more good than all the bad that may result from the use of those bombs.[20]

Reines touched on a central theme for many working with nuclear weapons—that their efforts were not just for destructive purposes but for the creation of new, beneficial uses of atomic energy.

Mary Palevsky, the daughter of Project Y veterans Harry and Elaine Palevsky, interviewed numerous nuclear scientists, from Edward Teller to Joseph Rotblat, to understand, first, how her parents could have helped create a weapon of mass destruction and, then, how people after Hiroshima and Nagasaki could continue to build more and bigger nuclear bombs. The wartime urgency, the nuances of nuclear deterrence in the Cold War, and the attraction of "technically sweet" science provide the backdrop for her book. In *Atomic Fragments*, Palevsky explores the moral and ethical implications of the bomb. For many of the nuclear pioneers, creating atomic bombs was not a black-and-white issue. Even a few of those people who worked long hours to create an atom bomb during World War II opposed further postwar development. Sometimes they returned to supporting nuclear weapons as tensions between the U.S. and the U.S.S.R. rose in the early 1950s. With some of the greatest physicists of the times working with atomic weapons, the justifications that Palevsky discovered are scientific, political, and even spiritual. As she quotes Freeman Dyson:

"We are struggling to come to terms with a drama too large for a single mind to comprehend."[21]

As the attempt to establish international control over nuclear energy faltered in the late 1940s, and the Cold War intensified when the Soviets blockaded West Berlin, residents at Los Alamos told reporters their mission was essential for national defense and indeed, world peace. Some reporters interviewed LASL personnel about these current events. One such story in the *Christian Science Monitor* summed up the workers' attitudes: "Disillusioned by the failure of the United Nations to get anywhere on the international control of atomic energy, these men are sure now that such security as the United States can have rests primarily upon their constant endeavor to create more powerful, more efficient, more advanced types of atomic weapons."[22]

The attraction for some of the scientists in working at Los Alamos went beyond technically sweet science, national security necessity, or belief in an atomic cornucopia. Richard Feynman offered another reason in his autobiography: "The same thrill, the same awe and mystery, comes again and again when we look at any question deeply enough. With more knowledge comes a deeper, more wonderful mystery, luring one on to penetrate deeper still. . . . With pleasure and confidence we turn over each new stone to find unimagined strangeness leading on to more wonderful questions and mysteries—certainly a grand adventure."[23] The mysteries and the power of the atom did provide unimagined strangeness for many scientists on the Hill. As these people witnessed the primal blasts of nuclear weapons' testing, many reverted to a mysticism like Feynman's to help understand the awesome forces unleashed. And for some, their belief in God grew stronger as they themselves acquired the godlike powers that could create an Armageddon.

Whatever the attraction of building nuclear weapons, work continued at the laboratory. However, after the Bikini tests in 1946, the United States did not explode another nuclear weapon until 1948. Partly because of the transfer from the U.S. Army to the AEC and partly because of a lack of plutonium, the U.S. atomic weapon stockpile remained small. Nevertheless, President Truman in July 1947 authorized a series of tests for the new weapons developed by Los Alamos, code-named "Operation Sandstone." As the AEC settled into its managerial duties, and with the British agreeing to augment America's raw nuclear material early in 1948, the United States planned a new series of atomic tests at the Eniwetok Atoll in the Marshall Islands of the South Pacific. Joint Task Force Seven, a multi-branch military organization, was created to construct the testing grounds and assist the AEC in conducting the tests in October 1947. In April and May 1948, three second-generation prototypes of atomic bombs gouged out huge craters in the Eniwetok Atoll. These more efficient bombs, designed at Los Alamos, dramatically increased the weapons' yields. Each bomb dropped on Japan in 1945 equaled twenty-five thousand tons of TNT (twenty-five kilotons), whereas the Sandstone models unleashed the explosive power of forty-nine kilotons. For the more efficient models, less plutonium was needed and, consequently, by 1950, the United States had manufactured approximately three hundred atomic devices.[24]

In spite of the success of the bombs, problems arose with Operation Sandstone. The nine-thousand-mile supply line from the States to Eniwetok hampered the testing of atomic weapons, so a continental test site was proposed. In response, recently promoted Rear Admiral William (Deak) Parsons, deputy commander of Joint Task Force Seven and the man who armed the Hiroshima bomb, noted: "There is no question that there will be difficult local and general public relations problems." The AEC would smooth over the public relation problems in the years to come, beginning with the published account of Operation Sandstone.[25]

In the United States, the attitude toward nuclear energy, especially atomic bombs, had changed in the three years since 1945. One can see this in two official publications, *Operation Crossroads* and *Operation Sandstone*. These books are mainly pictorial records of the two series of tests. *Operation Crossroads* chronicles the preparation, the detonations, and the effects of Tests Able and Baker in 1946 with numerous photos of the mushroom clouds. Graphic pictures show the destruction to ships and land caused by the Operation Crossroads' two shots. On the other hand, *Operation Sandstone* focuses on the construction and preparation for the tests in 1948 with hundreds of photos of men working and playing on the islands. On page 84 of the 104-page book, a picture of a swirling cloud is the only photo in the sequence that hints of the atomic blast. Following page 84, photos show the decontamination of planes and equipment and personnel leaving the site. No evidence of the destructiveness of the blasts exists in *Operation Sandstone*, and the only pictures of the full mushroom clouds are the frontispiece and eight photos taken from a distance that are inserted at the end of the book. In addition, the book does not mention how many shots were fired, nor what their code names were. If one took a cursory look at *Operation Sandstone*, one might conclude that this was merely a training mission on an exotic island, instead of a successful series of tests where new, more efficient bombs carved out large atomic footprints on the sands of Eniwetok.

After the initial flush of atomic exuberance in 1945 and 1946, more guarded feelings about atomic weapons entered into the national debate. Secrecy, in place to prevent atomic information from falling into enemy hands, was now adapted to protect American citizens from atomic fears. As noted above, the awe-inspiring photos of huge mushroom clouds and large-scale destruction showcased in *Operation Crossroads* gave way to the summer camp pictures in *Operation Sandstone*. In addition to enforcing secrecy in response to the escalating arms race, the AEC and the military clearly sanitized the reports coming back from Sandstone to defuse public fear and shield their operations.[26]

The effects of radiation on the human body is still one of the most hotly contested topics about atomic weapons. Health hazards concerning exposure to radioactivity surfaced again in the Sandstone tests. Several workers from Los Alamos received severe radiation burns during the shots. On one occasion, four men removing air filters from the air samplers that recorded the radioactivity after the blast were exposed to high levels of radiation. One man noticed a tingling and itching in his palms as he removed the filters at Eniwetok. Two hours later, his hands stiffened and a slight swelling surfaced. The next day, the swelling and redness had increased, and within a month, big blisters had formed on his hands. A Health Division report noted: "There was minimal healing during the third, fourth, and fifth months of the disease. Skin grafting of these lesions is to be performed in the near future. . . . It is felt that surgical repair will result in only poor final function."[27] Later reports noted that recovery of these men took from fifty days to seven months. Three of the men required plastic surgery to cover skin ulcers and to restore the use of their fingers. Despite the earlier fears about poor recovery, health officials later concluded that the results of the operations had "been surprisingly good."[28]

Back at Los Alamos, additional incidents involving radioactivity occurred on the Hill from 1947 to 1949. Several of these occurred in a series of open-air experiments called the RaLa (Radioactive Lanthanum) Program. In the tests, personnel attached quarter-sized pieces of radioactive lanthanum to conventional explosives and detonated the assembly. These experiments produced data on the explosive process. Between 1944 and 1961, 254 RaLa tests exploded in Bayo Canyon, two miles north of the town. In 1948, two workers received radioactive burns in the canyon, and in 1949 and again in 1950, fallout from the tests blew over parts of a housing area and Los Alamos's main road. Authorities closed the road, and men in respirators patrolled the contaminated stretch. Laboratory officials claimed no one was overexposed at the time of either incident.[29]

Additional exposure to radioactivity came from carelessness or arrogance. Beginning in 1943, a chemical sewer line that originated at the Tech Area dumped its toxic and radioactive liquid wastes into Acid Canyon, near Central School. At a town council meeting in August 1946, irate parents complained about Acid Canyon. According to the meeting's minutes: "It was reported that there was a dangerous contaminated area 1500 feet from the school grounds that needed fencing in. [Associate Director Darol] Froman will attend to this."[30] He did not. Despite additional memos from the health officials at LASL about the proximity of untreated radioactive liquid waste to the school, no fences went up. Almost a year later, in a July 1947 memo, Dr. Louis Hempelmann (group leader of the Health Division) warned: "The Health Division has disclaimed all responsibility for future consequences resulting from the continued delay in erection of such fences."[31] After this stern memo, a fence finally enclosed the dump site.

Close to the school and several housing neighborhoods, Acid Canyon connected with the larger Pueblo Canyon, which was a favorite play area for the Hill's children. Susan Tiano remembers feeling safe in the canyon, and Jack Bell made forts with his friends on the canyon floor. No memos have surfaced as to why laboratory officials delayed fencing off a radioactive portion of their children's play area. Perhaps the bureaucratic confusion and transfer to the AEC prevented timely action. Or maybe the authorities realized the futility of fencing off a small portion of the canyon from inquisitive youngsters. As Jack Bell recalled: "We'd go all over the plateau until we'd run into a fence, and then we'd jump over that fence until an M.P. would run us off."[32] Still, money for fencing the site was available, and the Zia Company had adequate staff for the job. During the war, initial conditions at Los Alamos permitted authorities to gloss over health concerns. After the war, the institutionalized neglect of atomic waste continued, despite evidence of its toxicity.

Children knew about such hazards in their own ways. A reporter for the *Christian Science Monitor* observed some children playing on the Hill. He wrote: "Children, playing hopscotch, call the squares to be jumped over, on the sidewalk, 'contaminated'—the word atomic scientists use to warn of a radioactive area."[33] Incorporating this term into their games and having a place nearby called Acid Canyon suggests that some type of knowledge about the toxic nature of the work at the lab permeated to the youngest members of the community.

In 1949, the AEC released a pamphlet on handling radioactive wastes. The guidelines for dealing with such wastes were clear: "At the Radiation Laboratory, Berkeley, California, concentrated liquid wastes are mixed with cement and stored in oil drums. Later these materials are dumped some 30 miles out at sea. No radioactive materials are dumped in the San Francisco Bay region."[34] The Los Alamos laboratory did fence in Acid Canyon but, contrary to the AEC's own published guidelines, continued to dump untreated liquid radioactive waste into Acid Canyon until 1953.

A series of questionable medical experiments at Los Alamos examined how various radioactive elements affected the body. In one group of tests, more than fifty individuals, including scientists' children, were given small doses of radioactive iodine, tritium, and other substances to see how quickly the material passed through their bodies.[35] Additional invasive experiments using radioactive elements on human subjects proliferated in the late 1940s. In one report, the Department of Energy estimated that sixteen thousand men, women, and children participated, knowingly and unknowingly, in experiments that put radioactive substances in their food and drink and submitted them to plutonium injections in a few cases. Pregnant women, mental patients, and prisoners received varying amounts of radioactive doses to see where the elements collected and how fast the body could expel them. The purpose of these experiments was to set safety standards for nuclear workers, and, indeed, many of the standards used even today derive from them. Unfortunately, some of the subjects of these experiments never gave their informed consent for the procedures. Besides the civilians exposed to radiation, some one million military personnel participated in operations that also exposed them to radioactivity and toxic materials. At the atomic sites in Japan, and during the 235 above-ground nuclear tests that the United States conducted, servicemen assisted in the blasts and conducted maneuvers to test the effects of nuclear explosions on combat readiness. The long-term health effects of exposure to both penetrating and lingering radioactivity continues to stir rancorous debate.[36]

In spite of the radioactive hazards, many residents of Los Alamos felt safe and secure in their town ringed by fences and patrolled by guards, and the natural beauty of the site enticed adults and children. Dave McKee, project manager for the Zia Company, bragged about the quality of life on the Hill: "Our city is, without a doubt, one of the finest places in which to raise children because of the absence of dreaded diseases which are encountered in larger cities and warmer parts of the country."[37] True, traditional urban diseases, like tuber-culosis, rarely showed up at Los Alamos, but with toxic elements pouring out of a sewer into Acid Canyon, and the disposal of other poisonous substances at sites on the Pajarito Plateau, Los Alamos was not entirely safe. In fact, worries about elevated risks of cancer due to radioactive exposure at the site surfaced over the years and continue to this day. However, the immediate danger for children at Los Alamos resided not in the unseen radioactive hazards but in a more tangible form.

The town, from its inception, blew up things. Because conven-tional explosives often initiated the atomic chain reaction in bombs, many experiments investigated the behavior of such a blast's shock waves. Residents routinely heard and felt non-nuclear explosions. Ellen Reid, whose father worked with high explosives, knew tests were scheduled regularly at 10 A.M., 12 P.M., and 3 P.M. At school, she could hear them. "If there were explosions at times other than those designated times, we worried. Everybody would sort of stop and go 'hmmm.' The other thing, we sort of got to be connoisseurs of explo-sions. We liked the really big ones. If they would go boom-Boom-boom-Ba-BOOM, aha, that was a good one."[38]

With shock waves rocking classrooms, some children sought out the source of the booms. Most of the testing of explosives occurred at S Site, south of town; however, during the war, research on the hydro-dynamic behavior of high explosives occurred all over the Pajarito Plateau. Some ordnance had failed to detonate and littered the wooded areas, unexploded. Children romping through these areas found the shells, and not surprisingly in a town known for explosions, played with the devices. One of Donald Marchi's earliest memories involves an accidental detonation when he was six. Donald's mother was baby-sitting twelve-year-old Leroy Chávez when some youngsters in the apartment above them tired of playing with a live bazooka shell they had found. They threw it off the balcony, it exploded as it hit the ground, and the shrapnel ripped open Chávez's abdomen. Marchi's sister, who had nursing experience, held Chávez together as they rushed him to the hospital. Miraculously, Chávez survived. Another ordnance accident also affected a child on the Hill. Vicky Mullholland either found a mortar shell while playing in the canyons, or her father picked one up and brought it home. It exploded while she was playing with it, and as a result, she lost one of her legs. Several schoolmates recalled seeing her in the halls of the high school in a wheelchair, disabled from the accident.[39]

In the town site and the wooded areas of the plateau, children also encountered fenced-off areas with prominent signs warning "Danger—Contaminated—Do Not Enter." For some children, this was an invitation. In 1949, police found four boys playing in a fenced-off area, sailing their boats in a radioactive pond. Health officials inspected and released the boys, asserting that "the children were found to be minus radioactivity" and echoing the police that "entrance to the area must have been through a disposal plant."[40] The article neglected to mention whether this site was Ashley Pond or Acid Canyon. As Tiano noted, Los Alamos was a dangerous place for children because of the unexploded ordnance.[41] One had to be careful in the atomic landscape surrounding Los Alamos because it held a treacherous beauty.

Not all the youth at Los Alamos broke rules or played with unexploded shells, but all of them attended school. Because the baby boom came early to Los Alamos, the resultant surge of children hit the elementary school in the late 1940s. By 1948, approximately 1,300 students jostled in the hallways and classrooms on the Hill. Construction struggled to keep up with the growth. As one magazine story noted, buildings were "hardly up before they [were] overcrowded."[42] New elementary schools popped up to relieve the pressure on the Central School, and in the fall of 1949, a new high school opened to wide acclaim. The local paper, under the headline "Pace-Setter for the Nation," proclaimed the high school "one of the most modern and beautiful school buildings in the country."[43] Even though the anticipated enrollment at the high school for the fall of 1949 amounted to only 200 students, the school could eventually accommodate 750 pupils as "the much greater number of students in the lower grades, increasing proportionately down to kindergarten, made a much larger high school building a necessity."[44] Already, two new elementary schools, Canyon and Mesa, augmented the elementary facilities and helped Central School handle the crush from the baby boom and the new families arriving at the town.[45]

Los Alamos's educational system continued to play a key role in attracting laboratory staff. In a 1947 handbook, new LASL employees learned: "The Los Alamos Public Schools are organized for the sole purpose of assisting in the development of emotionally secure, well trained American citizens. Because we are living in a democratic society, our philosophy and methods are democratic. . . . Great stress is placed on the so-called fundamentals of education: reading, writing, and arithmetic. As much attention is given to arts, crafts, music and physical education."[46] To create such a comprehensive curriculum, the AEC generously subsidized the Los Alamos Public Schools. In 1948, the school budget totaled $400,000, which, divided among the 1,300 students, came to $308 per pupil per year. The nationwide average at the time equaled $180 per student, but New Mexico allocated only $165. The 1949–50 school year had a budget of $516,641 for an estimated enrollment of 2,000 students, with $366,641 paid by the AEC and $150,000 from the state. The new total cost for each student amounted to $356. Los Alamos's school budget, subsidized by the federal government, paid for teachers' salaries, for construction of modern facilities, and for programs emphasizing math and science that were unusual for a town of its size in New Mexico.[47]

As Los Alamos moved toward official county status in 1949, problems mounted concerning the incorporation of the town's schools into the state's educational system. Difficulties arose over the budget, administrative support, and the classification of the schools. Eventually, Los Alamos organized as a rural school district because of the unique county status created for the atomic city; however, parents and school officials refused to accept New Mexico's rural school district requirements—not because they were too arduous, but because they were not rigorous enough. New Mexico set a maximum salary for a rural superintendent at $4,426. The Los Alamos school board wanted to pay its superintendent $8,100. County principals were limited to a reduced clerical staff, and no public kindergartens serviced rural school districts, which was unacceptable to Hill parents. New Mexico allocated $1 per pupil per year for supplies; the Los Alamos superintendent requested $12.75.[48]

Overcoming such discrepancies, the Los Alamos school board accepted state incorporation in the summer of 1949. While the state dictated minimum requirements for curriculum and teacher qualifications, the Los Alamos district usually surpassed these guidelines to satisfy the demands of parents on the Hill. To generate the funds needed for the enhanced programs, the AEC School Committee turned to creative bookkeeping because Los Alamos, being a federal reserve without private ownership of property, lacked the usual real estate taxes that supported public education. To rectify the absent tax base, the committee developed a formula that estimated the value of Los Alamos real estate at $82.5 million. Using half of that as a theoretical tax base, the AEC then contributed $375,431 to the Los Alamos school budget to make up the shortfall. Thus, the Los Alamos public school system, comparable to private schools around the nation, was mostly paid for by the federal government.[49]

The influx of families to the laboratory strained not just Los Alamos schools but nearby school districts as well. Senator Dennis Chávez (D–N.Mex.) angrily denounced the federal government's subsidizing of Los Alamos schools while ignoring the neighboring communities that suffered from overcrowding as a result of the children of commuting LASL employees. When pressured by Chávez, the AEC justified its generous support as being in "the best interest of the United States."[50] Following this congressional scrutiny, school board member (and LASL director) Norris Bradbury wrote the AEC that the board objected to publicity about Los Alamos's schools in national publications. He asked the AEC's public relations personnel to discourage any further requests from journalists in order to avoid criticism of Los Alamos's school system. The AEC tried to honor Bradbury's request. As a result, Congress and the country stopped learning about the superior schools and innovative programs on the Hill, and like the site's nuclear programs, the schools' achievements remained secret.[51]

For most children, Los Alamos's postwar schools lived up to their parents' expectations. Teachers and administrators sought to provide excellent educational programs. Youngsters who had attended schools elsewhere confirmed the better quality of Los Alamos schools. Kim Manley remarked: "A lot of the teachers were very good, and if you were motivated, they would bend over backwards to make sure that you had things to keep you interested, that you could do beyond regular assignments in their classes."[52] Ellen Reid agreed: "All the way through school, if you expressed any interest in anything, there was always someone there to sort of reinforce you or let you do it. I think it was a very good school system."[53] In the 1950s, Ellen and her friends requested a Russian studies program in the school, and they got one. Thus, as the Cold War with the Soviet Union intensified, students at Los Alamos High School took courses in Russian language and culture.

Superintendent F. Robert Wegner recruited teachers from across the nation to fill his classrooms. For example, in the spring of 1949, he crisscrossed the country searching for twenty-nine new teachers. Once at Los Alamos, teachers had to face the uncomfortable situation that sometimes their students knew more than they did. One magazine reported: "Intelligence tests have rated a number of the pupils in the near-genius class, a situation that challenges the professional competence of even their teachers."[54] Sam Miles, principal of Mesa Elementary school in 1949, had this motto: "Genius is common, and the circumstances fitted to develop it very rare."[55] To develop the abilities of his students, Miles offered not only the three R's but practical applications. Teachers set up stores in the second grade where children play-acted buying and selling goods. He also let sixth-graders run the store, selling school supplies and candy with the help of an adding machine. Second-graders used typewriters, and by the fourth grade, some students typed their English compositions. Beginning in first grade, shop class was required for all students. Miles explained these classes: "We've found that the higher the intelligence, the more creative the child can be. Children in the past often haven't had a chance to develop their manual skills. We . . . find it develops their skills as well as teaching them respect for manual

High school students learned typing at Central School. Courtesy of Los Alamos National Laboratory Archives.

workers. . . . The projects get the children to thinking. . . . That's the most vital part."[56]

Another reason for exposing children at an early age to shop class and machines sprang from the needs of the Atomic Age. At this outpost on the technological frontier, workers familiar with scientific equipment and ones who could manipulate various materials from wood to exotic metals were scarce in the immediate postwar years. To train a new generation of workers for the highly specialized work in nuclear enterprises, Los Alamos schools started in the elementary grades to acquaint students with such technical skills.

The national press increasingly focused on Los Alamos after the AEC took over. Publications like the *Denver Post*, the *Saturday Evening Post*, the *Christian Science Monitor*, *Life*, the *New Republic*, and the *New Yorker* ran stories about the atomic city. Some articles recounted

Manhattan Project tales, but others portrayed the Hill as a pacesetter for the nation, a modern city of the future. The *Saturday Evening Post* on December 11, 1948, ran a profile of Los Alamos in its "Cities of America" series, calling Los Alamos "part factory town, part college town, part a typical but highly progressive American community. There is in the dust and clamor of pneumatic drills and lumbering road machines something of the feeling of a boomtown, but there is elsewhere that sophistication and intellectual atmosphere of a university."[57] Part boomtown, part college campus, Los Alamos was nonetheless predominantly a factory town in the nuclear complex. It designed and provided assistance in assembling and delivering atomic weapons. Because of the secrecy of this enterprise, reporters could not write about the laboratory, so they focused on the burgeoning town instead. With the town erecting a Community Center and suburban neighborhoods, journalists concentrated on the invention of this atomic community on the frontlines of the Cold War.[58]

Los Alamos as a high-tech, Wild West boomtown fascinated the American imagination. Building on the frontier myth, nuclear weapons replaced six-shooters, and atomic cowboys rode to the rescue of the country, defending the nation and the free world from Stalin's gang of villains in black hats. Although barred from writing about activities in the Tech Area, a few journalists pointed out the explosions that rocked the community. Mason Sutherland in the *National Geographic* noted that a blast happened soon after he arrived at the site. An accompanying public relations' officer dismissed the explosion, saying it was an "ordinary construction blast. We have many of them. . . . However, when a construction blast raised a mushroom-shaped cloud, outsiders were convinced we were firing atom bombs. We faced a lawsuit by a farmer who said our 'bombs' made his hens stop laying."[59] Daniel Lang, writing for the *New Yorker*, heard a different explanation for the explosions: "When there is an especially loud bang, someone, availing himself of a local pleasantry, will say 'Thunder'."[60] At the time of these stories, construction projects did use dynamite for carving into the soft tuff of the plateau; however, the Ra-La experiments in Bayo

Canyon also detonated blasts that at times scattered radioactive particles over surrounding areas.

Notwithstanding the explosions that affected hens, benefits accrued to the region from the nuclear enterprises on the Hill. High-paying jobs, scarce in the small farming communities nearby, continued to attract workers from around the country to the site, as well as provide employment for local people. One reporter interviewed 104-year-old Geronimo Tafoya from nearby Santa Clara Pueblo, and wrote: "Los Alamos . . . has brought prosperity to the pueblos and to his people. His daughters and granddaughters [worked] on the Hill and he [was] fond of telling them that twenty-five cents was considered a good wage when the Indians started working for the white man in this country."[61] Pueblo governments used the income from Los Alamos jobs to improve their communities. Tesuque Pueblo, ten miles north of Santa Fe, installed indoor plumbing and electricity to all the homes surrounding their plaza in 1947. In 1948, San Ildefonso Pueblo, the closest village to Los Alamos, bought a new harvester, a new truck, and gave each tribal member $45 at Christmas from the income gained by renting reservation land to a construction company.[62]

Not everyone at San Ildefonso was happy, though. Edith Warner, who lived at Otowi Crossing (the place where the "Water Cuts Down Through"), told an East Coast reporter: "The Indians . . . are earning more money, but not enough to compensate them for what they have lost. They cannot get wood, water, or greens for their dances. . . . They used to go to certain canyons for that, but now they are shut off from those places by guards or by radioactive contamination."[63] The Hill, despite its well-paying jobs, adversely affected the pueblo in other ways. First, with men and women working on the Hill, farming was neglected. Second, the pueblo no longer had access to traditional hunting and sacred grounds on the Pajarito Plateau. Finally, people from Los Alamos intruded on what was left of pueblo land. Able Sanchez, a later governor of San Ildefonso, complained: "We tried to keep [people from Los Alamos] away from our reservation. It was pretty hard to do that. People that come from the East don't understand tribal regulations."[64] Newcomers not accustomed to tribal practices and puebloan sacred landscapes did intrude upon those traditions and places.

The intrusion of Los Alamos into northern New Mexico also challenged the lawmakers of New Mexico. In the spring of 1949, New Mexico legislators debated the legal status of Los Alamos. As a federal reserve appropriated by the army during the war, Los Alamos remained outside of state laws, and its relationship with New Mexico remained murky. For example, residents enjoyed no representation in the state legislature and could not vote as New Mexico residents in national elections. In response to these problems, President Truman, on March 4, 1949, retroceded Los Alamos to New Mexico, which opened the way for the New Mexico Senate to pass Senate Bill # 216. Approved on March 16, S.B. 216 established a new category of counties in New Mexico, the Class 6 county, which, among other stipulations, had to have a population of not less than five thousand and cover an area of not more than twelve square miles. Only Los Alamos County, in all of New Mexico, fit all these guidelines. On June 10, 1949, Los Alamos became New Mexico's thirty-second county, carved out of Sandoval and Santa Fe counties. Residents of the new county moved quickly, naming county commissioners, establishing a county government, and applying for school funds for the coming school year. To settle difficulties with the State Board of Education, specifically over the enhanced requirements and extra expense of the Los Alamos school system, the AEC agreed to "augment school funds as considered advisable."[65] At the same time that Los Alamos achieved official county status, an international event insured that the community would remain a permanent fixture in the atomic firmament.

Even though the United States held a monopoly on atomic weapons, scientists, politicians, and newspaper editors had warned from the beginning that the monopoly would not last. After Trinity, the world knew of the Manhattan Project and the successful application of atomic energy for military purposes. The binding energy of the atom was no longer a secret of nature, but one of man. Los Alamos had tapped atomic energy, and now the only secret lay in the details, which other nuclear scientists, with enough governmental support or through espionage, could repeat. Even before Trinity, the Soviet Union had gained access through Klaus Fuchs and David Greenglass to the Manhattan Project and received precise information about the secrets of the atomic bombs. The question was not whether another country could create its own atomic weapon, but when.[66]

The military complained about the lack of nuclear readiness. With the international situation deteriorating as the Berlin Blockade entered its second year, as Czechoslovakia fell to a Soviet coup, and as Chinese Communists moved toward victory in the world's most populous country, Secretary of Defense Louis Johnson warned Truman that "the National Military Establishment is gravely concerned over the need to expand our production facilities for fissionable material."[67] In the letter, Johnson and the Joint Chiefs of Staff requested $300 million over the next three years for construction of new plants to produce fissionable material for weapons and $60 million per year thereafter for operating costs. So, even before the detonation of the Soviet bomb, the military had sounded an alarm.

The alarm turned into a full-blown emergency in the fall of 1949. On September 3, 1949, a weather reconnaissance plane in the North Pacific took an air sample that showed a high level of radioactivity. After receiving extensive analysis from Los Alamos and the army, Oppenheimer, Parsons, Vannevar Bush, and Robert Bacher met in Washington, D.C., on September 19 to review the data collected, not just from the weather plane but from other sources around the Northern Hemisphere. They concurred with the conclusions of Air Force General Vandenberg's staff that the Soviets had detonated a plutonium bomb sometime between August 26 and 29 in eastern Russia. Indeed, on the morning of August 29, the Soviets had exploded their own atomic device in the province of Kazakhstan.[68]

Even before the test at Trinity in 1945, the Soviets knew about Los Alamos's bomb project from their spies at Site Y. Soon after the war, the USSR initiated its own nuclear weapons' program and in April

1946 chose Sarov, a monastery 240 miles southeast of Moscow, as its research laboratory.[69] Like Los Alamos, the Soviet's atomic city had many code names: Base-112, KB-11, Kremlev, Centre-300 (the Volga Office), and Arzamas-16. Arzamas-16, purposely named after a town forty-five miles to the north, became its official title. Andrei Sakharov, who invented the Russian hydrogen bomb and worked at Arzamas-16 from 1950 to 1968, called the place "the Installation." For Sakharov, the Installation was a "curious symbiosis between an ultramodern scientific research institute . . . and a huge labour camp."[70] Most scientists referred to the atomic city merely as Sarov and even humorously as Los Arzamas.

The nuclear scientists at Arzamas-16 struggled with many problems. As at Los Alamos, housing was bleak, with some of the structures obtained as war reparations from the Russian-Finnish War of 1940. Other buildings were quickly constructed out of wood without any foundation ditches. Some supplies were scarce and, as late as 1947, Soviet scientists had to cut flat rubber gaskets for their vacuum tubes out of inner tubes from car tires. Some of the workers at Arzamas-16 were prisoners, although no political prisoners were allowed at the site. Despite these difficulties, the Soviet bomb project progressed rapidly. In December 1946 at the Moscow Laboratory # 2, a small nuclear reactor went on-line. In July 1948, the Russians activated a more powerful reactor. By the middle of 1949, using information passed on from their agents at Los Alamos during the war, Soviet scientists started experimenting with critical assemblies.[71]

In August 1949, the Soviets were ready to test their bomb, which they dubbed "the Manufacture." On the train ride to the testing ground at Semipalatinsk, some of the personnel jumped onto the station platform during a short stop and started playing volleyball. A colonel went over to stop them, while a superior fumed: "They're supposed to be serious people. . . . They're on a responsible mission and they behave like a bunch of eighteen-year-old kids."[72] Using the blueprints that had come from Los Alamos, the Soviets detonated a bomb comparable to Fat Man at the end of August.

President Truman informed the American public about the Soviet bomb on September 23. In a statement from the White House delayed nearly a month by arduous verification and frantic consultation, he said:

> I believe the American people, to the fullest extent consistent with national security, are entitled to be informed of all developments in the field of atomic energy. That is my reason for making public the following information. We have evidence that within recent weeks an atomic explosion occurred in the U.S.S.R. Ever since the atomic energy was first released by man, the eventual development of this new force by other nations was to be expected. This probability has always been taken into account by us.[73]

The president concluded his statement with an appeal for international control of atomic energy: "This recent development emphasizes . . . the necessity for that truly effective enforceable international control of atomic energy which this Government and the large majority of the members of the United Nations support."[74]

Reaction to Truman's statement varied around the country. The stock market rallied as investors believed that a renewed arms race would boost employment and prevent a recession. *Life* magazine published this updated sentiment of "Praise the Lord and pass the ammunition" in its October 3 issue: "At 11:02 A.M. on September 23, 1949, . . . the long wait of the Western world came to an end. . . . What the atomic explosion means for the U.S. citizen was still uncertain. . . . Above all, the U.S. would go right on trusting in the rights as God gives it to see the right, meanwhile stockpiling its atomic weapons."[75] On the streets of Santa Fe, one man asked: "Why should we worry here in Santa Fe? We're all in danger wherever we are. I'd feel no different in Los Angeles or New York than I do here."[76]

Two days later, the Soviet news agency TASS released its own statement. After verifying that the USSR had exploded a nuclear bomb, it concluded with a statement similar to Truman's: "It must be said that the Soviet government, despite its possession of atomic weapons, still maintains, and in the future will continue to maintain, its former position on the unconditional banning of the use of nuclear weapons."[77] Two of the victorious allies from World War II now faced each other as potential enemies armed with nuclear weapons.

Calls for rapid and massive expansions of the nation's nuclear facilities came from the nation's capital. On October 4, rumors appeared hinting that the AEC would ask for additional funding beyond the $1 billion already appropriated. Senator Homer Ferguson, a member of the Senate Appropriations Committee, observed: "The Atomic Energy Commission has received just about everything it has asked for. . . . It seems doubtful that they could spend any more money wisely, but if they can, Congress probably would grant it."[78] Stories appeared in newspapers of Truman's signing bills to create new research facilities and to expand those already in existence. These and other reports in the press on the country's atomic installations assured the public that the United States would not falter in its race with the Soviet Union. However, top-secret Los Alamos avoided most of the press coverage.[79]

Publicly, officials from Los Alamos said little about the Soviet bomb. On the day the news broke, director Bradbury was in Washington for consultation, though the laboratory refused to say whether the trip had any relation to Truman's announcement. Frustrated by the lack of response, one reporter wrote: "The official mouthpiece in the Atomic Energy Commission's atomic center here was closed tighter than a Soviet underling."[80] This comparison revealed a new journalistic willingness to criticize government secrecy.

Despite the public silence, Los Alamos attracted official delegations from the government and the military. At the end of October, four members of the Joint Congressional Committee on Atomic Energy met at Los Alamos to investigate "a phase of weapon development."[81] At the same time, four other men, members of the AEC's Weapons Evaluation Group, arrived on the Hill. One person in this latter group, Rear Admiral Deak Parsons, was an old friend to Los Alamos. If the congressmen had questions about the military implications of Joe 1 (the American nickname for the Soviet blast) or the status of America's atomic arsenal, Parsons and the rest of his group could provide expert answers. After the meeting, Representative Chet Holifield, the chair of the Joint Committee, told reporters that the world situation revealed "an urgency just short of war." However, to reassure a worried public, Holifield praised the work done at the laboratory: "Experimental work in weapons conducted at Los Alamos is vital to the work done at the production centers of Hanford, Washington and Oak Ridge, Tennessee."[82] Los Alamos's experiments and research would help protect the nation in the escalating nuclear arms race.

Perhaps with permission from the Joint Committee, a week after the congressmen and military experts left Los Alamos, Santa Fe's *New Mexican* ran a front-page story on what to do in the case of a nuclear attack. Officials in Los Alamos discussed with reporters the possibility of an attack on the atomic city and the chances of surviving it. While admitting that Los Alamos might be considered "enemy potential target No.1," AEC officials argued that a nuclear war "will be a battle of short duration, with little point in wiping out the research center here."[83] Concerning the chances of surviving an atomic blast, a laboratory official somewhat flippantly suggested this scenario: "If you are within a half-mile of the point directly under an atomic explosion, you've had it. . . . From one-half to two miles from the explosion, it's all in the lap of lady luck. . . . At over two miles, the odds are way over on your side. So, generally speaking for Los Alamos, a bomb explosion over the present technical area here would raise the dickens with the tech area itself, the community center, and most of the residential area in the eastern end of Los Alamos."[84] His jaunty language was clearly an attempt to defuse public fear. The article continued: "Experts have recommended air raid warnings, bomb shelters, evacuations, dispersion, and organized disaster relief as much that can be done to cut down casualties and save thousands of lives."[85] Residents of Los Alamos probably took little comfort in this scenario for their community. With the two superpowers now possessing atomic weapons, the threat emerged more than ever in the United States that one's own backyard might become an atomic Ground Zero.[86]

As the nation, the state, and the Hill prepared their civil defense plans for atomic attacks, the laboratory also shifted into high gear to counter the Soviet advances with nuclear weapons. Los Alamos's mission put it once again in the forefront of national security, and the nation looked to the laboratory and the community for reassurance and hope in the face of an escalating arms race.

CHAPTER 5

A COLD WAR
COMMUNITY UP IN ARMS

COMPETITION AND
CONFORMITY

*"The longer one remains in this remote and
restricted government town . . . the stronger
becomes the impression that this is now the most
important point on the map of the United States
except for Washington."*
ROLAND SAWYER, "LOS ALAMOS: THE TOWN FEW
CAN SEE — BUT THE WHOLE WORLD WATCHES,"
CHRISTIAN SCIENCE MONITOR, NOVEMBER 8, 1949

After the Soviet Union exploded Joe 1 in 1949, the nation's attention
returned to the country's atomic facilities in the hinterlands. Los Alamos, Hanford, and Oak Ridge all held key positions in the nuclear
arms race. With the laboratories still off-limits to journalists, the
media focused on the atomic communities to help predict the country's nuclear future. And Los Alamos shone the brightest. With the
United States scrambling to stay ahead of the Soviet bomb program,
Los Alamos remained the nucleus of the nation's atomic defense
complex. After World War II, secrecy no longer completely shielded
the Hill from public view or from congressional oversight. Indeed,
the public looked to Los Alamos as a bulwark against potential Soviet
nuclear aggression and for assurance against the chilling of the Cold
War. As in any war, if one's opponent gains parity, one must look for
ways to regain the advantage. The United States turned toward the
creation of more powerful nuclear weapons, and the arms race that
had begun at the end of World War II escalated. As city planners
reenvisioned its urban landscape, Los Alamos reinvented itself once

again. Its new suburban image as an atomic utopia offered the nation an alternative to nuclear Armageddon.

On January 31, 1950, in response to the Soviet bomb and under pressure from the military and Congress, the White House released a terse statement announcing that President Truman had approved development of the hydrogen bomb. The statement also reasserted the nation's dedication to freedom and peace.[1] Los Alamos laboratory, which had investigated the possibility of a "Super" (or hydrogen) bomb during the war, now pursued the concept with renewed vigor.

Los Alamos stood to gain much from a decision to develop the new weapon; however, opinions differed there about the advisability of the project. Leading up to Truman's decision, debate raged over the merits of inventing a hydrogen bomb. Edward Teller, who had worked on the Super during the war, supported it. He offered to bet John Manley, an associate director at Los Alamos, that "unless we went ahead with his Super," he, Teller, "would be a Russian prisoner of war in the United States within five years!"[2] Manley disagreed with Teller and tried to rally the Hill's scientists against the hydrogen bomb. In a memo from the AEC's General Advisory Committee to the AEC's commissioners, Manley argued for rejecting the development of the new bomb because: (1) atomic bombs (as compared to hydrogen or thermonuclear ones) were adequately destructive; (2) information about the Super would inevitably find its way to the Soviets and assist the work on a Russian Super; (3) money for the hydrogen bomb project could be applied elsewhere and result in greater military potential in offensive and defensive arenas; and (4) the United States' "over-all national position would be weakened, not strengthened, by committing [itself] to a super-bomb program at this time."[3] The memo by Manley, an associate director at LASL, illustrates the reluctance of even some of the lab's key administrators and scientists to create a hydrogen bomb. The General Advisory Committee, which included Oppenheimer, sent an even stronger letter to the AEC, stating: "We believe a super bomb should never be produced. Mankind would be far better off not to have a demonstration of the feasibility of such a weapon until the present climate of world opinion changes."[4] Oppenheimer's opinion would return to haunt him.

Most of the people on the Hill, despite their misgivings about the hydrogen bomb, supported Truman's decision once he made it. Two events that occurred soon after the decision helped to advance the development of the Super. First, an easy solution to creating a hydrogen bomb surfaced, and many feared that the Soviets would also quickly discover it. Second, on June 25, 1950, the North Korean Army launched an attack on South Korea, and the Korean War began. As the oral historian Mary Palevsky observes: "Under the influence of these two events, many physicists who had previously expressed doubts about the H-bomb began to participate in its development."[5]

To carry out the president's decision, the AEC poured money into Los Alamos to support new research and development in the labs and to handle the influx of new personnel into the community. Thus, a new phase of expansion swept the Hill. A plan that had attracted some interest the year before—moving the laboratories to South Mesa, a plateau across Los Alamos Canyon south of the existing town—now gained official approval. In February 1950, the AEC announced that blueprints for a laboratory site on South Mesa would be available by the end of April with bids due on June 20. Completion of the project was expected by the summer of 1952. The budget for this round of construction at Los Alamos in 1950 totaled $74,517,340, which included $43,066,655 for new research and production facilities and $31,450,685 for more housing and community facilities. A further expenditure of $85 million was requested for the immediate future. This new plan sought to erase all World War II–era buildings as if they were scrawled equations on a scientist's chalkboard.[6]

With the push to create a hydrogen bomb, the AEC predicted that the population on the Hill would jump from 8,600 in 1950 to 12,000 within a couple of years. Plans to attract a new cadre of scientists were debated in Washington when Senator McMahon inquired whether the Congressional Joint Commission on Atomic Energy should assist. AEC acting chair Sumner Pike responded: "It is to be expected . . . that many of the scientists who have been approached would show some reluctance to sever their ties with their parent institutions and that it would take some time to make up their minds as to the wisdom or propriety of joining the staff at Los Alamos. These misgivings are, in our opinion, to be best resolved between the Laboratory and the individual."[7] Consequently, the laboratory recruited adequate staffing without any help from Congress.

In fact, from 1949 to 1952, population on the Pajarito Plateau increased from 8,643 to 12,800, an increase of almost 50 percent. Whereas 1,411 people worked at the Los Alamos laboratory as of January 1, 1950 (the largest contingent in the entire AEC program), that number doubled in response to the Soviet explosion. Of the 12,000 residents in 1952, approximately 2,800 worked at Los Alamos Scientific Laboratory (LASL), with 482 holding scientific degrees (257 doctoral, 96 masters, and 129 bachelor degrees) and 192 with engineering degrees (9 doctoral, 25 masters, and 158 bachelor degrees). The rest of the Hill's employees worked for the Zia Company, which managed the site and modernized the laboratory and the residential neighborhoods.[8]

As new residents scrambled for the scarce housing, the laboratory created a hydrogen bomb. Once President Truman approved the development of the Super, some predicted the task would take as long as four or five years. In February 1950, Los Alamos organized the "Family Committee," which had direct responsibility for and oversight of LASL's Super program. Edward Teller won the chairmanship of the Family Committee but had to report to the technical associate director, Darol Froman. Due to misgivings about Teller by the lab's leaders, a strategy was formed to control him. Froman recalled that strategy: "The idea was to get everything Teller could give, but not to let him run the thing."[9]

Teller contributed much to the activities of the Family Committee, but Stanislaw Ulam made the key breakthrough. Françoise, Ulam's wife, recalled her husband standing by their window on Bathtub Row one noon in December, peering into their wintered garden. He told her he had found a way to make the Super work. Ulam's way used an atomic bomb to ignite the hydrogen bomb, thus staging the explosions to obtain a dramatic increase in the detonation. He added: "It is a totally different scheme, and it will change the course of history."[10] As a result of Ulam's insight, the laboratory now had a viable way to create a thermonuclear explosion.

The work on the Super gained success on November 1, 1952, when an island in the South Pacific vaporized as the "Mike" bomb of the *Operation Ivy* series of tests detonated with the power of 10.4 million tons of TNT. Little Boy's explosion had yielded an equivalent of only 12,500 tons of TNT. Thus, Mike multiplied the destructive power of the atom by almost a multiple of one thousand. The first H-bomb fireball rose to 57,000 feet within a minute and a half after detonation, and the cloud passed above 100,000 feet in just two and a half minutes. The stem of the mushroom cloud eventually grew to thirty miles across and the canopy of the cloud spread out over one hundred miles. As nuclear historian Richard Rhodes wrote: "Mike's fireball alone would have engulfed Manhattan; its blast would have obliterated all New York City's five boroughs." The Los Alamos radiochemist George Cowan witnessed the Mike shot and recalled: "I was stunned. I mean, it was big. . . . As soon as I dared, I whipped off my dark glasses and the thing was enormous, bigger than I'd ever imagined it would be. It looked as though it blotted out the whole horizon, and I was standing on the deck of the *Estes*, thirty miles away."[11] LASL had succeeded in creating a hydrogen bomb earlier than most thought possible. By doing so, the laboratory also succeeded in securing a nuclear trump over the USSR. The U.S. had raised the stakes in the arms race.

The success of the hydrogen bomb vindicated many people in the atomic weapons field. Bradbury and the commissioners of the AEC applauded the scientists and technicians who delivered a thermonuclear device in less time than the Manhattan Project took to create an atomic bomb. In spite of the success, however, concern about the wisdom of creating such a powerful weapon leaked out of the Tech

Area and into the homes and families on the Hill. Some residents, like Françoise Ulam, were appalled at the possibility that a Super could work. Their daughter Claire had a more accepting attitude about her father's work. She recalled: "I knew my dad played an important part of the H-bomb. . . . I just thought that was normal, that was what people do. . . . I just thought that was the way it was. It never struck me that was odd or unusual."[12] Carson Mark's daughter Joan also remembered the controversy about the Super: "The only thing I remember much about hearing any controversy or discussion was when there was a lot of push and pull between Teller and other people up there when he wanted to proceed with the hydrogen bomb. My father was very much against a lot of things that Teller was up to. They had been friends and colleagues for a long time and then there was a bitter split."[13] Joan recalled that her father thought the H-bomb was technically feasible, but that enough harm had been unleashed with the atomic weapons, and there was little need for bigger weapons. Despite his reservations, Carson Mark did contribute to the project. In fact, the Los Alamos engineer Jacob Weschler praised Mark's knowledge and instinct about the physical behavior of radiation in a thermonuclear explosion. Like others on the Hill, Mark worked on the hydrogen bomb and at the same time fretted over its creation.

An article about Oppenheimer illustrates this paradox. Featured in *Life* magazine in October 1949, right after the revelation of the Soviet bomb, Oppenheimer talked about a theory in physics called complementarity. He explained: "One of the first things that the student of atomic structure must come to understand is . . . the principle of complementarity, which recognizes that various ways of talking about physical experience may each have validity and may each be a necessary and adequate description of the physical world and may yet stand in a mutually contradictory relationship to each other."[14] Any examination of the United States during the Cold War, especially in relation to nuclear weapons development, reveals the contradictory interplay of science, policy, and emotions, of both nuclear hubris and atomic fear. People at Los Alamos supported the development of the H-bomb at the same time that they believed they were securing peace. As contradictory as it sounds, the labs at Los Alamos sought to prepare for war and secure peace at the same time.[15]

Ellen Reid's family learned of the Super despite the security and secrecy. Ellen, whose father worked with high explosives, recalled discussing the hydrogen bomb at home: "One day Daddy came home for lunch and said, 'You know, there's a chance we may set the atmosphere of the world on fire.' And I remember thinking, 'I don't think that this is a very good idea.' I think that is the only time that I remember him saying anything. He was worried that maybe they weren't sure enough of what they were doing."[16] Ellen went back to school that afternoon and talked with her friend Mike Haley, and they agreed that the laboratory should not continue with the Super until they knew more about what they were doing.

The work on the Super revitalized Los Alamos and brought new families to the Hill. This influx of families, at the height of the postwar baby boom, almost overwhelmed Los Alamos. As at Site Y during the war, the birthrate on the Hill rose above the national average. During 1952, the hospital at Los Alamos delivered 339 babies for a birthrate of 26 per 1,000. The national average during the pregnant fifties equaled 24 per 1,000. The birthrate may have been even higher since some women, like Susan Tiano's mother, chose to leave the Hill for the births of their children. Tiano recalls: "My mother didn't much like the doctors in Los Alamos. . . . She had a Los Alamos doctor, but they delivered me at St. Vincent's [Hospital] in Santa Fe." In 1951, babies and children up to four years old composed 14 percent of the population at Los Alamos, and children aged five to nine totaled 11 percent. Thus, one quarter of the Hill's residents were under ten. To accommodate the baby boom, new houses and schools had to be built and essential family services expanded. As usual, Los Alamos's officials turned to the federal government to provide the funds.[17]

In testimony before the House Appropriations committee in spring 1950, AEC officials acknowledged that the government spent $160 million annually to operate its outpost on the Pajarito Plateau. Of that total, $10,846,000 went to running the town itself. In a congressional hearing to investigate the spending, Representative Frank Keefe grilled Carroll L. Tyler, the AEC manager in New Mexico (and responsible for overseeing Los Alamos): "Your budget would scare any municipality that I know of. . . . It would scare them to death." Tyler replied: "It frightens me a bit at times, too."[18] To justify the expense of operating Los Alamos, AEC Chairman David Lilienthal told the congressmen that the top-secret town was not run like any other city: "I think if you could see this place a good deal of the mystery would be gone. . . . This is a spot on top of this mountain that was picked for isolation purposes. . . . This place would never have been picked except that it is isolated."[19] Testimony from these hearings led one editor in Atlanta to observe: "These [police] have built a fence around Los Alamos and nobody gets into town unless he has a special pass; so it is that the 8,500 residents live in a twentieth-century Shangri-La more isolated than a medieval monastery on a mountain top."[20]

The funding to upgrade Los Alamos augmented an already generous budget for operating expenditures. Largely in response to Joe 1, money poured into the laboratory. In 1951, LASL received $45.4 million to run its scientific facility. The amount increased in 1952 to $63.4 million, and in 1953 the laboratory received $95.3 million, nearly doubling the 1951 level of funding.[21] This figure (which comes from a report to the Congressional Joint Commission on Atomic Energy in 1959) does not agree with the $160 million operating budget quoted in the congressional hearings in 1950. Totaling up the cost of operating the town of Los Alamos and LASL is like a shell game where money appears and disappears under the hulls of construction, town operating costs, or laboratory operating costs. Total budgets gleaned from the various hearings or governmental offices rarely equal each other. Shielded by the cloak of national security, Los Alamos enjoyed generous, at times even lavish, support from taxpayers and the federal government.[22]

At the national level, the AEC capitalized on the fears resulting from the Soviet bomb, the Korean War, and the nuclear espionage trials in both England and the United States and increased its capital investments budget from $1.7 billion in 1947 to $9 billion in 1955. As a result, Oak Ridge and Hanford doubled in size, and by 1957, AEC facilities consumed 6.7 percent of the total U.S. electrical power output. As the AEC rushed to increase its production of atomic weapons, Los Alamos invented a new array of weapons. In addition to bombs delivered by planes, nuclear weapons now included depth charges, torpedoes, cannon-fired projectiles, and ballistic missiles. In 1950, the U.S. had 298 bombs. Five years later, the nation's nuclear arsenal contained 2,422 weapons.[23]

With an increased arsenal, new testing grounds were needed. On January 11, 1951, President Truman authorized the AEC "to use part of the 5,000 square-mile Las Vegas (Nev.) Bombing and Gunnery Range for experiments necessary to the atomic weapons development program. . . . The use of the Las Vegas Bombing and Gunnery Range will make available to the Los Alamos Scientific Laboratory a readily accessible site for periodic test work with a resultant speed-up in the weapons development program."[24] The location of the Nevada Test Site (NTS), seventy miles northeast of Las Vegas, simplified the laboratory's program to test new nuclear-weapon prototypes. Travel time, logistics, and accessibility were much easier with the test site only hundreds of overland miles away instead of thousands of miles overseas. Between the Pacific Proving Grounds at Eniwetok and the NTS, the AEC spent almost $89 million in operational costs to fund all the nuclear tests, from Operation Sandstone in 1948 to Operation Upshot in 1953. Additional expenditures accrued in building base facilities at the two test sites (which cost $23.7 million) for a grand total of almost $113 million over the five-year period. To supply the nuclear material for the burgeoning stockpile, a new mining boom swept the West as prospectors ranged over the deserts and mountains looking for raw uranium deposits for this massive increase in nuclear weapons.[25]

As seen at the national nuclear laboratories and during the uranium mining boom in the early fifties, atomic energy was a growth industry, and nuclear weapons were a Cold War priority. Thus, cost accountability disappeared from the atomic balance sheet. Not surprisingly, problems arose. Journalists expressed amazement over the

The Los Alamos laboratory assisted in experiments like these at the Nevada
Test Site, where Marines participated in maneuvers that tested the battlefield
readiness of atomic soldiers. Courtesy of National Archives II, College
Park, Md.

large expenditures revealed at committee hearings. Citing costs like
$500,000 for janitors and salaries for 675 police for Los Alamos, an
admittedly crime-free city, an editor from Atlanta cried foul: "The
Government intends to spend next year $750,000 on new streets,
grass plantings, and a sprinkler system to keep 'em green. I'd surely

like to get my paws on one of those police passes and see Los Alamos for myself. I might even run into some of those expensive janitors at work."[26] Expensive janitors did work at Los Alamos; they had to be specially trained to clean rooms containing radioactive and toxic materials.

Other problems concerning the expenses of operating Los Alamos attracted the attention of Congress. At first, congressional attention focused on the contract with the Zia Company. A hearing of the Committee on Expenditures on January 3, 1949, issued a report that stated: "The operation of the Zia Co. is far more expensive than warranted and the Zia Co. should be terminated. . . . A change in this set-up will save the Government hundreds of thousands of dollars each year because of excessive numbers of employees, extravagance, and waste."[27] This report also looked at the new houses in the Western Area: "It would appear many of the buildings have required an unusual amount of repairs, which in some cases has [sic] been due to faulty designs and insufficient inspection by the architect."[28] The most serious defects of the Western Area housing concerned ceilings that collapsed, but problems with the foundations also appeared.

In a congressional hearing in June 1949, Santa Fe Operations manager Carroll Tyler was questioned about deficiencies in these three-year-old houses in the Western Area built by the Zia Company. The major problems consisted of "improper roofing, overloading of structural members . . . and the waiving of the moisture content of the lumber."[29] Responding to the grilling by congressmen, Tyler minimized the inconvience and expense: "The ceilings in one bedroom in a number of houses began to give away. As a matter of fact, only two families had to move out of their houses during the repair periods. Only 27 families lost the use of one room of the 350 houses. . . . The total repair bill of 350 houses was $250,000."[30] These deficiencies in design and construction aggravated the problems caused by the rapidity of construction of the Western Area in the summer of 1946. The congressional inquiry into the Zia Company and the housing problems at Los Alamos might have caused Zia to lose its lucrative contract, but the Soviet detonation of an atomic bomb shifted the focus away from such problems at AEC installations as they rushed to develop a hydrogen bomb. As the fallout from the Soviet bomb reinvigorated the U.S. atomic program, these other problems were quickly forgotten since any disruptions caused by a change in site management might lose the arms race.

Nonetheless, charges of economic mismanagement continued to surface. In the summer of 1953, two security guards, Andrew Sobien and O. M. Hernandez, wrote a letter to President Eisenhower complaining of a variety of problems at Los Alamos. They charged that "large amounts of government property [are] being stolen or used illegally because this is one of the few government installations that does not allow searching of vehicles leaving the project."[31] Other problems listed in the letter touched on low morale within the security forces, questionable disbursement of government money, approval of inferior construction, and the immorality of many of the employees on the Hill. Frustrated because their confidential letter to the president quickly found its way to the AEC, the very organization responsible for allowing the problems to happen, Sobien and Hernandez "refused to answer questions put to them by the investigators because they were convinced that the probers had been assigned to 'whitewash' their charges."[32] The two men were subsequently relieved of their badges and guns and removed from active duty.

Even though the federal government dominated Los Alamos, privatization of some services occurred. In February 1950, a nonprofit corporation, the Los Alamos Medical Center, Inc., assumed control and responsibility for the hospital, dental, and public health services. Under contract with the AEC, the Los Alamos Medical Center planned to build a new facility for a January 1952 opening. The new hospital would also contribute to the Hill's mission to investigate the medical uses of nuclear energy. Prior to the establishment of the Los Alamos Medical Center, the laboratory's Health Division had explored the medical aspects of atomic enterprises. The Health Division employed 125 workers divided into five groups: Occupational Medicine, Radiological Safety, Industrial Hygiene, Safety, and Biomedical Research. In a building adjacent to the new hospital, a $1.5 million laboratory would "provide modern and centralized facilities for the biomedical and industrial health research activities of the Los Alamos Scientific Laboratory."[33] A new branch of medicine, called Health Physics, arose to deal with the radioactive and toxic effects of atomic energy.

As the health physics laboratory and the new hospital rose on the north rim overlooking Los Alamos Canyon, new scientific laboratories emerged across the canyon on the top of South Mesa. To connect the existing labs and residential town site with the new technical area to the south, an open-spanned steel bridge arched over the deep canyon. The Los Alamos Canyon Bridge, one of the longest in the Southwest with a 422-foot span, took sixteen months to build and cost $704,781. Its simplified design was awarded honorable mention for aesthetic excellence by the American Institute of Steel. With the bridge open, the laboratory began its move to the South Mesa, and after 1951 construction at the original laboratory area, Tech Area 1, tapered off. Initially, the new Tech Area (TA-3) on the South Mesa held the Administration Building, the Chemistry, Metallurgy, and Physics buildings; a Van de Graaf accelerator, a steam plant, and other shops and laboratories.[34]

The built environment of the Pajarito Plateau again underwent a drastic transformation in the early fifties as new bridges, hospitals, and technical facilities were constructed in response to the arms race. Residential areas also expanded to accommodate the rush of talent to the site. By the end of 1949, 584 new homes in the North Community were completed. In 1950, an additional 442 homes were built, and in 1951 the North Community added another 234 houses. Some of the older structures in the Eastern Housing Area escaped the wrecking ball as school systems from New Mexico, Arizona, and Colorado purchased the units and moved them off the Hill. Private contractors as well as the federal government's Bureau of Indian Affairs also bid on and bought these relics from the Manhattan Project.[35]

To replace the wartime structures, construction workers built more residences in the early fifties, erecting 344 one-bedroom apartments and 232 kitchenette apartments. Most of these apartments lay near the new Community Center and replaced the dormitories left over from the war. After the initial rush to accommodate the hydrogen bomb

As the Western Area aged, the instant suburb lost some of its glitter. Courtesy of Los Alamos Historical Museum Photo Archives.

development, expansion cooled, and no new residences were built in 1953. The pace picked up again in 1954 as construction began on 120 new houses. These two-, three-, and four-bedroom homes replaced 198 structures left over from the Manhattan Project that had been razed in the Eastern Area between the Community Center and the community's small airport. Slated for completion by the spring of 1955, these houses epitomized the suburbanization of Los Alamos. With attached carports, space for clothes washers and freezers, and forced-air heating systems, they offered amenities only dreamed of during the war and comparable to those of ranch-style homes, which were popular in the new suburbs of postwar America. Thus, to attract personnel to the Hill, houses barely ten years old were erased and replaced by the latest in suburban living.[36]

Officials turned to another area of the plateau to meet the housing demands attending the renewed arms race. The community of White Rock, built to house construction workers during the hectic days of the late forties, now hosted families who could not find accommodations in Los Alamos. By the middle of 1950, 325 families lived in White Rock. As the pace of construction intensified, the population at White Rock skyrocketed. Looking back on the summer of 1950, the *Los Alamos Herald* noted: "World events destined the community of White Rock for bigger things. Before the summer had ended, there were some 2,000 residents living in this community."[37] An elementary school opened for the children of the families moving to this suburb of Los Alamos. Because of the temporary nature of the construction jobs on the Hill, families moved into and out of White Rock at a prodigious pace. As a result, the turnover rate of children at the elementary school neared 50 percent, with 150 having left the school since the beginning of the 1950–51 term, only to be replaced with 150 newly arrived youngsters. The local newspaper commented: "It is not uncommon to have eight or ten children leave or transfer out of the school on Friday afternoon and on Monday morning to have approximately the same number of eager new faces waiting to enroll."[38] White Rock once again sheltered the migrant families of the construction workers at Los Alamos.

With this new round of expansion, including 120 new residences in the Eastern Area and new administrative offices and labs on the South Mesa, the boom at Los Alamos again challenged the community's ability to provide services and housing. Despite the strain, the atomic city continued to reinvent itself as millions of federal dollars helped upgrade the technical and residential facilities. And laboratory workers continued to wrestle with the contradictory activities of nurturing marriages and raising children while developing weapons of mass destruction.[39]

The reinvention of Los Alamos became obvious to anyone who had lived there during the war. One of the Manhattan Project's original participants, Laura Fermi, returned to Los Alamos in 1951 and described the changes on the Hill. She commented: "I was quite prepared to find the Mesa (as Los Alamos is often called) in its well-known state of everlasting building. . . . But for one feature of present day Los Alamos

I was not prepared: All the houses in the Western Area are surrounded by unbelievably green lawns. Water is now pumped to the Mesa in great abundance. . . . I remember the period during the war when no water at all came out of the faucets."[40] She also noted this change: "Now that the military administration has surrendered its power to the civilian Atomic Energy Commission, Los Alamos tends to become similar to any small town. Most of the socialistic features have been abandoned. . . . In Los Alamos, apart from their essential participation in the nation's defense effort, men live as men do in any suburban community."[41] Fermi commented on a final shift in the political attitudes of the men on the Hill who are "vocal on political issues. . . . They give lectures, hold debates, and write articles for newspapers and magazines. This seems to be the reverse of their attitude during the war. The men may say that they were always interested in politics, that they foresaw the implications of the Atomic Age for humanity. If so, I was not aware of it."[42] As the wife of a Nobel prize winner and a keen observer of Los Alamos, Fermi saw a community different from the war years as it became suburbanized and normalized.

Change swept through much of the West in the early postwar period. In the West, growth and mobility often have been abiding components, and this trend continued as the nation placed many of its nuclear facilities in the region. Westerners welcomed the economic prosperity and population growth brought about by defense-related industries. In fact, community boosters competed with each other throughout the West and elsewhere in the nation for a slice of the atomic pie as they encouraged the AEC and the military to establish nuclear facilities in their region. The urban historian Roger Lotchin addressed the union of urban boosters and the military-industrial complex in his exploration of the defense industry in California. Regarding President Eisenhower's warning about a monolithic military-industrial cabal, Lotchin writes: "Eisenhower was correct about the use of undue political influence on behalf of military contracting, but wrong in his description of it. [The military-industrial complex] was not a unitary institution . . . but a nation full of Darwinian urban areas, heavily dependent upon defense spending."[43] Defense-dependent cities mushroomed during the Cold

War with local boosters aggressively pursuing military installations and contracts for economic development as well as from patriotic motives.

The social history of postwar America also revolved around the confrontation with the Soviet Union. As social historian Elaine Tyler May observes, families assumed new roles: "A home filled with children would create a feeling of warmth and security against the cold forces of disruption and alienation."[44] Concerning the arms race and the Cold War containment policy of the State Department, May notes: "It was not just nuclear energy that had to be contained, but the social and sexual fallout of the atomic age itself."[45] The containment of despair and promiscuity in the atomic age could be accomplished through an emphasis on the family: "The family seemed to offer a psychological fortress that would protect them against themselves."[46] Since they could do little against the external atomic threat, families found security within the home.

At Los Alamos, with fences and armed guards protecting the town, families felt safe from the disruptive forces of the times. Los Alamos's overriding mission—to safeguard the United States by building bigger and better bombs—also bound the community together. Jack Bell, a teenager at Los Alamos during the 1950s, recalled: "There was actually almost a sense of pride that you were involved in nuclear weapons."[47] For some residents, a closeness developed that paralleled the traditional habits of small-town America. Donald Marchi observed: "We were unique being raised in that community up there. If I was raised in California, Los Angeles, or Denver, I don't think we'd have the same closeness. I think it'd be lost. But you could take a small community and have the same closeness."[48] On the front lines of the Cold War, Los Alamos combined a small-town atmosphere with responsibility as the defender of democracy. The effect was to bind the community together.

Living in this small town that created nuclear weapons, women in Los Alamos adapted to the demands of raising nuclear families. As during the war, many women on the Hill were still caught between the two fences. To be sure, clubs, schools, and social activities occupied their time not spent working or keeping house; however, for some, frustration came from the confining roles of housewives and mothers. Brant Caulkin, who arrived in Los Alamos as a boy in 1943, remembered it as a "hard-drinking town" that was "symptomatic of other things. . . . What you had basically were nonparticipatory families where one member, usually the male, was totally absorbed. The isolation for some people was pretty complete. They could not visit where their husband worked. The husband appeared at the house at the end of a very long day and left again the next morning."[49]

Some of the women were unhappy with the town. Tom Ribe, who grew up on the Hill, observed: "I think life was extremely difficult for the women, because they were bright and bored to death. It caused a lot of frustration and as a result, there was a lot of alcoholism, and I understand that there was a lot of infidelity."[50] Ellen Reid also remembered that some women at Los Alamos drank a lot, and Susan Tiano recalls that her mother was "bored out of her mind. She did a lot of things like winning duplicate bridge tournaments and participating in Dale Carnegie courses and winning all of the awards. She was a brilliant woman who excelled at everything she did, but without a work role, she was totally miserable. . . . But the norm in Los Alamos in general was for women not to work, and I think that contributed to the divorces and extra-marital affairs and the craziness that went on in that sector of the population. She and all her friends were having affairs. From the time I was little, I was aware of these things."[51] Containment on the Hill isolated some of those residents who were caught between the fences. Just as people found ways to circumvent the Hill's policy of enforced secrecy, they escaped domestic containment through extramarital affairs and alcoholism.

Containment, like secrecy, is rarely absolute. The threat from Russia was real, and the protection of U.S. citizens against a Soviet nuclear strike occupied both federal and local authorities. Even though the Soviet atomic bomb caught many in the United States by surprise, the official investigations of Trinity, Hiroshima, Nagasaki, Operation Crossroads, and Operation Sandstone had taught officials much about what atomic bombs could do.

This civil defense expertise quickly came forward immediately after the Soviet detonation as the nation's magazines began telling Americans how to prepare for an atomic attack. In a January 1950 article in the *Saturday Evening Post*, "How You Can Survive an A-Bomb Blast," navy Lieutenant Commander Richard Gerstell drew from his experience at the Bikini tests. He advised "that relatively few direct injuries are caused by the blast of the actual 'squeezing' of the bomb's pressure wave. Most injuries and fatalities are results of the blast's indirect effects—from being thrown against something or struck by a falling object."[52] To protect against these shock waves, Gerstell suggested that people lie flat or find any type of shielding. The second major cause of injury came from heat and fires. Removing inflammable material around a house and shutting off pilot lights and oil burners would help counter that threat, according to Gerstell. Having discussed those effects of an atomic bomb in a little over a page, Gerstell moved on to the hazards of radioactivity: "This radioactivity, which is perhaps the atomic bomb's only basic added hazard, is, for the layman, perhaps the most widely feared of all its forces. . . . Actually, radioactivity is the least of the nuclear bomb's threats. . . . "[53] The remainder of the article's four pages were devoted to suggestions for protecting against this "least danger."

Gerstell first explained radiation's effects on humans and then explored how communities could organize radiological monitoring teams to find the "hot spots" after an explosion. He separated radiological hazards into two categories: prompt and lingering. Prompt radiations "consist of X-rays, gamma rays, and neutrons that are thrown off at the very second of explosion and last only as long as the detonation itself."[54] To protect against prompt radiation, one needed to be, at Ground Zero, in a shelter made of one foot of steel or three feet of concrete or five feet of earth. The effects of prompt or penetrating radiation brought on "radiation disease," as seen at Hiroshima and Nagasaki and at Los Alamos with the accidents involving Daghlian and Slotin.

Lingering radiation came from the undetonated radioactive particles, suspended in the mushroom cloud that then fell to earth downwind

from an explosion. According to Gerstell, this lingering radiation consisted of "invisible hot bits of unexploded uranium and plutonium
atoms that failed to undergo fission when the weapon was detonated.[55]
This low-level radiation could not even penetrate skin, but if ingested
or inhaled into a human body, could result in long-term health threats.
Gerstell suggested that defense against non-penetrating, lingering radiation centered on not swallowing suspected contamination or getting it
into cuts. Gerstell concluded his article thus: "Actually, there is nothing
that is new or mysterious about radioactivity. . . . More, for example, is
known about radiological injuries than is known about polio or the
common cold. Basically, radioactivity is no greater a threat in wartime
than are typhoid fever and other diseases that often follow the ravages
of a bombing."[56] This attitude—that after the initial release of the penetrating radiation of X-rays, gamma rays, and neutrons at the moment of
detonation there is little to fear from the lingering radioactivity—was a
common theme in many civil defense announcements of the 1940s and
early 1950s.

Fearing that Soviet bombs might begin falling on American soil,
the federal government instituted a public information campaign centered around civil defense. The protection of urban Americans against
a nuclear war could come only through a radical transformation: the
building of underground cities. Apart from that, little could be done to
shelter urban dwellers from a concerted nuclear attack. However grim
that scenario, the public's will to support nuclear weapons remained
vital to American interests. As historian Guy Oakes observed: "The
policy of containment by means of deterrence required the public to
exhibit credible expressions of determination to fight a nuclear war. . . .
This plan was a comprehensive system of emotional management
designed to suppress an irrational terror of nuclear war and foster in
its stead a more pragmatic nuclear fear. Once the passage from nuclear
terror to nuclear fear had been completed, civil defense organizations
could be in a position to employ nuclear fear in their programs of
human resource management."[57] To effectively wage the Cold War in
the 1950s, the American people had to support nuclear weapons and
believe that, if the worst happened, many of them would survive an

exchange of such weapons. Thus, civil defense was part mobilization to protect citizens and also part public relations to blunt the terror of a nuclear attack.

The Office of Civilian Mobilization (OCM), the official civil defense organization, responded to Joe 1 by intensifying its preparations for a nuclear attack. The *New York Times* reported: "An organization is being set up to cope with disaster on a scale neither this country nor any other country has before dreamed possible. All previous concepts of defense have been swept aside for the newest concept of defense against nuclear explosions. The newer organization, when completed, must deal with all phases of such things as emergency housing, sanitation, rehabilitation, fire fighting and radiation detection and treatment."[58] Spurred on by the OCM, civil defense for northern New Mexico went into high gear in the summer of 1950.

Los Alamos had plans for civil defense dating back to World War II. Evacuation routes and procedures for evacuating the Tech Area first existed in 1944, but exercises to abandon the town or efforts to construct bomb shelters were not considered at the time. By 1948, a disaster plan for both the town and the laboratory included an evacuation procedure as well as respirators and protective clothing in case of a radiological disaster. To help implement this plan, a Committee for the Preparation and Maintenance of the Disaster Plan began in 1949 under the direction of James Maddy of the AEC's Safety and Fire Protection Division. In August 1950, almost a year after the Soviet bomb was tested, AEC manager Carroll Tyler appointed Lloyd Kersey as project officer for Defense and Disaster Planning. That same year, community volunteers organized an auxiliary to the police force to assist with civil defense. These volunteers served in all the test evacuations and in case of a real emergency would remain on duty to direct fleeing cars away from the Hill.[59]

In response to the Soviet Union's detonation of an atomic bomb, the U.S. Congress authorized the replacement of the Office of Civilian Mobilization by the Federal Civil Defense Administration (FCDA) in December 1950. The FCDA moved quickly and initiated its "Alert America" campaign in June 1951. Three separate caravans of ten large trucks each carried exhibits that showed the dangers of an atomic attack. Over one million people visited the Alert America convoys as they crisscrossed the country in 1952. As part of the campaign, "Operation Alert" staged mock atomic attacks beginning in 1954 on hundreds of American cities to test civil defense preparedness. Upon completion of the annual exercises, the FCDA predicted the number of "casualties." For example, in Operation Alert 1956, an estimated eight million people "died" from the attack, with over six million "injured" and twenty-four million "left homeless."[60] To emphasize the nuclear danger, the *Annual Report for 1951 of the Federal Civil Defense Administration* stated that the new dimension of atomic weapons "makes our backyards of today the potential front lines of tomorrow."[61] In fact, during the war, Edward Teller had speculated on a wide range of ideas for nuclear weapons. The code name for the largest one simply read "Backyard." As the physicist Robert Serber explained: "Since that particular design [Backyard] would probably kill everyone on earth, there was no use carting it elsewhere."[62] With America's backyards targeted by newer, more powerful bombs that would make one's barbecue pit a Ground Zero, civil defense officials struggled to find a balance between a realistic response to the nuclear threat and one that would not scare the American public.

In northern New Mexico, a local civil defense network organized to help prepare civilians for a nuclear war. On January 10, 1951, Civil Defense directors assembled in Los Alamos and agreed to form a mutual aid committee "to work out problems involved in the event of an attack on any of the critical target areas of the state."[63] The next night, another civil defense meeting occurred, this time in Española, to set up an emergency evacuation center. The meeting also called for volunteers to survey the housing of the Española Valley "to determine how many people could be fed and housed in case of emergency."[64] Before the end of January, another meeting in Santa Fe also ordered a survey of housing in the event of an evacuation. Since only Los Alamos in northern New Mexico could be considered a critical target area, neighboring communities prepared to receive the atomic refugees from the Hill.

The Los Alamos City Council wasted little time in supporting the organization of civilians involved in preparing the community for a nuclear attack. On January 26, 1951, it created a Civil Defense and Disaster Corps to explore the ways the community could protect itself. Residents received a jolt in late February when a civilian airplane violated the restricted air space above Los Alamos and buzzed the town before landing at the airstrip. The occupants of the plane had no diabolical plans to attack the laboratory or the community, but could easily have bombed key installations. If residents had thought they were safe behind the fences and in the hinterlands, this joy ride rudely awakened many of them.[65]

A flurry of stories appeared in local newspapers in January of 1951 on ways to survive an atomic bombing. Santa Fe's Civil Defense Public Information chairman, Joe M. Clark, advised: "Fall flat on your face. More than half of all wounds are the result of being bodily tossed about or struck by falling and flying objects."[66] In another article, Clark assured readers that "people are not very likely to be exposed to dangerous amounts of [radioactivity] in most atomic raids."[67] Returning to the claim that lingering or low-level radiation presented little danger, Clark denied that any health hazards resulted from blasts at high altitudes since most of the radioactivity rode upwards on the violent surge of super-hot gases. Despite his assurances about the lack of danger from fallout, another of Clark's stories warned the public to keep doors and windows closed in the event of an attack because "it [was] far easier to prevent radioactive pollution of a household than it [was] to remove it."[68] Clark's advice created the impression that surviving a nuclear attack relied on planning and common sense.

Clark's articles in the *New Mexican* reiterated a national civil defense strategy. In January 1951, the Office of Civil Defense published *Survival under Atomic Attack*. Within a year, twenty million copies were distributed touting the main thesis that the dangers of nuclear attack were wildly exaggerated. As historian Guy Oakes notes: "Civil Defense theorists attempted to replace this apocalyptic view of nuclear war with a very different conception designed to check American anxiety about the bomb."[69] Not surprisingly, the community of Los Alamos experimented with civil defense strategies early on.

In March 1951, a new initiative addressed a key component of any civil defense for a community of families. A disaster plan for schoolchildren won tentative approval. In a front page story, the *Los Alamos Herald* announced the new policy for the schools: "If the 'yellow' alert changed to the 'red,' room monitors would quickly open the windows and drop the blinds to block flying glass. All children would put on any available extra clothing, then file out of their rooms into the 'structurally strongest' portions of the building and lie on the floor, eyes shielded in the crook of the elbow until an 'all-clear' signal sounds."[70] With this warning system in place, civil defense officials addressed one of the most pressing issues in any civil defense planning—how to protect children, especially when they are at school, from an atomic blast.

Surprisingly, the civil defense initiatives in New Mexico did not receive funds from the FCDA, although it had benefited from knowledge abtained at Los Alamos. Edward Oakley, assistant director of New Mexico's Office of Civil Defense, complained in a 1951 letter to the FCDA: "Since it is evident that a very modest sum of Federal funds have been allocated to New Mexico . . . I cannot but wonder if I have over-estimated the importance of the Civil Defense program for the state and instead of further expansion, we should not now limit our activities."[71] The FCDA did indeed neglect New Mexico from 1951 to 1955, since it was the only state in the union that received no funds from the agency.[72]

In spite of the lack of financial support from the FCDA, civil defense in northern New Mexico did receive federal monies. In March 1951, the local civil defense organization "began pumping blood into what was heretofore a plan on paper."[73] The Los Alamos Civil Defense and Disaster Corps' budget totaled $75,000. This money came not from the FCDA but from the AEC. With Los Alamos one of its key facilities, the AEC took care of its own. In March, Los Alamos used these AEC funds to purchase new high-frequency radios and medical supplies, as well as a large number of warden armbands. Officials also called for volunteers to organize as neighborhood wardens. Training of the wardens was aided by the arrival of ten instructional films on civil defense.[74]

To test the feasibility of civil defense at Los Alamos, a mock evacuation was held in November 1952. Residents drove away from their homes and offices but did not leave the Hill. The Los Alamos Disaster and Defense Planning Committee announced: "All check points where cars will park are outside target areas and are considered safe for Civil Defense Parking areas."[75] At Los Alamos, eight thousand residents loaded into three thousand cars, clogging the escape routes away from the city. This exercise occurred right after Operation Ivy detonated the world's first hydrogen bomb at Eniwetok.[76] As one of the first towns to hold community-wide civil defense drills, Los Alamos amplified its role as a national center for the research and development of nuclear enterprises, only this time by testing federal civil defense strategies.

A country-wide program of studies and civil defense drills began two years later in 1954, and in 1955 communities across the country evacuated en masse. On April 26, 1954, a test exercise called "Operation Walkout" focused on the evacuation of a seventy-block downtown area of Spokane, Washington.[77] The next evacuation of the Hill happened June 1954 when Los Alamos, along with fifty-four other communities, participated in "history's first continental air raid drill."[78] Thus, in November 1952, Los Alamos had paved the way by conducting a community-wide evacuation almost two years before the rest of the nation did.

Were officials on the Hill serious about defending against a nuclear attack? To be sure, civil defense precautions, like evacuations away from a target area and duck-and-cover drills, might have helped in the event of an atomic bomb like the one dropped on Hiroshima. But with the increased destructive power of hydrogen bombs, those measures no longer proved effective. Additionally, the health hazards of the lingering radioactivity in fallout, warned about by Frisch and Peierls in a memo before the war, were ignored in the early 1950s. In 1951, the

Columbia Broadcasting System, in collaboration with the Civil Defense Commission of New York State and the American Red Cross, published the *Homemaker's Manual of Atomic Defense*. Under the heading "What You Need to Know about Radioactivity," the booklet claimed: "Radiation last [*sic*] 90 seconds after an air blast. There is no danger of contamination after such a burst." It concluded with this admonition: "If you are the mother in your family, you naturally become the Chief of Staff in your home. . . . Both panic and apathy will prevent you from meeting a crisis adequately. The calm courage which comes with knowledge will be an effective life-saving weapon in preserving our families and ourselves in the event of an atomic attack."[79] To counter atomic panic, misinformation about the dangers of radioactivity appeared in print, on radio, and even in this companion booklet to an early television newscast about civil defense.

At Los Alamos, one of the few towns in America where the true consequences of nuclear weapons were minutely studied, some people knew better. Civil defense was a response to a grim necessity, but after the Soviets detonated their own hydrogen bomb in November 1955, the strategies of duck-and-cover no longer protected the American public. With the use of ballistic missiles to deliver nuclear weapons in the late 1950s, community evacuations also lost their usefulness. These drills acted more like a placebo, given to citizens in a target area to help reduce their fears. Indeed, short of dispersing urban America to the countryside or moving it underground, little could be done to protect the nation's population against hydrogen bombs.[80]

Federal civil defense initiatives against hydrogen bombs were not really about survival. They perpetuated the delusion of survival by appealing to the American faith in action, any kind of action. As Guy Oakes has observed: "The Cold War conception of nuclear reality represented an attempt to think about the unthinkable, to conceptualize an unintelligible event and rationalize a world that seemed to be irrational, by reducing the apparently unimaginable experience of nuclear war to a set of routines."[81] Replacing nuclear terror with a set of easily followed routines like duck-and-cover and community evacuations, civil defense allowed the American public to continue to support the arms race. To assist with the publicity campaign, the AEC used the newly popular medium of television.

In the spring of 1952, a hydrogen bomb detonated at Yucca Flats in the Nevada Test Site. Millions of people around the country saw it live on their television sets. Charter Heslep, chief of the Radio-Visual Information Service of the AEC, coordinated with the KTLA television station in Los Angeles to bring the live-feed 275 miles over the mountains and deserts that separated the test site and Los Angeles. Working under strict security and a tight time schedule, Heslep and the technicians from KTLA used marine helicopters to place the necessary transmitting gear at 8,000 feet above sea level on the sides of mountains. The television crew even worked through a blizzard. They also had to attempt a single 140-mile relay across the desert—something that had never been accomplished. At 9:30 A.M. on April 22, television audiences witnessed the nuclear blast. Heslep estimated that several million schoolchildren saw it, and the headline from the *Chicago Sun-Times* read "BOOM! Millions See a Bomb on TV." In the *Dayton News*, an editorial summed up how many people felt: "We were watching happen, at the moment that it happened, what could happen in Dayton, Ohio, any day that the Russians decide to launch atomic aggression. It hits us in our living rooms." Heslep concluded his account with this thought, taken from the Dayton editorial: "No one could have left his television set without a redoubled conviction that somehow, through still untapped resources of human wisdom and moral strength, this force must be made to work for constructive and not for destructive ends."[82] As civil defense efforts prepared the nation for an attack, research into the constructive and destructive uses of nuclear energy continued at Los Alamos.

Despite the possibility that the laboratory might be attacked by the Soviets, Los Alamos's residents felt safe and secure behind their fences. After the AEC reviewed the closed status of the Hill in the early fifties, the fences remained up. In the midst of the accelerated program to develop a hydrogen bomb during the summer of 1950, the AEC responded to a congressional initiative to turn the towns of Los

Alamos, Oak Ridge, and Hanford over to their respective residents. The acting chairman of the AEC, Gordon Dean, spoke against the plan: "To introduce such distraction and confusion in the personal lives of the individual workers of every sort would inevitably, we believe, slow down the progress they could individually and collectively make in the important work they perform."[83] Furthermore, Dean warned: "We feel it only fair to advise that Congressional action requiring it [a conversion to local government in Fiscal 1951] would, in our judgment, slow down output of fissionable materials, A-bomb production and H-bomb development."[84] To prevent such a disruption at the Los Alamos laboratory, the transfer was put on hold for the moment.

A congressional panel headed by Dallas lawyer Richard G. Scurry toured the atomic communities and issued a report recommending self-government and private ownership at Oak Ridge and Hanford to create more "normal" communities. When panel members visited Los Alamos in June 1951, they heard that Hill residents, contrary to the citizenry in their sister cities, actually wanted a closed town, fenced off from the rest of the world and sponsored by the federal government. The resulting Scurry Report listed four obstacles to private ownership at Los Alamos: (1) the municipal government would be hard-pressed to support itself because of its location; (2) Los Alamos's residents held a negative attitude to incorporation; (3) with much of the housing composed of multi-family dwellings, private ownership could be complicated; and (4) with the Tech Area still centered around Ashley Pond, security considerations prevented opening up the site until the laboratories moved to South Mesa.[85]

The federal government moved slowly on this issue, with the AEC taking two years to decide on its course of action regarding the privatizing of its nuclear communities. In June 1953, the AEC decided to open up the towns of Oak Ridge and Hanford but to keep Los Alamos a closed community. In offering this plan to Congress, Dean noted that "Los Alamos for the moment is in a separate category."[86] However, the decision delayed the opening of the residential area of Los Alamos only a few years.

In spite of the local resistance, the AEC continued with its plan to remove the gates to the Hill. On Sunday, April 18, 1954, Santa Fe's *New Mexican* ran a front-page story that upset many Hill residents. It disclosed that AEC officials expected quick approval of their recommendation to remove the fences surrounding Los Alamos within the year. Citing the $118 million relocation of the laboratories to South Mesa, AEC officials told the *New Mexican*: "There is no justification for further maintaining the guard gates and requiring passes to enter the community."[87] Additional justification for removing the fences focused on the youngsters on the Hill. An anonymous AEC official explained: "This is not a happy situation . . . especially to those who are raising families. Many Los Alamos children have known no other home than the atomic city and their attitudes have been formed in the environment of secrecy, guards, and concealment."[88] The official anticipated little resistance from residents for the move, saying he believed that "opening up the town [would] lead to better feeling within the city. 'And happy residents make for good workers'. . . ."[89]

Los Alamos inhabitants quickly showed how unhappy this prospect made them. Their calls flooded the *New Mexican* offices protesting the AEC's announcement. The newspaper conducted personal interviews and telephone surveys to ascertain the depth of opposition to the proposal and found that it ran deep. Nobody that the newspaper contacted liked the idea of getting rid of the fences. Some of the concerns included the following: "It will become a sight-seeing place"; "We've all been investigated and our backgrounds checked so that we know and trust one another. But open up the town and everyone will be allowed in"; and "We can send our kids out on the bus every day and know that they are all right. But if they open up Los Alamos, our daughters might get attacked, and you can't tell what might happen to grandmother."[90] As the debate erupted in the local newspaper, the safety of Los Alamos's women and children figured prominently in the protest.

An editorial in the same issue of the *New Mexican* conceded that Los Alamos had to open up sooner or later. Interestingly, a major part of the editorial focused on the effect that bringing down the gates might have on the children of the Hill. Somewhat sarcastically, the editor speculated: "For it will mean an end to the spic-and-span test-tube life of the younger generation on the Hill. There are some children . . . who don't know what non-Los Alamos people look like; who never have seen a tourist or a California driver; and who have grown to their present state in life deprived of other similar pleasures. . . . Sooner or later the little tykes must face the realities of life and learn that there are things other than neutrons and protons in this vale of tears."[91] But to Los Alamos parents, protecting the children seemed as important as protecting the laboratory's secrets.

Residents quickly rallied to counter the challenge to their gated community. At a town council meeting on April 26, an overflow crowd voted in favor of keeping the gates closed. Only one person voted to open up the city. Disagreement with the AEC's plan spread throughout the community. For instance, Joe Connors, representative of the mechanics union, stated that his group opposed opening the gates "now or any other time."[92] Reflecting the alarmist fears of the times, councilman Kenneth Walsh expressed qualms about his own personal safety: "I, as a chemist, feel that if we have an open city my family might lose me . . . and that applies to many more here. Let's keep our gates closed."[93] In a world made more dangerous by nuclear weapons, the fences surrounding Los Alamos provided a sense of safety and security.

As a result of the protests, residents created a committee to present the community's view to the AEC. That August, the AEC polled 10 percent of the Hill residents and found that most people did not want the outer fences torn down. The AEC's Santa Fe Operations Office manager, Donald Leehey, noted: "I am also informed that some other residents favor retaining the existing outer guard arrangement, so that they can continue to enjoy a certain feeling of security from annoyance or encroachment by outsiders who do not possess the credentials necessary to obtain an entry pass."[94] In early September, Leehey released the results of the poll, which showed that of the 262 respondents, 212 (81 percent) wanted the city kept closed. Only thirty-nine people voted to tear down the fences, and eleven did not care. Los

Alamos's residents offered many reasons for keeping the town behind fences. Not only the safety of children and grandmothers but also the annoyance of salesmen, even the threat of kidnapings and assassinations, were quoted to persuade the AEC to keep the fences up. As in the past, the morale of staff and families trumped the wishes of the government, and the expensive access control to the residential areas continued.[95]

Fenced in, residents often claimed that Los Alamos was classless; however, classes did exist there. During the war, with the army in control of Site Y, a rigid military class system existed. After the war, with housing scarce on the Hill, class status revolved around the type of residence one secured. In the hierarchy of neighborhoods in Los Alamos, the newer the subdivision, the better the houses. Each new wave of construction incorporated more modern features and more square footage in the houses. Immediately after the war, senior personnel coveted the new homes in the Western Area. Then the North Community assumed the privileged position as the most desirable location on the Hill, a status it held through most of the fifties. Houses left over from the war became substandard as these clapboard structures noticeably aged. With scientists and administrators moving into the more modern residences, class structure revolved around one's employment position, symbolized by where one lived.

Children understood this inequality. Carlos Vásquez, who was twelve when his family arrived on the Hill in 1956, noticed a difference between Los Alamos and his hometown of Santa Fe: "There was a distinction [in Los Alamos] as to where you worked. Everyone was very conscious of that fact. But it was interesting that people very rarely out and out said; 'Where do your parents work?' Rather: 'Where do you live?' It was shorthand for what you did."[96] Single houses were scarce in the fifties, and the growing families of the Hill coveted them. Susan Tiano, whose father operated the sporting goods store (one of the first private businesses in the town) remembered: "You had to work in a certain capacity for the government to qualify for certain types of housing. And my father, since he was a merchant . . . wasn't really qualified for the kind of housing that the high level scientists got. . . . So he put his name on the list for a single and waited and waited and waited."[97] After a long wait, the Tiano family secured a coveted house, the only single residence in that neighborhood. Susan explained: "It was a mixed neighborhood in that most [houses] were quadruplexes with security guards and working-class people, but we were one of the two more middle-class people. [There was] this residential segregation. We were certainly part of that."[98]

Residential segregation also affected other children in the town. Suzanne Ray noted: "I was a peon. My father wasn't a scientist or a doctor. Yes, he worked for the labs, but he was just a guard."[99] Jack Bell's father was a machinist and tool-and-die maker. Arriving in 1947, the Bell family was assigned to a trailer close to the Otowi Bridge over the Rio Grande. Bell knew he was from a poorer part of town because in grade school, "they used to call us 'trailerites.'" Despite the ridicule, Bell denied there was any class structure at Los Alamos. He echoed a theme of other people who grew up on the Hill: although residential areas conformed to a class hierarchy that revolved around employment at the laboratory, little prejudice existed on the playground. For children, Bell noted, it "seemed like everybody accepted everybody for what they were."[100]

As Los Alamos's residents in the early fifties scrambled for scarce housing, dealt with residential segregation, and protested the removal of access controls, the dormant issue of Oppenheimer's leftist politics resurfaced and almost derailed the work on nuclear weapons. With Senator Joseph McCarthy accusing various officials from the State Department and U.S. Army of being Soviet agents, the Red Scare of the 1950s eventually focused on the nuclear establishment and targeted J. Robert Oppenheimer. Oppenheimer continued to hold influence at Los Alamos, within the AEC, and with the public, where he emerged as the liberal conscience of nuclear scientists. He was chosen to appear on the magazine covers of *Time* in November 1948 and *Life* in October 1949. While on the AEC's General Advisory Committee, he had vigorously opposed the secrecy surrounding nuclear matters. In a *Foreign Affairs* article in 1953, Oppenheimer lamented: "I must tell [about the arms race] without revealing anything. I must reveal its nature without revealing anything."[101] He also warned that the nation's economy was destined to be skewed by an arms race and that "security" would be used to cover up instances of malfeasance, pay-offs, and blunders. In another article, Oppenheimer questioned the sanity of the arms race, comparing the U.S. and the USSR "to two scorpions in a bottle, each capable of killing the other, but only at the risk of his own life."[102] Most incriminating, however, was the fact that as chairman of the General Advisory Committee in 1949, Oppenheimer had argued against the development of the hydrogen bomb. Those in the government and AEC who supported hydrogen bombs focused on Oppenheimer as a powerful opponent of their atomic policy. They bristled at Oppenheimer's questioning of the policy of secrecy and at his opposition to the Super and decided to revoke his security clearance.

As the AEC Chairman, Lewis Strauss led the attack on Oppenheimer. Strauss, who had recommended building the Super in 1950 while he was an AEC commissioner, had left the commission and then returned as its chair in 1953. Under his reign, security became the predominant issue. Harold Green, an AEC lawyer who conducted security checks, witnessed the transformation in 1953 and thought that Strauss was conducting a purge of the commission. Soon after Strauss became chairman, a close friend of Oppenheimer received a call from a colleague on the staff of the AEC. He warned: "You better tell your friend Oppie to batten down the hatches and prepare for some stormy weather."[103]

After reviewing his FBI security file (the same file that had been cleared in 1947), the AEC informed Oppenheimer of their intention to revoke his security clearance on December 21, 1953. To support its allegations, the AEC handed Oppenheimer a list of charges detailing his association with Communists in the 1930s and his supposed hindrance of the development of the hydrogen bomb. One former executive director of the AEC and a key opponent, William Borden, wondered: "In the 1940–42 period, did Dr. Oppenheimer have any close friends who were *not* identified with Communism?"[104] The FBI began wiretapping Oppenheimer's phone calls on New Year's Day, and by listening in on conversations between him and his lawyers, the government knew the defense's strategy.[105]

Another prominent opponent, Edward Teller, had privately told the FBI in May 1952 that Oppenheimer had unpatriotically opposed the Super since the war. Teller also suggested to the FBI that, without Oppenheimer as an impediment, the hydrogen bomb would have been a reality eighteen months earlier. A week before the revocation hearing, Teller warned Charter Heslep, a speech writer for Strauss, that because Oppenheimer was so powerful "politically" in scientific circles it would be hard to "unfrock him in his own church."[106] But Teller insisted that it "must be done or else . . . scientists may lose their enthusiasm for the [nuclear weapons] program."[107] Thus, the proceedings against Oppenheimer had two objectives: to remove Oppenheimer's access to classified documents about nuclear weapons and, more importantly, to remove him as a powerful voice of opposition to the official policy of the AEC. As a dissenting voice on nuclear weapons policy, Oppenheimer had to be silenced.

McCarthyism and the Red Scare of the 1950s put many people under suspicion. Looking back, Oppenheimer remembered his surprise over the turn of events: "Given the circumstances and the spirit of the times, one knew that something like this was possible and even probable, but still it was a shock when it came."[108] Others also were shocked. Complaining about this attack on a conscientious and patriotic person, Albert Einstein remarked: "The systematic and widespread attempt to destroy mutual trust and confidence constitutes the severest possible blow against society."[109] Other scientists also rallied around Oppenheimer. The chair of the AEC's General Advisory Committee, I. I. Rabi, informed Strauss that all the members of the committee would testify at the revocation hearings in support of Oppenheimer.

The hearings began on April 15, but perhaps the most damaging testimony came on April 28 when Edward Teller told the board: "I would like to see the vital interests of this country in hands which I

understand better, and therefore trust more. . . . I would feel personally more secure if public matters would rest in other hands."[110] On
May 23, after hearing other witnesses for and against Oppenheimer,
the security board voted two to one that, although Oppenheimer was a
loyal citizen and that "no man should be tried for the expression of
his opinions," his security clearance should not be reinstated.[111] On
June 29, the AEC accepted the security board's recommendation and
voted 4 to 1 to revoke Oppenheimer's clearance. The decision on the
matter of J. Robert Oppenheimer moved out from the hearing rooms
and openly erupted on the Hill.[112]

The first response to the AEC's decision came from the Federation
of American Scientists (FAS): "Many of us who know Robert Oppenheimer can only respond by doubting the good judgment of the majority of the board. . . . There can be little respect for their conclusions."[113]
Commenting from Los Alamos, David Hill, the retiring chairman of
the FAS, warned: "A suspicion will persist, in light of the committee's
recommendation, that Dr. Oppenheimer is being penalized for giving
his honest opinion several years ago against the advisability of a 'crash
program' to build the H-bomb."[114] Oppenheimer's attorneys, while
appealing to the commission to reverse the ruling, asked: "How can a
scientist risk advising the government if he is told that at some later
day a security board may weigh in the balance the degree of his enthusiasm for some official program?"[115] Like Oppenheimer, many scientists on the Hill had been guilty of opposing the Super.

Reactions from the Hill took over the front page of the *New Mexican* on June 17th. Approximately five hundred lab personnel (about
half of the lab's scientific staff) signed a petition protesting Oppenheimer's revocation, including five of the seven division heads at the
laboratory. The petition, which was sent to President Eisenhower, Representative Sterling Cole (chair of the Joint Congressional Committee on Atomic Energy), and the five AEC commissioners, informed
Washington that scientists on the Hill were "deeply disturbed" by the
recommendations of the security board, adding: "It is inexcusable to
employ the personnel security system as a means of dispensing with
the services of a loyal but unwanted consultant."[116] Dr. David Hill

released another statement criticizing the AEC: "Political crimes of the sort committed against (Dr. J. Robert) Oppenheimer and our country must not be possible in the government of a free country."[117] Hill predicted that the consequences of such a policy, "if continued, will eliminate the men of independent mind from our defense establishment."[118] Lab director Bradbury speculated that this was "not going to make it easy to draw people into classified work."[119] Several scientists talked to the *New Mexican* on the condition that their names not be used. According to one, "the general effect of the Oppenheimer hearing at Los Alamos . . . was a crystallization of the attitude: There-but-for-the-grace-of-God-go-I."[120] The message was clear for the staff. If you disagreed with official policy, your work at the lab could be terminated and your career ruined.

David Hill fired a last salvo at the AEC before he stepped down as the president of the FAS. Hill argued that the policy that resulted from Oppenheimer's revocation, "if persistently applied . . . will tend to drive the more imaginative and creative individuals from the atomic energy program."[121] Hill further denounced this "un-American doctrine" as contradicting "the belief in the dignity and worth of the individual upon which our nation has been founded."[122] As outgoing spokesman for FAS at Los Alamos, Hill represented the dissenters at the laboratory who protested the curtailment of dissent to official policy and who feared the specter of Red Raids upon the Hill.

Another casualty of Oppenheimer's security revocation was Admiral Deak Parsons. One of the atomic pioneers during the Manhattan Project, Parsons and his family had lived next door to the Oppenheimers on Bathtub Row. The Parsonses had long left Los Alamos, but Deak was still deeply involved with nuclear weapons and had served on the Military Liaison Committee of the AEC. The night that Parsons heard about the decision, he suffered pains in his chest. His daughter, Peggy, recalled: "He was so agitated, thinking about how he could prevent this [security revocation] from happening." Parsons died the next day from a heart attack.[123]

To help quell the disgruntlement among the scientists at Los Alamos, Chairman Strauss visited the town in June. To counter Teller's charge that Los Alamos's role in the making of the hydrogen bomb was "greatly exaggerated," Strauss brought a citation from President Eisenhower that clearly acknowledged Los Alamos as "the Nation's principal institution for the development of atomic weapons." The president noted that "the Laboratory's momentous success in the field of fission weapons has been followed by equal accomplishments in the fusion field."[124] Eisenhower attempted another effort at damage control when he sent a personal note to Strauss. The president asked Strauss whether Oppenheimer would be interested in working on the desalinization of water, adding: "I can think of no scientific success of all time that would equal this in its boon to mankind."[125] Neither the citation honoring Los Alamos nor the presidential query about Oppenheimer's future settled the tempest.

In September, several insiders at the laboratory, including Carson Mark, the director of the Theoretical Division, continued to express publicly their bitterness over the Oppenheimer hearing. Mark warned: "It should not be forgotten that by far . . . most scientists continue to regard that decision [against Oppenheimer] as damaging to this country's security and good name." Mark also likened the "Oppenheimer affair . . . to a nasty—though ever so formally correct—assassination."[126] David Hill was also blunt: "I know that the indignation of many scientists and others has increased in the past two months." Directing his criticism at the AEC, Hill admonished: "If now the commission appears defective, as in its pious abuse of the security system in the Oppenheimer case, the effect is discouraging, and will damage the future of the program."[127] Although the Red Hunts of the McCarthy era never charged directly up the Hill, Oppenheimer's security revocation put lab personnel on notice and possibly discouraged some potential employees from applying.

Despite the resentment by lab personnel toward the AEC, it is uncertain how many scientists actually left the laboratory. Many of those who were troubled by weapons work had already left for research or work elsewhere. Those who remained at the lab had already made their decision long before the Oppenheimer security revocation.

Even though hostility toward the AEC simmered, nuclear weapons research and development continued at Los Alamos. The country had poured vast sums of money to upgrade the site since Joe 1, and now Los Alamos had become an atomic utopia, a nuclear city on a hill where many scientists and their families lived the good life. The country had invested too much in the community to allow anything to disrupt the arms race. Thus, even though the AEC had fired a warning shot across the bow of dissenting personnel with the Oppenheimer revocation, the vocal residents of the Hill registered their protests with the commission and prevented any further raids against the talent at the laboratory.

Another consequence of the Oppenheimer affair was connected to the scientists' outcry. Newspapers rarely had access to stories from the Hill that reported dissent behind the fences. Most articles focused on the community or described the progress made at the laboratory in the development of the various non-military applications of atomic energy. That this matter erupted onto the front pages of the *New Mexican* shows the discontent of the scientists and the power they wielded if they wanted to talk to reporters. The newspaper coverage offers a rare glimpse into the opinions of lab personnel apart from official press releases and shows a community where silence was the official policy but where protest did brew and could erupt in public.

Predictably, the detonation of a Soviet atomic bomb in 1949 intensified the Cold War. The laboratory at Los Alamos responded by creating an even more powerful nuclear weapon. At the same time, money flowed up to the Hill for community improvement. Los Alamos was made more attractive for its families while it became a showcase to highlight the benefits of nuclear energy. During this scrambling to counter the nation's loss of its atomic monopoly, Los Alamos served as a test community for federal civil defense strategies. As a symbol of the future promise of nuclear energy and a place to prepare for the peril, Los Alamos prospered on the front lines of the Cold War. The country anxiously looked to the Los Alamos Scientific Laboratory for reassurance that its backyards were safe. Since the lab was off-limits, what the country saw was the residential community on the Hill, a beacon of better living through science.

CHAPTER 6

TOWARD NORMALIZING LOS ALAMOS

CRACKING THE GATES

"The destiny of all nations during the twentieth century will turn in large measure upon the nature and the pace of atomic energy development here and abroad."
PRESIDENT DWIGHT EISENHOWER IN A PRESS RELEASE FROM THE WHITE HOUSE, FEBRUARY 17, 1954

The public furor at Los Alamos over the revocation of Oppenheimer's security clearance subsided in the fall of 1954. Although Hill personnel still revered Oppenheimer, the laboratory continued its research into the various applications of atomic energy, the community advanced its modernization drive, and families pursued the postwar American dream. All this occurred in an atmosphere of suspicion and apprehension about the Soviet Union's intentions in the Cold War. Los Alamos's mission remained vital to the nation's security, and so this unique town continued to invent itself as a modern suburb in order to adequately recruit and retain personnel.

The process of normalizing Los Alamos could be applied to the secrecy at the site. Cracks in the secrecy that surrounded the residential section and even the Tech Area began to appear. In commemoration of the tenth anniversary of Trinity, LASL sponsored an unprecedented event. It opened the Tech Areas to newsmen, staff, and the family members of its work force. On July 17 and 18, 1955, thousands of people toured the technical areas that now spread over the plateau tops and among the canyons and viewed top-secret experiments. At Omega

West in the bottom of Los Alamos Canyon, visitors saw nuclear reactors. As one reporter observed: "The three machines, christened in the curious, grimly humorous jargon of atomic scientists are called Topsy, Godiva, and Jezebel."[1] The Godiva model fissioned at a rate of a billion atoms a second. A Manhattan Project veteran, associate director Ralph Carlisle Smith briefed reporters and explained Godiva's name by saying it was a bare reactor like the Englishwoman horse rider. When the critical assembly attained a chain reaction, a warning sign flashed "Route 2," telling the visitors the safest path away from the building if something went wrong. Smith told the journalists: "Always run into the wind." But he insisted: "Only a human consciously trying to make a series of mistakes could get this reaction out of control."[2] Like all careful scientists, laboratory officials plotted escape routes in case the worst happened.

One journalist, after visiting the previously closed labs, reported that two things impressed those around him: "the hugeness of the entire installation and the safety precautions taken."[3] Detection equipment for monitoring radioactivity was seen "all about the area," and laboratory officials emphasized that all radioactive material was handled by remote control. Indeed, some visitors tried the remote control arms, but none could compete with the resident operator who maneuvered the mechanical hands to unscrew an eyedropper from a bottle and squeeze three precise drops out of it.[4]

In addition to the influx of journalists and visiting scientists, spouses and children toured the workplaces of their partners and parents for the first time, some after more than ten years of living on the Hill. With open access to the Tech Areas, families thronged through the various sites on the Pajarito Plateau to see what went on behind the closed doors. Interspersed among the mute assemblies of technical equipment were exhibits that entertained. In one area, Elizabeth Graves, wife of Alvin Graves (who survived the Slotin accident and went on to direct the Nevada Test Site), demonstrated an electrical current passing through her body and discharging out through her fingertips and her hair. In another building, an exhibit called "cooking your dimes" allowed visitors to put dimes into a counter that measured radioactivity. The units of measurement were "rare, medium, or well-done, according to how much radioactivity they had picked up."[5] How the dimes picked up their radioactivity was not disclosed. Other exhibits included playing peek-a-boo through the holes in the water-boiler reactor and observing a monkey in the medical research laboratory.

Families wandered through the Tech Areas with different expectations. Some children, although intrigued with the interactive exhibits, were more impressed by entering parts of the plateau that had been off-limits to them. Visitors came from the entire range of workers on the Hill. Mrs. Marvin Anna, whose husband had electrically wired many of the laboratory buildings for the Zia Company, stated that she and her two children enjoyed "seeing the places where [*sic*] he had so often spoken about."[6] Suzanne Ray, whose father was a guard, felt strange going through the labs. She said: "Growing up there, I never really thought that was where they had the bomb made."[7] A journalist concluded: "Although foot weary from the tour, most families decided it had been well worth their while 'seeing where Daddy works.'"[8] Visiting where a spouse or parent worked brought new realizations to some and a feeling of normalcy to others.

The laboratory's Open House, which allowed families and journalists into the technical areas for the first time, exhibited no nuclear weapons. Thus, the real work at LASL remained hidden from these guests. Instead, the Open House offered a sophisticated science fair with nuclear reactors, remote-controlled arms, particle accelerators, and "cooked" dimes. The safety in the Tech Areas impressed many of the visitors who saw the numerous radiation monitors positioned throughout the workshops. With the Open House such a success, especially with the families on the Hill, it became an annual event at LASL.

Another trend helped create a more ordinary community. Individual churches acquired their own buildings of worship as a wave of church expansions swept Los Alamos. For many people on the Hill, acquiring church buildings contributed to permanency. At the same time, distinct denominations branched off from the ecumenical observances that had existed since the war. In October 1951, the old Theater #1 from the Manhattan Project became the Baptist Church, the first exclusive single denominational building at Los Alamos. The Baptists bought the theater as surplus material and then moved it onto a plot of land they had leased on Diamond Drive in the North Community. During the same time period, the United Church, which had enjoyed healthy attendance at its multi-denominational services, acquired a permanent chapel. However, Episcopalians, Lutherans, Mormons, Jews, Catholics, and Methodists all wanted their own separate facilities to draw the faithful.[9]

The Methodist Church, after years of meeting at the United Church, in school rooms, or at various private residences, finally acquired its first permanent building. Its new facility, former dormitory T-236 built during World War II, was on Trinity Drive. The parishioners had to move the building to another site almost two miles away. To facilitate the move, T-236 was cut in two. The moving of the first half went well; however, an ice storm struck the plateau, and the contractors hired to move the building could not complete the job right away. The Methodists on the Hill worshiped at Central School for several weeks until the weather warmed up enough to allow the second half to be moved. One of the church members recalled that interval of exposure as a time when "we were like birds in the wilderness."[10] Once the divided building reunited, the Methodist flock came in from the wilderness and worshiped in their own chapel.

The upsurge in religion at Los Alamos mirrored a national trend. As religious historian Winthrop Hudson wrote: "By the 1950s, it was evident that the United States was in the midst of a religious revival. . . . The uneasy peace of the 'Cold War' . . . with its recurring crises and continuing conflicts, heightened the sense of anxiety and insecurity."[11] Another historian of religion, Sydney Ahlstrom, tabulated the rise in postwar church construction in the United States and found that in 1945 only $26 million was spent on building new churches; in 1950 the amount rose to $409 million; and in 1956, construction costs soared to $775 million.

Other indications of the religious revival sweeping the country were the addition of "under God" to the pledge of allegiance in 1954 and the adoption of the official motto "In God We Trust" in 1956.[12] Ahlstrom offered two reasons for the religious revival: first, being a church member affirmed the "American way of life," especially since the USSR was officially committed to atheism; second, "being an active church member became a way to avoid suspicion of being a subversive influence."[13] As Billy Graham said in his revivals: "If you would be a true patriot, then become a Christian. If you would be a loyal American, then become a loyal Christian."[14] For many Americans, the religious revival was fueled by the anxiety of the Atomic Age, the fear of Communism, or a response to the Red Scare of the early fifties.

An additional reason for religious devotion motivated some nuclear scientists. As these scientists manipulated the very fabric of the universe, a turn to religion helped some of them with their work. One engineer at the Brookhaven National Laboratory in New York, a sister facility to Los Alamos, told a *Time* magazine reporter: "Up in the [atomic] pile we see mass disappearing and becoming energy, but nowhere can we add to or subtract from the total mass and energy. Where did mass and energy come from? . . . There must be a Higher Power who can make it."[15] At nuclear facilities and throughout the country, religion comforted many in the new age.

A final issue concerning the spiritual needs of residents resolved itself in 1955. From its beginning, Los Alamos lacked a cemetery. In February 1955, the County Commission organized a committee to study the possibility of a formal burial site on the Hill. The Atomic Energy Commission was willing to provide the initial funding to establish a cemetery, but asked the County Commission to manage the place. Thus, after over a decade as a town, Los Alamos residents finally obtained Guaje Cemetery, a local final resting place.[16]

Progress toward making Los Alamos a more typical town also focused on the school system. By the opening day of classes in 1953, the Los Alamos public school system had expanded to include nine schools. Elementary students attended Aspen, Little Forest, Canyon, Central, Mesa, Little Valley Mountain, and Little Poplar. Pupils above the elementary grades went to Pueblo Junior High School and then Los Alamos High School. Almost two thousand children filled the elementary schools, and seven hundred students attended junior high and high school. Most schools were close to the neighborhoods they served, so the district had only four school buses and a single driver. In the morning, the bus driver transported youngsters from White Rock to the high school, "but all other students had to walk to school."[17]

Dedicated to excellence, the Los Alamos schools adopted this mission statement: "We have committed ourselves to the ideal that every American citizen deserves just as much education as he can personally benefit from. In order to provide adequate challenge both for the fast as well as for the slow learner, our curriculum and methods must be sufficiently flexible to interest all students."[18] As mentioned in previous chapters, such a flexible curriculum included a variety of subjects, but emphasized math and the sciences.

In spite of the institutional commitment to a superior system, dissatisfaction existed among many teachers. Toward the end of the 1953–54 school year, this tension came into the open as the *New Mexican* reported that 40 percent of the teachers on the Hill would not return the next year. Complaints from the teachers focused on Superintendent Lewis Allbee's managerial style. Allbee had come to Los Alamos in 1949 with a Ph.D. from Yale and a Certificate d'Etudes from the Sorbonne in Paris. He was a principal at Los Alamos High School and then an assistant superintendent on the Hill until he succeeded Robert Wegner as superintendent in May 1953. Thus, Allbee had been the top administrator for less than a year when complaints surfaced, specifically that he used "irregular tactics" and that merit raises were granted only to those teachers who conformed to Allbee's "way of doing things."[19] So, at the same time that Oppenheimer's security hearings took place, dissent erupted over Los Alamos's schools. Some teachers complained that the pressure of teaching under him had made them incapable of doing their best work. Since so many instructors were quitting their jobs, school officials warned that "a shortage [of teachers] might result at the high school and a few of the elementary schools."[20] For a community that prided itself on the quality of its educational system, this presented a serious challenge.

The Los Alamos School Board responded to these charges at a public meeting on April 20th. More than two hundred parents and teachers listened to board member and LASL director Norris Bradbury talk for an hour defending Allbee and addressing the specific charges against the superintendent. Bradbury said he did not ordinarily respond to "unsigned charges," but then added: "Because we want the best school system possible, let's take a survey of the public statements bandied about."[21] Bradbury admitted that about one-third of the 150 teachers were not returning, but this was the same percentage as the previous year. He then listed the reasons that the teachers gave for leaving their jobs. They included: marriage, four; pregnancy, ten; transfer of husbands, eight; career change, eight; dissatisfaction with Los Alamos, four; and desire to return east, six. Bradbury did concede that "other miscellaneous reasons . . . might have been given to cover some of the real dissatisfaction with the present administration."[22]

An editorial in the *New Mexican* on April 21 disagreed with Bradbury's defense of Allbee: "The charges against the administration were made by teachers and school administrators who, for obvious reasons, preferred to remain anonymous. Even those who are leaving the system—and this is a not inconsiderable thirty-two percent—do not chose to risk being 'branded' as potential troublemakers."[23] The editorial concluded by suggesting that the teachers and the administrators "bury the hatchet and start afresh in a cooperative spirit."[24] Because of the defection of teachers, schools at Los Alamos opened in the fall of 1954 with slightly more crowded classrooms.[25]

Nonetheless, the controversy over Allbee did not die. Less than a year later, he quit as superintendent, citing one of those miscellaneous reasons himself. He and his wife had wanted for a long time to buy their own home. "But since we cannot do this here in Los Alamos, we have finally decided to move at the end of this school year."[26] Another source on the Hill disputed this reason, saying that Allbee was not completely satisfied with his new contract. The Los Alamos school board president, Leslie Hawkins, reassured parents that the board was conducting a "search for a leading professional educator to continue the fine work that Dr. Allbee has established."[27] The board did move quickly to find a replacement for Allbee. By the middle of May, they had considered forty-four candidates and had unanimously selected Dr. Clarence W. Richard from Wyoming.[28] The change in administration evidently corrected the problem of high teacher turnover since only twenty-seven teachers left in 1955, compared to fifty-one the previous year.[29]

In the midst of an arms race, Los Alamos schools continued to emphasize scientific training for all grades "to help meet the nation's soaring need for scientists."[30] By the third grade, students on the Hill had explored the solar system, studied magnetism and electricity, and observed various plants and animals. In fourth grade, using classroom "Science Kits," they experimented again with magnetism, electricity, and air pressure. The introduction of a hands-on science program at the elementary schools of Los Alamos continued the trend begun in the 1940s to expose children to science at an early age.[31]

The science program accelerated at Pueblo Junior High School. Utilizing a new science laboratory, all junior high students took a twelve-week course in science. The course explored physical science, energy conservation, and general areas of chemistry with experiments such as growing bacteria, exploring the principles of acid and base, and examining the forces of air pressure. The new classroom lab had gas and compressed air outlets for all students, and a mirror hung over the instructor's desk so that students could observe the experiments without crowding around the teacher's table.[32] This preparation in science paved the way for advanced courses in high school.

In 1958, Los Alamos High School (with an enrollment of 1,189) was the only secondary school in the nation that offered five separate years of math and an advanced science program with prerequisites in chemistry, physics, and biology. By comparison, in 1957 only 9 percent of New Mexico's high schools had a four-year math program, and only Los Alamos offered four years of laboratory science beyond general science.[33] Three days a week in the chemistry laboratory, students heard lectures on electron theory, famous chemists, metallurgy, colloids, plastics, and other areas of organic and inorganic chemistry. In the other two class periods each week, they attended a laboratory where they conducted their own experiments in chemistry. For a portion of the final exam at the end of the year, each student received an "unknown" substance and had to determine its chemical composition.

Laboratory time extended to the other sciences as well. In physics class, high school students experimented with heat, light, sound, electricity, magnetism, and other elements in a lab designed to "enable a student to enter a course of college physics with assurance or to allow him to be able to understand better the world around him."[34] A biology lab equipped with microscopes, prepared slides, dissecting equipment, and hand lenses also allowed students to explore in depth various plants and animals. By taking these advanced courses, some students graduated early. Ellen Reid and her friend Tina Herland decided to skip their senior year: "We were able to do that because we [had been] taking high school courses since we in the Eighth grade."[35]

To be sure, curriculum development was not unique to Los Alamos. At the same time that Los Alamos inaugurated these advanced programs in science and math, a wave of educational reform swept the United States. Early in the 1950s, new subjects were introduced into grade schools across the country that included more classes in art, music, drama, dance, and student government. When the Soviet Union exploded its own thermonuclear weapon in 1954 and then launched Sputnik, the first manmade satellite, in 1957, many Americans worried that the Russians had surpassed the United States in science and technology. Consequently, an urgent shift toward more math and science occurred in the country's public schools. In fact, prior to Sputnik, most of New Mexico's schools experienced declining enrollments in their physical science courses. One science teacher complained: "Many of our children, and adults, consider a scientist as at least 'slightly odd,' [and believe] that a scientist does not and cannot be a normal member of society living a normal home life."[36] After Sputnik, as the country turned to places like Los Alamos to respond to the new Soviet threats, scientists became more ordinary members of society. And science and math education became vital in winning the arms race as classrooms around the nation began training future Cold Warriors.

Beginning in the fall of 1955, a series of articles appeared in the *New Mexican* explaining the public school system of Los Alamos. The weekly articles highlighted the science and math programs of the schools but also covered student government and the school libraries. Glowingly prepared by "personnel of the Los Alamos Schools," the columns reversed Bradbury's edict against publicity. Much had happened in the atomic empire since the Soviet Union had detonated its own atomic bomb in 1949 and thermonuclear weapon in 1954. Perhaps the Los Alamos School Board did not feel so vulnerable as the town solidified its status as a model community. The strong school system at Los Alamos was an advertisement for the promise of the atom and an atomic utopia.[37]

In January 1958, Dr. Bradbury welcomed representatives from New Mexico's schools to a "Conference on the Secondary Schools of the Future" held at Los Alamos. In a speech entitled "New Responsibilities of the Secondary Schools for the Future," Bradbury sounded a familiar theme: "The chief overall responsibility of the secondary school . . . is to educate each individual to take an effective role, the one most meaningful to him, in the society of which he is a part."[38] The society that Los Alamos had created, one engaged in a nuclear arms race, required youngsters trained from an early age in the mental as well as manipulative skills of the theoretical and applied sciences. Not surprisingly, the Hill's educational system prepared some of its students to become atomic scientists and nuclear technicians.

Curriculum reform was not the only change sweeping the nation's schools in the fifties. Beginning with the 1954 Supreme Court decision of *Brown vs. Board of Education of Topeka*, the country confronted inequality in the education of minority children. During the summer of 1957, plans to integrate the high school at Little Rock, Arkansas, progressed. When nine black teenagers sought to enter the high school on opening day, September 3, crowds of white parents and teenagers vehemently protested. Over the next decade, scenes like this were repeated across the United States as discriminatory practices were demonstrated and challenged in school halls, at lunch counters, and in bus stations.[39]

At the Los Alamos schools in the 1950s, segregation was not a legal issue. The children of the only two African-American families on the Hill attended the town's schools. Hispanic-Americans at Los Alamos were more numerous than African-Americans, and the children from these families also attended the school system. Still, cases of blatant racism occurred. Nelson Martínez recalled one incident when a boy called him "every name in the book: scuz, scum, spick." This boy told Martínez: "Elvis Presley would rather kiss a jack-ass than marry a Mexican."[40] Carlos Vásquez, who arrived in Los Alamos from Santa Fe in 1956 and attended seventh grade, was singled out in class by one of his teachers. This teacher "made it a point to point out in class (this is your first year in junior high and you're vulnerable) that [I was] a character from Santa Fe. Of course, everybody knew how rowdy people were down in Santa Fe . I was a straight 'A' student in Santa Fe. . . . For the first time in my life, I got 'C's."[41] Among his peers, Vásquez commented: "Socially, I had a good set of friends. There was distinction, but it wasn't segregation anymore. It was occupation, class."[42] Vásquez's stepfather worked as a security guard, and so they lived in the part of town reserved for the service personnel. Segregation at Los Alamos revolved around occupation in the laboratories or with the Zia Company, and not directly with race or ethnicity.

In contrast to the incidents of racism that some experienced at Los Alamos were the friendships that developed between youngsters from different ethnic backgrounds. Jack Bell, who was in high school in the late fifties, recalled: "Seemed like everybody accepted everybody for what they were."[43] In 1952, Secundino Sandoval, who had arrived on the Hill as an "Arizonian" during the Manhattan Project, was co-captain of the football team and senior class president. Proof of this acceptance of minority teenagers at the high school is evident in the 1957 Los Alamos High School yearbook. The student body selected the following teenagers: for Homecoming Queen, Rose Maestas; for Senior Class favorite, Anna Mae Naranjo; for Junior

Class favorite, Helen Archuleta; and for Sophomore Class favorite, Joe Ruiz. The large Hispanic representation in these elected positions occurred in a student body of which approximately 10 percent had Hispanic surnames.[44]

When not in school, many Los Alamos teenagers enjoyed the outdoors. Terell Tucker spoke for them when he said: "The countryside around it was such an incredible area, with all the old ruins. I spent a lot of time in the country, which was a salvation for me. . . . I think living that close to a pretty virgin kind of wilderness served me in good stead." Suzanne Ray walked her dog in Pueblo Canyon and saw deer there. She also went with her friends to the reservoir where they "would pretend we were fishing, but we had no fishing poles." Don Marchi camped at Bandelier with his friends. He and Terell started a motorcycle club and rode in the Jemez Mountains. Kim Manley remembers: "We were always out in the canyons and in the woods and down in the bottom of the canyons. I think that that kind of freedom was very, very nice. . . . We had a lot of imagination but it was tied in with the physical environment." With her friends, Kim went on backpacking trips: "We'd go up into the Valle Grande in the summer and hike all around this area." She recalled that living at Los Alamos meant "being able to go higher to ski, lower to hike, sideways to hike—a wide variety of outdoor activities."[45]

Like teenagers throughout the nation, those in Los Alamos took to the outdoors for another type of social activity. Young couples necked all over the Hill. Some of the favorite places were in the cemetery, down near White Rock, and up on Sawyer Hill near the ski runs. Jack and Kathy Bell recalled one time when they had parked and were "making out" in the woods near Sawyer Hill. They noticed a bear looking at them through the car windows. Nelson Martínez recalled a tunnel under the high school as a popular spot. Teens got into it through an entrance near the swimming pool.[46]

As Los Alamos accumulated the trappings of a typical community, from improved schools to teenage spooning spots, a milestone was passed with the graduating class of 1955. Three students graduated from Los Alamos High School who had received their entire education on the Hill. Mary Frances Olivas, Dimas Methardo Chávez, and Elizabeth Joan Allen had all arrived on the Hill with their families in 1943 and attended the fledgling school system during the war. Olivas's family came to Los Alamos from Santa Fe in August 1943. Her father became a technician in the laboratory's P-3 group (Physics Division, Van de Graff/Cockroft-Walton Accelerator group). Chávez arrived on the Hill in March 1943 from Santa Fe when his father was hired to clear the plateau top with a bulldozer. Allen came to Los Alamos from New York City with her family in May 1943 when her father was hired to serve as the chemical purchasing agent for the Manhattan Project.[47]

With more teenagers graduating from the high school, what did young adults do on the Hill? A survey of the seventy-one graduating seniors of the class of 1954 showed that thirty-two attended institutions of higher education around the country. Most of the rest were employed, had joined the military, or were homemakers. Only eighteen of the seventy-one graduates remained at Los Alamos. Indeed, with many of their peers gone and laboratory employment enhanced by advanced university degrees, remaining on the Hill offered little enticement for most graduating seniors. Commenting on what the town was like after graduation, Donald Marchi recalled: "Once you got to be eighteen, [Los Alamos] was not a neat place anymore. You were almost an outcast if you were single or not off to college somewhere. . . . If you didn't get on at the labs, you were almost a lost sheep."[48] The lack of opportunity forced many young adults to fly off the Hill like charged electrons.

A more forbidding aspect of the future for the area's students involved preparing them for a possible nuclear attack. By 1953, the school's operating procedures offered two plans in case of a "disaster." Plan A was contingent on an early warning of an impending disaster. If such a warning arrived in time, students were to go directly home and then evacuate the Hill with their parents. Plan B addressed the possibility that "the warning received indicated insufficient time . . . for evacuation." Under Plan B, students would be instructed by their teachers to move all of the desks to the outside wall of the room, collect all available clothing in the room for covering and protection,

In 1956, civil defense officials on the Hill evacuated elementary school
children in preparation for a community evacuation drill. Courtesy of Los
Alamos Historical Museum Photo Archives.

climb under the desks, drape themselves with the available clothing,
and cover their heads with their arms. Students were to remain under
their desks until the "All Clear" signal sounded.[49] Although a nuclear
attack was not mentioned as a possible disaster, Plan B could only
have had that in mind.

In January 1956, Los Alamos again led the nation in civil defense
planning. Parents received written instructions from administrators
outlining the procedures that both students and parents should follow
in an upcoming test evacuation of the schools at Los Alamos. This
was the first community-wide test evacuation of children from the
schools at Los Alamos. The exact date and time of the test, unannounced beforehand, occurred at 2:40 P.M. on January 19, 1956, when
sirens wailed an alert. Elementary students ran home, and even the
larger schools cleared out within five minutes. Some high school
students disregarded the seriousness of test and "went to nearby stores

Teenagers file out of the new high school as part of the civil defense exercises in 1956. Courtesy of Los Alamos Historical Museum Photo Archives.

for their usual after-school refreshments" instead of to their homes.[50] After the students left the classrooms and supposedly went home, the test ended.

Beginning with the trial evacuation of the schools in January, the year 1956 started an active period for civil defense preparedness. On May 1, an evacuation surprised Hill residents. This was the third community-wide test evacuation held at Los Alamos. A first-alert siren sounded at 1:13 P.M., followed by a Red Alert warning at 2 P.M. Prepared by the January exercise and in accordance with Plan A of the school's operating procedures, students ran home. A high school baseball game between Los Alamos and Española was suspended as the teams loaded onto buses and were driven away from the town. The game resumed after the All Clear signal sounded at 3:06 P.M. Area newspapers carried conflicting reports of the test. The *New Mexican* noted

Cars clogged the intersection of Ninth Street and Central Avenue as residents participated in a community-wide Civil Defense evacuation drill in 1956. Courtesy of Los Alamos Historical Museum Photo Archives.

that the test "was marred only by the lack of resident interest, estimated at less than sixty percent of the total population."[51] The *Albuquerque Journal* more positively reported: "The test in general went off well with the exception of a few expected traffic jams and the locked gate at the exit of Guaje Road."[52] Perhaps those residents who did not participate in the evacuation felt immune because of the community's distance from the coasts, or perhaps they refused to join because they suspected the futility of evacuations in the event of thermonuclear explosions. Taking into account the poor showing for the evacuation, a later newspaper article estimated that "there would be 2,600 casualties, who . . . would be caught within the area of total destruction."[53] This estimate of casualties equaled about 15 percent of the town's population.

Several federal Civil Defense officials observed the Los Alamos evacuation in preparation for the national "Operation Alert" to be held

Radiation monitors inspect the feet of a Hill worker as part of the Civil Defense evacuation drill of 1956. Courtesy of Los Alamos Historical Museum Photo Archives.

in July. James D. Maddy, director of civil defense for Los Alamos, stated: "The information and observations recorded during the third community evacuation held on May 1 of this year will be used as feeder material for forwarding to civil defense organizations at state, regional, and national levels."[54] Thus, Los Alamos was used as a test case in May for the nationwide "Operation Alert" maneuvers several months later.

Operation Alert in July spared Los Alamos an actual evacuation since it had already undergone one in May. Nonetheless, the Hill (for the purposes of this alert) was hit by a "one-megaton hydrogen bomb" with only an estimated 2,600 fatalities. Hypothetical hydrogen bombs also fell on seventy-five other cities, towns, military installations, and AEC facilities in the United States.[55]

The final event in 1956 at Los Alamos occurred in September in conjunction with National Civil Defense Week. Preparedness exhibits and displays were erected at the Community Center, in storefront windows, on the football field, and in the theater lobby. Comic books on civil defense were distributed to third, fourth, and fifth graders in all of the Hill's elementary schools. Perhaps the most unusual activity involved the Borror family, who voluntarily lived for that week on a seven-day emergency rations regime recommended by the Federal Civil Defense Administration. The supply kit included canned meat and fish, canned vegetables, canned fruit juice, dried fruit, cereal, instant coffee, cocoa, powdered and canned milk, chocolate bars, crackers, and dog food for the Borrors' pet. The idea for the experiment originated in Los Alamos and was sponsored by the Los Alamos Civil Defense Organization. A doctor examined Violet and Kenneth Borror and their two sons before and after their trial and found them to be in good health and not suffering from any vitamin deficiency. But the experiment by the Borrors avoided dealing with some of the more serious issues concerning protecting one's family in the aftermath of a nuclear attack. Would seven days after a nuclear attack be enough time before one could venture out? What type of shelter would provide safety from the shock waves, fires, and radioactive dangers of a nuclear blast? After only seven days, would fresh food be readily available? Even though a doctor declared the Borror family healthy after their experiment, vitamin deficiency from canned foods seemed to be the least of a family's worry after a nuclear attack.[56]

Avoiding a public examination and debate of the acute dangers of a nuclear attack seemed to be the goal, at least at times, of the FCDA. In Operation Alert 1957, Civil Defense authorities estimated that a sixty-kiloton bomb dropped on Los Alamos would kill only 153 people. Another example of avoiding the truth about nuclear weapons is seen in a trucking industry publication that reprinted a statement by Dr. Edward Teller. Teller assured the public that after a full-scale nuclear attack: "We can be back in business within a few hours."[57] Similar nostrums were offered in a Civil Defense film showing a family calmly retreating to their basement to seek shelter from an imminent attack. A little while after the explosion had rattled their shelter, the father calmly decided that the danger had passed and that they ought to go up and see what had happened.[58] Those Los Alamos personnel who surveyed the destruction of Hiroshima and Nagasaki and who attended the test shots in the Pacific and at the Nevada Test Site knew that the lethal effects lasted more than just a couple of hours or even a couple of days after an attack.

By the latter part of the 1950s, public awareness of nuclear dangers shifted. In a survey completed in April 1955, only 17 percent of the respondents knew about fallout from hydrogen bombs. By the time of a May 1957 poll, 57 per cent of those questioned were concerned about fallout. This reflected the growing controversy over fallout from above-ground testing. In Operation Alert 1958, civil defense officials revised their optimism concerning public policy and public perception of nuclear attacks. Acknowledging the increased destructiveness of hydrogen bombs, Los Alamos civil defense director James Maddy told a journalist: "Residents are urged to consider their individual capability to care for themselves and their families, should the real attack ever come. Food, clothing, medical attention and supplies would be difficult to obtain, if available at all. It might be necessary to live under very trying conditions for weeks, and even months."[59] After years of planning for an attack without distinguishing between atomic and hydrogen bombs, the nation's civil defense network now shifted to confronting the realities of a thermonuclear war. In the coming decade, officials looked more to underground shelters to protect citizens from the hydrogen bomb's quantum leap in destructiveness.

A more realistic appraisal of another fundamental characteristic of Los Alamos also occurred during this time. After years of debate and heated public hearings, the fences and checkpoints surrounding the town's residential areas came down, and people entered and left the town without special security passes. The planning for this event originated with the Master Plan of 1948, which transferred the laboratories and technical areas to the South Mesa. Los Alamos's sister city at Oak Ridge had opened up its gates and taken down its fences in 1949, but, as seen in the previous chapter, the Hill's residents resisted such a move. Nonetheless, in 1953, Ralph Carlisle Smith (who was now an assistant director at LASL) chaired a long-range planning committee to evaluate opening the town site. Other members of the committee included Paul Wilson, local manager of the AEC; Chalmers C. King, legal counsel for the Los Alamos Field Office of the AEC; and H. Frank Brown, vice president of Zia Company. The committee concluded that the security reasons for keeping the residential part of Los Alamos closed disappeared when the laboratory moved to South Mesa. The planning committee then stated: "Maintenance of access controls is expensive, a nuisance to private lives of residents and business opportunities, and a major obstacle to a 'normal' community."[60] Could Los Alamos truly sustain anything like normal living if it remained surrounded by fences like a military post or a prison camp? Access control for residential Los Alamos had to go.

In 1954, a bill was introduced into the U.S. Congress by Senator Clinton P. Anderson (D-N.Mex.) and Representative Carl T. Durham (D-N.C.) that proposed to allow private ownership of land and residences at the AEC towns of Hanford, Oak Ridge, and Los Alamos. That year, the Joint Committee on Atomic Energy halted the bill, but it was reintroduced in 1955. The bill rattled many people at Los Alamos, who strongly resisted the opening up of their community to the outside world and even the opportunity to purchase their own homes. Consequently, the AEC issued this opinion: "After giving full consideration to the security, economic, and community relations aspect of a plan to alter community access controls at Los Alamos, the Atomic Energy Commission concluded that present procedures should not be changed at this time."[61] However, plans to permit the residents of Oak Ridge and Hanford to purchase property proceeded.

A public hearing at Los Alamos on September 6, 1955, attended by Senator Anderson and Representative Jack Dempsey, also of New Mexico, allowed Hill inhabitants to voice their opinions about the legislation. Los Alamos's residents raised concerns over taxation, appraisal of existing homes, and federal support for community institutions like the schools and library. Many people cited the survey done in August 1954 that polled 10 percent of the Hill's population. Eighty-one percent of those questioned wanted the fences kept up.

However, the minority who favored opening up the community also were vocal in their position. A Mrs. Briscoe told Senator Anderson:

> I would like to say that not all of the citizens of Los Alamos expect to be on a milk diet all of their lives. Quite a lot of us have reached the adult point where we are willing to take responsibility of a normal community along with the privileges of a normal community. . . . I would definitely like to see the gates left if it could be done . . . but if they have to go, it is a small price to pay to be able to paint my living room the color I want, plant a rose bush and see it bloom, and live in a house that I own.[62]

Over the next several years, despite the recommendations by the long-range planning committee and the removal of access control at the other AEC towns, people at Los Alamos still fought to keep their site closed and the fences up. Residents were not bothered by door-to-door salesmen, crime remained low, and parents were happy with the security provided for their children. However, the gated nature of the town irritated some of the teenagers on the Hill. Ellen Reid recalled the difficulty of getting past the guards at the gates: "It did make it harder for kids to go drinking or buy alcohol. . . . If the guards at the gate thought that you were going somewhere, they would say 'Where are you going? Does your mom know that you're going down there?'"[63] Other, more serious, arguments in support of the removal of the fences began to be heard.

Richard M. Bidwell, a chemist at the laboratory, complained about the "creeping socialism" at Los Alamos and asked:

> Who are we . . . to have the taxpayers protect us from peddlers, vagrants, and unwelcome in-laws? We can do this ourselves, individually and as a community. . . . This asking an outside force to run our affairs is not the American way of doing things. . . . America and the West were not settled by people who wanted to be taken care of. Unwillingness to take responsibility for their own affairs has gradually led more than one people to a welfare state and dictatorship.[64]

Indeed, people at Los Alamos enjoyed the amenities of postwar suburban living with few of the problems. Subsidized by the federal government, Los Alamos residents paid no property taxes for the community services of their model town. Despite invoking the western myth about rugged individualism, Dr. Bidwell's reference about the independence of those who settled in the West rings hollow. The federal government has a long tradition of helping people settle in the West. As western historian Patricia Limerick said: "Independent living is hard work, after all; one needs all the help one can get."[65] Nonetheless, the myth of an independent frontier West continued to help the atomic pioneers on the Hill in inventing their world.

In accordance with the AEC's desire to get out of the residential real estate business at Los Alamos, Barranca Mesa, an area north of the North Community, was slated for private ownership. In 1953, the long-range planning committee had suggested a private development within the federal reserve, and at the public hearing in September 1955, the suggestion was raised again. To satisfy the demands of those Hill residents who wanted to own their own homes, the AEC conducted more public meetings, engineering surveys, and meetings with the Federal Housing Authority to plan for the construction of private residences on Barranca Mesa.[66]

After years of reversing its policies to accommodate the residents' desires, the AEC shocked the people of Los Alamos. On Friday, February 15, 1957, the AEC announced that on the following Monday, February 18, the residential areas of Los Alamos would lose their access control. After that Monday, the gates would open and people would not need passes to enter the town. Indeed, the security guards would leave the gates they had monitored twenty-four hours a day since January 1943 and be reassigned to the Tech Areas. There was little advance warning of this decision, and many Hill residents expressed dismay. Ed Grilly, a chemist at LASL, was chagrined: "It will make my wife lock the door and we will have to be more careful about the house belongings and the children, but I suppose we have been rather careless up here."[67] Ruth Haley, who had lived at Los Alamos for thirteen years, said: "It really doesn't make too much difference but I would rather have seen them shut."[68] However, others in the community were delighted. Mrs. Herman Hoerlin told a reporter that she was "100 percent in favor of it" and "very, very happy about the whole thing."[69] The police chief, Ralph Kopansky, commented: "There undoubtedly will be many friendly taxpayers who will wish to visit Los Alamos to see how their tax dollars have been and are being spent."[70] Whatever their feelings about access control, residents could do nothing to prevent the loss of their guards, gates, and fences.

The AEC gave several reasons for reversing their previous policy of keeping the residential areas of Los Alamos behind fences. The announcement listed four advantages to removing the gates: "1. The recruitment of scientific personnel will benefit. 2. Private financing of home sites on Barranca Mesa will be facilitated. Action has been taken to opening these home sites for privately owned homes. 3. Private interest in leasing Government owned land and buildings for commercial purposes will be enhanced. 4. Removal of the gate controls will save approximately $100,000 a year in direct costs."[71] After the transfer of the main technical areas to South Mesa, there were few security reasons to justify access control to the town, except to accede to the wishes of residents. Since World War II, the AEC often had followed the policy begun by General Groves of deferring to the wishes of the people of Los Alamos to keep up morale. Now, however, the AEC's overriding concern about cutting costs and its wish to create a more "normal" community at Los Alamos forced final removal of the access controls.

At noon on February 18, 1957, under an overcast sky and lightly falling snow, the guards at the main gate were relieved of their duties, and New Mexico's Governor Edwin L. Mechem became the first person to enter Los Alamos without a pass. Paul Wilson, manager of Los Alamos for the AEC, escorted Mechem into the town and addressed the assembled crowd with these remarks: "To me, this little ceremony is symbolic of several things. First, it indicates the continued desire and effort to make Los Alamos part of New Mexico and to make it a more normal community. Second, it is symbolic of [the] continuing effort on the part of the AEC to make available for public use information pertaining to the peaceful uses of atomic energy. Third, it is symbolic of the freedom of the American people and their desire to live without unnecessary restrictions."[72]

Reactions to the loss of controlled access to the Hill varied. The town's merchants took out a large advertisement in the *New Mexican* stating that "The Gates Will Be . . . OPEN" and inviting readers "to come to Los Alamos to shop and look over our world famous city."[73] Years of debating the issue had left some of the town's residents afraid that criminals might target the Hill. Roger Corbett, who operated Corbett Cleaning Company at Los Alamos, recalled: "People up here were terrified. . . . On about the tenth of March, we had our first safecracking. Somebody broke into the old Golf Club safe and also got the high school. About April 8th or 9th, my safe was stolen."[74] Corbett explained that the Golf Club and high school safes were broken into by the president of the student body and the captain of the basketball team. The Corbett Cleaner's safe was stolen by one of his delivery men. For Corbett, "the first two big crimes didn't come from off the Hill, they were right in the middle of [our] own people."[75] Donald Marchi, who attended Los Alamos High School in the fifties, also remembered the crime committed by his classmates. Marchi recalled that the two teenagers were attending a Boys State conference in Las Cruces, New Mexico, over three hundred miles to the south of Los Alamos. After the day's proceeding at Las Cruces, the two teens drove up to Los Alamos, robbed the safes of several hundred dollars, and returned to Las Cruces. The crimes had taken place on a federal reservation, and so the Federal Bureau of Investigation handled the case. The two teenagers were caught and, though they thought they had a solid alibi, were sent to the New Mexico Boys' School, a detention home for wayward youth.[76]

A year later, in an article surveying the changes since the gates had opened, many of the residents of Los Alamos acknowledged the lack of any major infractions, aside from the two cases mentioned above. No crime wave hit the town. Visiting sports teams enjoyed freer access to their games on the Hill. Fuller Lodge, the only hotel at Los Alamos, had little if any increase in overnight stays and experienced only a minor increase in meals served to tourists passing through. Most of the residents contacted for the article said they had experienced no changes in their lives since the gates were opened, but a few

An aerial view of Los Alamos looking southeast shows the bridge (center) that linked the old Tech Area and the residential area on the left with the new laboratory area on the South Mesa to the right. Courtesy of National Archives II, College Park, Md.

replied that their lives had become more convenient with the open access.[77] Perhaps most important for the teens on the Hill, the pass control building at the East Gate became the "Gate Drive-in," a popular eating spot. Claire Weiner recalls the drive-in: "The main social activity of the weekend was, you'd get into a car if you had a friend with one. You drove to the gate which was now a drive-in and then you didn't cruise like they do now but you drove back and forth to see who was there and who was with whom."[78] From security passes to shakes and fries, the reinvention of the East Gate guardhouse showed the movement toward a more normal community.

So the opening of the gates ended an era. Los Alamos was the last of the nation's atomic communities to take down the security fences that surrounded the residential areas. The people of Los Alamos weathered this change to their town as they had the previous ones. From 1943 to

1957, change had transformed the Pajarito Plateau several times. Los Alamos residents, driven by the urgency of the arms race, had invented and reinvented their community in the glare of the national media and, in doing so, had focused attention on what a model Cold War community should be. Even though the town of Los Alamos struggled to create a recognizably normal community through Open Houses, church building, and conversions like the Gate Drive-in, it could not escape its unique status. Federal officials used it as an experimental community to test civil defense strategies. Curriculum reform emphasizing math and science swept the Hill's educational system to better prepare students for a nuclear and technological world. The fences did come down, and Los Alamos became more like an ordinary place than ever before, but the community remained a company town, dependent on the federal government for funding, personnel, and guidance.

CHAPTER 7

ATOMIC CITY ON A HILL

LEGACY AND
CONTINUING RESEARCH

From 1943 to 1957, Los Alamos grew from an isolated school for a hundred boys to a booming, world-famous community of twelve thousand residents. Having fulfilled its mission to create an atomic weapon that would end World War II, the town also invented a new age. After World War II, the personnel at the laboratory served the front lines of the Cold War. These Cold Warriors worked on the frontiers of nuclear physics, nuclear medicine, computer technology, and atomic energy production, and transformed the world we live in. It is time to evaluate the legacy and impact of Los Alamos. That means going to the source—to those people who grew up in families on the Hill. Finally, this chapter will look at some of the research and development programs now being carried out at the renamed Los Alamos National Laboratory.

In 1957, the town of Los Alamos opened up to the world, and its families adapted to the loss of their fences and security guards. For outsiders who finally visited Los Alamos, what type of community did they see on the Hill? Most tourists saw a town that functioned well and supported the ongoing efforts of the lab to win the arms race for the United States. Schools taught, stores sold goods, the hospital administered to the sick, and the lab created nuclear weapons. In an isolated part of the country, the nation's premier nuclear weapons research laboratory invented a modern suburb with many of the amenities of postwar living. In contrast to how outsiders viewed the town, how did residents feel about their community? One way to answer this is to look at how those who grew up at Los Alamos now feel about their hometown and its historic legacy.

Coming of age in Los Alamos was a unique experience. Living in a privileged enclave and a pristine setting and being enrolled in one of the best public school systems in the country, many Los Alamos children thrived in the fifties. Advanced classes were offered in a wide range of courses, from mathematics and science to a Russian Studies' program. With such training at school often reinforced at home, students learned to use their minds. Ellen Reid learned that if "you think about something hard enough and long enough . . . you can probably do it." Jim Graebner agreed: "The ideas that I got there and didn't anywhere else was the imminent sense that everything could be fixed rationally." For Jim, this rationality extended to debates on nuclear weapons: "You were seen as being stupid if you couldn't rationalize nuclear defense. . . . If your mind doesn't get to the level where you could see the complexity behind it, then you must be an idiot."[1] Not surprisingly, many who grew up on the Hill believed in the power of the intellect.

Coming of age at Los Alamos provided children with unique opportunities. Nelson Martínez commented: "It helped because there were so many different cultures in Los Alamos, not only Hispanics from northern New Mexico, but other parts of the country. African-American, Japanese. It gave me a good variety of personalities with whom to contend." Martínez attributed at least part of his subsequent success to growing up in Los Alamos: "I saw how they [the scientists' families] lived. . . . I thought, these people do real well here and I'd sure like to tap in." Immersed in Los Alamos but with roots in the traditional Hispanic village of Chimayó, Nelson learned to code-switch among cultures. He joined the audiovisual club at Los Alamos High School and eventually became a news anchor at an Albuquerque television station.[2]

For Carlos Vásquez, life radically changed at Los Alamos. His widowed mother remarried a man who worked as a security guard on the Hill, and the family moved there from Santa Fe. With his stepfather's salary supporting the family, young Carlos did not have to work: "It was the first time in my life I was a kid. . . . There [were] two or three years in my life where I could afford to be a kid." As an oral historian, Carlos has returned to Los Alamos and conducted an oral history project called "Impact Los Alamos" about laboratory workers who lived off the Hill and commuted to Los Alamos from their traditional villages in northern New Mexico.[3]

Growing up at Los Alamos left deep and, at times, conflicting impressions. Jack Bell commented that there was a strong sense of pride that one's family was involved with nuclear weapons. Claire Weiner acknowledged "that feeling that you're so special, insulated from the real world. I think you spend a lot of time making up for that afterwards."[4] While on the Hill, life smiled on the children of Los Alamos like the sun on the desert. Sometimes warmed, sometimes baked, Los Alamos children skied, camped, and enjoyed the outdoor pleasures that came to typify the lure of western living in postwar America; however, as in much of small-town America, once teens graduated, there was little for them to do on the Hill. They needed further schooling and advanced degrees before they could return to the lucrative jobs at the laboratory.

When young people left the Hill, they experienced a world alien to the one they knew, where nuclear weapons sometimes evoked negative reactions. Ellen Reid recalled that she avoided telling people that she came from Los Alamos: "I can remember thinking [in the 1960s] 'hey, this is too much trouble. I'm not going to say.' No one needed to know and you're not responsible for what your father did." Upon leaving the Hill, Los Alamos's progeny carried the blessings of the community but, beginning in the 1960s, faced a changing public opinion about nuclear weapons.[5]

Women greatly influenced the invention of Los Alamos. In addition to working at the laboratories and in their homes, women on the Hill formed clubs and churches, organized parent-teacher associations, and advocated for better schools and a family-friendly community. They did this by resisting the enforced silence of the government, and by contesting the policies they disliked. Upon occasion, the women won. Women on the Hill also assisted the Association of Los Alamos Scientists and, later, the Federation of Atomic Scientists in opposing the May-Johnson bill and helping to pass the McMahon bill, which removed nuclear weapons from military control and created the civilian AEC. Thus, at times, the women of Los Alamos helped change governmental policies, both on the Hill and in Washington, D.C.

Upon the foundations of the wartime clapboard city, Los Alamos reinvented itself after the war. City planners chose to build a model suburban community with modern houses, an attractive shopping center, and a superb school system. Granted, the primary motivation was to attract new personnel and their families to the site; but, additionally, whenever nuclear enterprises needed good publicity, they featured the town. Articles about the laboratory itself were rare because the secrecy that surrounded nuclear weapons precluded such publicity. Instead, photographs of the new post office and of children frolicking on green lawns extolled the good life brought about by atomic living.

Residents of Los Alamos faced daunting realities. The first issue concerned safety. To begin with, toxic elements experimented with and manipulated in the laboratories posed health threats. Safeguards within the work places made the Tech Areas the safest places on the Hill, but outside the inner fences, families dealt with dangers that included live ordnance that littered the Pajarito Plateau and radioactive wastes that flowed into Acid Canyon. The danger that came from penetrating radioactivity, clearly seen at Hiroshima and Nagasaki and brought home by the nuclear accidents of Daghlian and Slotin, were readily acknowledged. The hazards from lingering or low-level radiation are still debated, since exposure might take decades to create an illness and ascertaining cause and effect from invisible particles is difficult. However, even though Groves and Oppenheimer insisted that the only radioactive danger came from penetrating radiation released at the moment of a detonation, these two men wore booties over their shoes when they visited the Trinity site in the fall of 1945 to dispose of any lingering radioactive particles they walked through. By examining how Los Alamos's scientists protected themselves as they worked with nuclear explosions, one can see that they were wary from the beginning about even low-level radiation.

In the fifties, danger also came from possible nuclear strikes launched by the Soviet Union. To counter this threat, Hill officials initiated civil defense drills that emphasized the rapid evacuation of Los Alamos and organized the towns and villages in northern New Mexico to care for the atomic refugees. One site selection criterion that helped locate the nuclear weapons laboratory at Los Alamos—that it was removed from the coasts and thus was protected from enemy attacks—changed in the Atomic Age. Due to its research and development of nuclear weapons, Los Alamos, like everywhere else, became a possible nuclear target.

Federal officials also used Los Alamos as an experimental community to develop the national civil defense strategies implemented in the 1950s. These strategies changed as the Los Alamos Scientific Laboratory collected and analyzed new evidence about the effects of atomic and hydrogen bombs. The new understanding about the bombs' effects came from the research and experiments done at the Tech Areas and from the explosions at the test sites in Nevada and the Pacific. The new civil defense strategies emanating from the Federal Civil Defense Administration in Washington, D.C., were often tested on the community of Los Alamos first. School and community evacuations originally practiced at Los Alamos helped create some of the civil defense plans later used in the nationwide Operation Alert drills. The exercises in Los Alamos provided information for federal officials to "fine-tune" their community, regional, and national civil defense strategies. Los Alamos's impact on science and technology and, therefore, on political and military affairs is obvious. As an outpost on the Cold War frontier, the town also influenced the nation's cultural responses to nuclear weapons as the community experimented with civil defense strategies in the 1950s and exemplified the virtues of suburban living enhanced by nuclear science.

Like the issue of safety, the secrecy of the laboratory impacted everyone on the Hill. Conversations between husbands and wives and parents and children often steered away from what was done at the office that day. The social achievements of Los Alamos, especially regarding the innovations in the school system, were at times cloaked in secrecy to defuse criticism about the privilege that existed on the Hill at taxpayers' expense. And, finally, secrecy prevented the families of Los Alamos, as well as those in the surrounding communities, from receiving information about the health and environmental hazards emanating from the laboratories on the Hill.

Furthermore, secrecy shielded the Manhattan Project and the AEC from accountability and public scrutiny. Governmental oversight came from the same agency created to promote nuclear energy—the Atomic Energy Commission. The time-honored restraint, enacted in the U.S. Constitution, of checks and balances to prevent the abuse of power failed in the handling of atomic matters because of the double duties of the AEC. Granted, it is unfair to criticize past generations using present-day standards, but the creation of the AEC flaunted the originating principle of checks and balances in the U.S. Constitution. During the 1960s, criticism about the dual roles of the AEC mounted and resulted in 1974 with the Energy Reorganization Act that split the AEC into two agencies—the Department of Energy, which promotes and manages the development of nuclear enterprises, and the Nuclear Regulatory Commission, which regulates and monitors the civilian use of nuclear materials to protect public health and safety.

The oversight of the billions of dollars that fund Los Alamos continues to raise questions about waste and fraud. In 2001, the Los Alamos National Laboratory (LANL) facilities manager, Jaret McDonald, complained to the FBI about improper purchases by Peter Bussolini and Scott Alexander that included John Deere tractors, snow-blowers, rototillers, and even a customized Ford Mustang. The initial estimate that $50,000 was misused has now grown to between $200,000 and $400,000. The FBI brought in Glenn Walp and Steven Doran to investigate, and after these two reported missing computers worth $2.7 million and other stolen property, as well as the misuse of lab-issued credit cards, they were fired by LANL. Walp said that the lab was more interested in protecting the contract with the University of California (what he called the golden calf) than uncovering malfeasance: "They knew about it but did nothing about it. Then when I tried to do something about it, they shut us down." Walp added that managers told him that going after the theft problems would damage the lab's image and, if he continued, they would "level me with both barrels."[6]

A subsequent report by Gregory H. Friedman, the inspector general for the Department of Energy, found that upwards of $3 million in equipment was classified as lost at LANL between 1999 and 2001. Losses of equipment valued at less than $5,000 were not even reported. Whether any of the missing computers contained secret information is unknown. The effect on future whistle blowers is chilling. Peter Stockton, a consultant for the Project on Government Oversight out of Washington, D.C., said: "There are horror stories all over the place where whistle blowers have all kinds of protections, allegedly, but man do they get creamed. . . . Very, very few come out the other end half together, and that's why these guys are hiding their identity" when they complain.[7]

After Walp and Doran were vindicated by Friedman's report, they were rehired to guide the university's investigation of Los Alamos. Walp believes that part of the problem comes from the staff's loyalty to the University of California, to the lab, and to superiors. He commented: "I believe in being dedicated to your boss, but there's a line you don't cross . . . and they crossed that line and began to perceive wrong as right."[8] Both LANL and the University of California have committed themselves to correcting the problems of accoutability but some congressional representatives have expressed concerns about LANL's ability to protect homeland security if they cannot safeguard their own operations.

Another recent controversy has involved alleged espionage. In 1999, physicist Wen Ho Lee was arrested on charges that he gave nuclear secrets to the People's Republic of China. Jailed for nine months, part of that time in solitary confinement, Lee was released in September 2000 after the lab failed to produce conclusive evidence that he transmitted sensitive information about nuclear missiles to China.[9]

In a changing world, Los Alamos has played a major role. Many participants have realized the importance of their work. As David Hawkins, Manhattan Project veteran, reflected: "There was one kind of development I must mention, a subjective one, which took place in parallel with the technical work of weapon development. . . . Everyone's life was being changed, changed radically I think, and irreversibly. . . . We all did know we were involved in something which would alter the nature of the world."[10] The harnessing of atomic energy has indeed revolutionized science, weaponry, diplomacy, business, popular culture, and society since 1945.

Today, what goes on at Los Alamos continues to revolutionize aspects of science, business, and society. The lab still specializes in nuclear weapons development under the "stockpile stewardship" program. Begun in 1996 by the Department of Energy, this program monitors, maintains, and refurbishes the U.S. stockpile of nuclear weapons. From 1945 to the middle 1980s, the nuclear laboratories in the United States designed and built over 23,000 nuclear weapons, capable of killing everyone on the planet several times over. Above-ground testing of these weapons went underground in 1961 with the Nuclear Test Ban Treaty, and the underground testing of nuclear devices at the Nevada Test Site continued until 1992. In the post–Cold War era, the U.S. stockpile has declined from a high of 23,500 nuclear weapons in 1985 to an estimated 8,000 in 2003, with Russia destroying a similar number of its nuclear weapons. Insuring the safety and reliability of the U.S. weapons involves monitoring and periodical upkeep by the military and the laboratories, especially since plutonium ages quickly. As one nuclear scientist quipped, these weapons have a short shelf life. Such upkeep is expensive.[11]

Other nations in addition to the U.S. and Russia have joined the once exclusive nuclear weapons club. Great Britain, France, China, Pakistan, India, Israel, various nations that used to be part of the USSR, and possibly South Africa all have nuclear weapons. As this is written in the winter of 2003, North Korea has restarted its nuclear reactor that produces weapons-grade plutonium. Despite the reduction of nuclear tensions between the U.S. and Russia since the fall of the Soviet Union, weapons of mass destruction proliferate as the world totters toward potential nuclear exchanges between belligerent countries like Pakistan and India or sneak attacks by nuclear terrorists. As the nuclear stockpiles between the U.S. and Russia have shrunk, the threat of a nuclear detonation continues to figure prominently in national security deliberations and actions.

In addition to stockpile stewardship, personnel at LANL work in other high-tech fields. The new generations of high-speed computers needed to simulate the testing of nuclear weapons continue to be developed at the labs. Since the United States halted the underground testing of nuclear weapons in 1992 in compliance with the Comprehensive Test Ban Treaty, computers have taken over the task of predicting how aging weapons as well as new designs might work. As a result of the reliance on high-speed computing, LANL has helped advance the science and practice of high-speed computing.

A difficulty similar to that which Oppenheimer faced also has resurfaced for the lab's administrators. Attracting new personnel to LANL is getting harder. Because of the controversies concerning corruption and subsequent firing of whistle blowers and the lure of more lucrative jobs in the private sector, potential employees shy away from lab work. As Paul Robinson, director of Sandia National Laboratories, noted at a hearing for U.S. Representatives Heather Wilson (R-N.Mex.) and Joe Barton (R-Okla.) in the fall of 2002: "We can't say, 'We'd like you to come, with your advanced degrees, to be the maintenance workers for the nation's doomsday machines."[12] Although working at the labs might not appeal to scientists and technicians as much as in the past, the high level of funding continues to attract scientists and technicians from around the world.

The federal government continues to lavish generous financial support for the laboratories at Los Alamos; however, as in the past, exactly how much money flows up to the Hill is difficult to decipher. One report states that the annual budgets in 2004 for the laboratories of Los Alamos and Sandia are projected to equal more than $2 billion, the same amount when adjusted for inflation as the largest nuclear weapons budget in history (which occurred during the Reagan buildup in 1985).[13] In another news article, a reporter stated that the budget just for Los Alamos alone has risen $800 million since 1990: "With a budget approaching $2 billion, the world's first nuclear weapons lab has nearly doubled its expenditures since 1991, the year our Cold War foe, the Soviet Union, dissolved."[14] Overall, the Brookings Institute estimated that the nuclear weapons program from 1940 to 1998 had cost $5.5 trillion nationwide.[15] As always, the true figure for monies that fund nuclear weapons enterprises is elusive.

Such generous funding supports a variety of research efforts in both nuclear weapons development as well as other spin-offs from high-energy physics and health physics. Non-weapons research has grown over the decades at Los Alamos. Some of the many areas that LANL has focused on are environmental issues, human health and DNA, and the creation of new materials. In regard to the environment, a LANL publication notes: "Our expertise spans a wide variety of environmental technologies, from advanced materials synthesis, processing, and fabrication to waste minimization and pollution prevention, process and quality control, and environmentally conscious manufacturing."[16]

How much impact does this lavish federal spending have on northern New Mexico? According to the 2000 census, Los Alamos County is the fifth richest county in the United States. Median income per household on the Hill equals almost $79,000. One study estimated that the federal government has spent $50 billion over the last six decades in New Mexico alone to fund the nuclear weapons program. For a state that ranks at the bottom of many indices on poverty, this is obviously a lot of money; however, debate continues about how much of that spreads out to the rest of New Mexico. For example, in Rio

Arriba County, which neighbors Los Alamos, median income per household equals only $29,400.[17]

Close at home, the laboratory continues to mitigate the legacy problems from the early days of the Atomic Age. Liquid radioactive waste flowed into Acid Canyon, and Omega West, the nuclear reactor at the bottom of Los Alamos Canyon, leaked tritium for years, if not decades. In 1992, LANL scientists discovered a leak in underground pipes when the reactor was shut down, but the system continued to lose water. Further testing revealed a plume of tritium contamination 350 feet below ground level, a mile downstream from Omega West. At another site in Los Alamos, a well dug to test water in the under-lying aquifer located more subsurface tritium contamination approxi-mately 200 feet below the lab's radioactive liquid waste treatment plant.[18] These plumes might eventually reach the aquifer that supplies Los Alamos with its drinking water. The environmental legacies from the decades of Cold War nuclear waste management will take many more decades to remediate.

The Human Genome Project, a national effort to map the approxi-mately 100,000 human genes, has a center at LANL. Gene mapping is a natural progression from the research begun during the Manhattan Project on the effects of radiation on human cells. Other research into single cell analysis, the production of non-radioactive and radioactive isotopes for diagnostic purposes, computer modeling, and other topics concerning the human body have led LANL personnel to create "a new frontier in science: biotechnology."[19]

On another frontier, LANL's scientists are excelling in advanced materials development. Although mainly devoted to defense and energy solutions, the labs have produced a multitude of new materials, including carbon-carbide and ceramic composite materials; micro-crysstalline alloys and textured alloys; ultra-light material based on metallic, ceramic, and polymer foams; intermetallics and light-weight structural composite materials; and chemical sensors.[20]

All of the research and development in high-energy physics, biology, and medicine has transformed our world. The inventions that came from Los Alamos, from nuclear weapons to high-speed computers, from mapping the human gene to creating composite materials, have changed how we live, work, and play. Donald Marchi, who graduated from Los Alamos High School in 1960 and now is a nuclear weapons technician at Sandia National Laboratories, said: "I feel like [we were] going from the beginning of mankind to the adulthood of mankind and that was the era." Ellen Reid added this: "I think that the atomic bomb is probably one of the great turning points in history." For Kim Manley, the legacy depended on who was talking: "To a lot of people, the legacy is nuclear weapons and the end of the war. . . . Some people say 'I'm alive today because of the end of the war. Otherwise I would have been a part of the invasion of Japan.' With younger people, it's changing."[21]

The relief felt at the end of the war with the deliverance of U.S. soldiers from an invasion of Japan has given way to other evaluations of Los Alamos's legacy. When asked about that legacy, Terell Tucker commented: "Ask Oppie what he thinks. It weighed heavily on him. . . . How much is enough? They had enough [nuclear bomb] material to do the job a long time ago. . . . They haven't had very good responsibility with what they've done with the by-products either. That's a real problem and will continue to be a problem. It's a strange bird that fouls its own nest."[22] Susan Tiano also talked of Los Alamos's legacy by looking at what has happened since then. She observed:

> It has much to do with bequeathing a really terrifying situation on the world. I think it [Los Alamos] didn't do anywhere near as well as it could have with the human capital that it had available. In other words, I was amazed at my high school reunion that I was the only person in my class that had reached a [professorship]. A couple of the guys were mentioned that had a Ph.D. in physics and had stayed there and were working there still, and there were some doctors and there were some lawyers. But I was appalled that given the incredible education that they'd gotten, how limited their aspirations were.[23]

Susan and Terell expressed their disappointment in the legacy of Los Alamos by looking at what people had done, or not done, with the privileged life and opportunities afforded to them.

Interviewed after the fall of the Berlin Wall and the end of the Cold War, Donald Marchi commented: "We've got 50 to 60,000 nuclear weapons which we never hopefully will use. That's just the legacy of the Atomic Age. And being part of it is a strange, strange feeling."[24] With the birthplace of the Atomic Age as one's hometown, growing up in the shadow of the bomb was a strange experience.

Despite the long-term legacies of the nation's nuclear weapon's industry, a complimentary paradox must be recognized in the aftermath of the fall of the Soviet Union. One can simultaneously prepare for war and for peace. The birth of the Atomic Age at Los Alamos saw the end of World War II in August 1945. The establishment of a nuclear weapons deterrence policy during the Cold War possibly averted an atomic Armageddon from destroying life on the planet as we know it, although the verdict of history is still out. Once the Pandora's Box of atomic energy was opened, one could at the same time work on destroying life while trying to preserve one's country and its citizens. Within Los Alamos, one could create a modern, suburban community with amenities for the family and also work on weapons of mass destruction. And one could keep earth-shattering secrets from one's spouse and children and still raise youngsters similar to those in the rest of the country. With the reduction of nuclear weapons in the superpowers' arsenals, the Cold War ended without any nuclear attacks. The fact that these weapons of mass destruction still proliferate in hot spots around the world is deeply troubling.

The Atomic Age thrust new life styles on the American people and required them to confront the threat of nuclear war as well as to envision the promise of atomic utopias. In the baby-boom fifties, Los Alamos represented a utopian dream of the Atomic Age. Generously funded by the federal government, Los Alamos prospered in the fifties and offered families the material comforts of suburban living in a beautiful region of the country. The community weathered the pressures of World War II, survived the immediate postwar uncertainty, and then re-invented itself on the forefront of a technological and suburban frontier. To attract personnel to wage the arms race as well as to offer a hopeful alternative to the frightening possibility of nuclear Armageddon, the town complimentarily became both an atomic utopia and a "normal" postwar suburb.

Los Alamos rode the wave of its power, prestige, and privilege to create a unique community, derived from the boomtown tradition of the Wild West but also rooted in the chaotic dash for nuclear and technological advancement in time of war. Families adapted to the new age and to the helter-skelter race at Los Alamos, and a new generation grew up with the bomb. In the 1940s and 1950s, Los Alamos offered families a model community with superb schools, a nearby wilderness, and a high standard of living. Families adapted to the secrets of the community and raised children much as families did elsewhere. Despite its uniqueness, Los Alamos continued the traditions of American families and the American West. It offered a distinctiveness and an abiding unity, as well as a threat and a promise.

The community of Los Alamos basked in the national spotlight during the 1940s and 1950s. By insuring national security through nuclear weapons development, the Hill secured power, prestige, and money that gave the community an aura of authority and excitement. Atop a remote plateau, circled by fences, the secrecy of the site lent an intrigue to the Hill. The mystique of the Atomic City combined with the vital national security role of the laboratory to attract the nation's attention. With access to Los Alamos controlled, the AEC censored the image of the site by focusing on the residential part of the town. Searching for the atomic bomb and being prevented from seeing it because of the shield of security, the country's citizens saw the atomic community instead. In the development of an atomic culture, the ultimate code-switch was inserting the suburban utopia of postwar Los Alamos for the terrifying image of a bomb capable of annihilating whole cities.

NOTES

KEY TO ABBREVIATIONS

AEC   Atomic Energy Commission.

AHC   American Heritage Center, University of Wyoming, Laramie, Wyoming.
          —Charter Heslep Collection

CSWR   Center for Southwest Research, UNM General Library, Albuquerque, New Mexico.

DDEL   Dwight David Eisenhower Library, Abilene, Kansas.

FCDA   Federal Civil Defense Administration.

HSTL   Harry S. Truman Library, Independence, Missouri.

JRO   J. Robert Oppenheimer Papers, Manuscript Division, Library of Congress.

LAHMA   Los Alamos Historical Museum Archives, Los Alamos, New Mexico.

LAHS   Los Alamos Historical Society, Los Alamos, New Mexico.

LANL   Los Alamos National Laboratory, Los Alamos, New Mexico.

LANLA   Los Alamos National Laboratory Archives, Los Alamos, New Mexico.

LASL   Los Alamos Scientific Laboratory, Los Alamos, New Mexico.

LC   Library of Congress, Washington, District of Columbia.
          —GRRD-LC: General Reading Rooms Division, Library of Congress.
          —MD-LC: Manuscript Division, Library of Congress.

NACP   National Archives II, College Park, Maryland.
          —RG: Record Group at the National Archives.

NMSARC   New Mexico State Archives and Record Center, Santa Fe, New Mexico.

NSC   National Security Council.

OHP   Oral History Program.
          —OHP-CSWR: Center for Southwest Research, UNM: General Library, University of New Mexico, Albuquerque, NM. All OHP citations refer to OHP-CSWR unless otherwise noted.
          —OHP-UCLA: University of California, Los Angeles.

237

RCS   Ralph Carlisle Smith Collection, CSWR, UNM General Library, Albuquerque, NM.

WHO   White House Office, Dwight David Eisenhower Library, Abilene, Kansas.

WSP   William S. Parsons papers, Manuscript Division, Library of Congress.

INTRODUCTION

1. Marjorie Bell Chambers wrote an exhaustive history of the development of the community of Los Alamos from 1942 to 1968 as a Ph.D. dissertation for the University of New Mexico. Her work provides part of the foundation for *Inventing Los Alamos;* however, since she wrote "Technically Sweet Los Alamos: The Development of a Federally Sponsored Community" in 1974, new research methods, especially oral history, and new information of Los Alamos have surfaced and have altered our understanding of the community.

2. Casey, *History of the Family*, 3.

3. These books contain more scholarship on family studies: Copeland and White, *Studying Families*, and Elder, Modell, and Parke, eds., *Children in Time and Place*.

CHAPTER 1

1. Badash, Hirshfelder, and Broida, *Reminiscences of Los Alamos*, 3, 4, 14, 15; Rothman, *On Rims and Ridges*, 215; Smith and Weiner, eds., *Robert Oppenheimer*, 238–39; Hales, *Atomic Spaces*, 43.

2. New Mexico Highway Department, "Maintenance Map of New Mexico, 1941"; New Mexico Geological Society, *Guidebook of the San Juan Basin*, 15.

3. Writers' Program of the WPA, *New Mexico*, 283.

4. Burns, ed., *In the Shadow of Los Alamos*, 26.

5. De Buys, *Enchantment and Exploitation*, 86; Peter Hales Bacon, "Topographies of Power: The Forced Spaces of the Manhattan Project," in Franklin and Steiner, eds., *Mapping American Culture*, 280–81.

6. Jane Lenz Elder, "Promise and Failure of a Territorial Economy," 17; Lamar, *Far Southwest*, 95.

7. Rothman, *On Rims and Ridges*, 116–17, 217; Marjorie Bell Chambers, "Technically Sweet Los Alamos," 37–39, 39–41.

8. List of alumni in exhibit at the Los Alamos Historical Museum; Morgan, *Literary Outlaw*, 43, 44, 45–46.

9. Truslow and Thayer, *Manhattan District History*, 3; "Map of Los Alamos Ranch School," MSS 149, box 2, RCS, CSWR.

10. Badash et al., *Reminiscences*, 5, 14–15; Chambers, "Technically Sweet Los Alamos," 46, 59; letter from Oppenheimer to Ernest Lawrence, May 12, 1942, "Los Alamos—Correspondence, 1942–1946," box 182, JRO.

11. Badash et al., *Reminiscences*, 5.

12. Ibid., 5; Bartimus and McCartney, *Trinity's Children*, 75; Rothman, *On Rims and Ridges*, 220, 222; "Founder of Los Alamos Ranch School Honored

Today," *New Mexican*, February 15, 1970, B6; "Conversion of Boys' Ranch School to U.S. Government Facilities," *Los Alamos Newsletter*, no. 5 (November 20, 1945): 1, in Adjutant General Files, Armed Services and Other Government Activities, NMSARC.

13. Hoddeson et al., *Critical Assembly*, 13–14.

14. Ibid., 8, 14–15, 19; Hans A. Bethe, "The Story of the Los Alamos Laboratory," *LASL Community News*, June 30, 1960, 4; Hewlett and Anderson, *New World*, 15–21; "Eugene Wigner Won Nobel Prize for Physics," *Albuquerque Tribune*, January 5, 1995, A-12. This is Wigner's obituary.

15. Hoddeson et al., *Critical Assembly*, 29–30; Hewlett and Anderson, *New World*, 81–82; Marjorie Bell Chambers, "Technically Sweet Los Alamos," 48.

16. Hewlett and Anderson, *New World*, 81.

17. Sanger, *Working on the Bomb*, 18–20.

18. "The Eternal Apprentice," *Time* (November 8, 1948): 71.

19. Ibid.: 71–72; "Biographical sketch of Dr. J. R. Oppenheimer to be released with the general story," Los Alamos—Correspondence, 1942–1946 file, box 182, JRO.

20. "Oppenheimer Replies," *Bulletin of Atomic Scientists* 10, no. 5 (May 1954): 177–81; "Eternal Apprentice": 76.

21. Herken, *Brotherhood of the Bomb*, 56–57.

22. Ibid., 31–32.

23. Ibid, 30–31.

24. Ibid, 102.

25. "Oppenheimer Replies": 177–81; "Oppenheimer, Noted Atomic Scientist, Dies," *Albuquerque Journal*, February 19, 1967, 1; Weart, *Nuclear Fear*, 96.

26. "Eternal Apprentice," 77.

27. Rigden, *Rabi*, 149–50.

28. Fermi, *Atoms in the Family*, 226.

29. Groves, *Now It Can Be Told*, 164.

30. Brandt, "Artist Remembers Some Special Teachers," *Los Alamos Monitor,* June 6, 1993, C16.

31. Brandt, "Artist Remembers"; Kathleene Parker, "A Special Place, A Secret Place," *Santa Fe New Mexican*, December 28, 1992, A-1; Mason, *Children of Los Alamos*, 16.

32. Dorothy McKibbin's personnel cards of all arrivals at Site Y for the Manhattan Project, LANLA; Kim Manley, interviewed by author, February 23, 1991, at Los Alamos, N.Mex., OHP.

33. Brandt, "Hudgins: the First 'SED,'" *Los Alamos Monitor*, June 6, 1993, C-8.

34. Wilson and Serber, eds., *Standing By*, 21.

35. Ibid., 27.

36. Hoddeson, et al., *Critical Assembly*, 60–61, 100; Mason, *Children of Los Alamos*, 36–37; Wilson and Serber, *Standing By*, 24.

37. Feynman, *"Surely You're Joking, Mr. Feynman,"* 110.

38. Joan Neary, interviewed by author, April 19, 1991, at Santa Fe, N.M., OHP.

39. Ferenc Morton Szasz, *British Scientists and the Manhattan Project*, 148–49.

40. Howes and Herzenberg, *Their Day in the Sun*, 13–14; Wilson and Serber, *Standing By*, 57, 59; Jette, *Inside Box 1663*, 29.

41. Manley, "One Atom and Many," *Scientific Monthly*, vol. 66, no. 1, (January 1948): 49.

42. Brandt, "Love of Horses Leads to Lifetime in Los Alamos," *Los Alamos Monitor*, June 6, 1993, C-18; Sundt and Naumann, *M. M. Sundt Construction Company*, 18–22; Lindsay F. Root, "'Hill' Road Project Had Tough Puzzles," *Santa Fe New Mexican*, n.d., RCS.

43. Bell, *Los Alamos WAACs/WACs*, 16–18, 26–27; Ellen Wilder Bradbury Reid, interviewed by author, January 27, 1991, at Santa Fe, OHP; Robert Jungk, "Los Alamos—Life in the Shadow of the Atomic Bomb," 4, RCS.

44. Roensch, *Life within Limits*, 12,13,15,19.

45. "Bencés Gonzáles Recalls 62 Years of Hill Development," *LASL Community News*, January 1959, 5.

46. Badash et al., *Reminiscences of Los Alamos*, 143; Jette, *Inside Box 1663*, 72; "Personalities on the Hill," *Los Alamos Times*, December 6, 1946, 2; Sando, *Pueblo Indians*,182; Los Alamos Historical Society, *Behind Tall Fences*, 124.

47. Jette, *Inside Box 1663*, 42; Marjorie Bell Chambers, "Technically Sweet Los Alamos," 117; Norris Bradbury, "Los Alamos—the First Twenty-five Years," in Badash, et al. *Reminiscences,* 162.

48. Letter from Oppenheimer to Ernest Lawrence, May 19, 1942, Los Alamos—Correspondence, 1942–1946 file, box 182, JRO.

49. Truslow, *Nonscientific Aspects*, 3; letter from Oppenheimer to Ernest Lawrence, May 19, 1942, Los Alamos—Correspondence, 1942–1946 file, box 182, JRO; Marjorie Bell Chambers, "Technically Sweet Los Alamos," 63; Sundt, *Sundt Construction Company*, 17–19; Boyd Pratt, "A Brief History of the Architecture of Los Alamos County," 7, a 1985 report found in the Bevers Collection, (RL) 5464/86 939, LAHMA.

50. Sundt, *Sundt Construction Company*, 20.

51. Pratt, "Brief History," 7, 9.

52. Lemoyne Frederick, "Sundt Apartments Leaving Hill Scene After 22 Years," *Santa Fe New Mexican*, n.d., Lucien File Papers, NMSARC.

53. Pratt, "Brief History," 9–10.

54. Jette, *Inside Box 1663*, 59, 76; Badash, et al., *Reminiscences*, 162.

55. Bryan C. Taylor, "Remembering Los Alamos," 88 and Elsie McMillan, "Outside the Inner Fence," both in Badash et al., *Reminiscences,* 41–49.

56. Brode, *Tales of Los Alamos*, 7; memo from Oppenheimer to civilian employees, Subject file: Atomic Project 1944–45, box 10, John von Neumann Papers, MD-LC.

57. Brode, *Tales from Los Alamos*, 9–10.

58. Jette, *Inside Box 1663*, 15; Marjorie Bell Chambers, "Technically Sweet Los Alamos," 127; Rudolf Peierls, interview by Ferenc Szasz, January 13, 1988, T-88-014, LANLA.

59. Wilson and Serber, *Standing By,* 35.

60. Peggy Titterton, interview by Ferenc Szasz, January 14, 1989, T-89-90, LANLA; Szasz, *British Scientists*, 32; Badash, et al., *Reminiscences*, 139.

61. Marshak, "Secret City," in Wilson and Serber, *Standing By*, 2.

62. Webb, *The Great Plains*, passim; Limerick, *Legacy of Conquest*, passim; White, *"It's Your Misfortune,"* passim.

63. Groves, *Now It Can Be Told*, 415.

64. Fisher, *Los Alamos Experience*, 49; Truslow, *Nonscientific Aspects*, 89–90.

65. Groves, *Now It Can Be Told*, 166.

66. Wilson and Serber, *Standing By*, 92.

67. Rabi et al., *Oppenheimer*, 26.

68. Wilson and Serber, *Standing By*, 16.

69. Serber and Rhodes, *Los Alamos Primer*, 3.

70. Ibid., 4.

71. Ibid., 13.

72. Ibid., 10.

73. Ibid., 57–63. For more detailed accounts of the harnessing of atomic energy for military applications, see Rhodes, *Making of the Atomic Bomb*; Hoddeson et al., *Critical Assembly*; and Hawkins et al., *Project Y.*

74. Hewlett, *New World*, 212; Hoddeson et al., *Critical Assembly*, 95–96; Serber and Wilson, *Standing By,* 54; Jette, *Inside Box 1663*, 33.

75. Jette, *Inside Box 1663*, 34, 64; Marie Kinzel, "The Town of Beginning Again," *Survey Graphic* (Oct. 1946): 355, RCS.

76. Jette, *Inside Box 1663*, 129–32.

77. Hales, "Topographies of Power," 280.

78. Ibid., 281.

79. Laura Fermi, "Los Alamos Revisited," Printed Material, 1951 file, box 3, WSP.

80. Jette, *Inside Box 1663*, 24; Reid, interview.

81. Fisher, *Los Alamos Experience*, 99–100.

82. Feynman, *Surely You're Joking!*, 114–18; Sykes, ed., *No Ordinary Genius*, 55; Jette, *Inside Box 1663*, 34, 87.

83. Claire Ulam Weiner, interviewed by author, March 17, 1991, at Santa Fe, OHP.

84. Reid, interview.

85. Ibid.

86. Oppenheimer, Noted Scientist, Dies," *Albuquerque Journal*, February 19, 1967, A-1.

87. Serber and Wilson, *Standing By*, 51–2.

Chapter 2

1. Memo from Eric Clarke to Stafford Warren, August 8, 1944, "Mental Hygiene Survey of 'Y'," 1, in Los Alamos Correspondence, 1942–46 file, box 182, JRO.

2. Ibid.

3. Ibid., 2.

4. Brode, "Tales of Los Alamos," in Badash et al., *Reminiscences,*137.

5. Wilson and Serber, *Standing By*, 16; Truslow and Thayer, *Manhattan District History*, 106; Marjorie Bell Chambers, "Technically Sweet Los Alamos," 128, 133–40; Eleanor Jette, *Inside Box 1663*, 67–68.

6. Chambers, "Technically Sweet Los Alamos," 130–32; Fermi, *Atoms in the Family*, 229.

7. Chambers, "Technically Sweet Los Alamos," 134; Brode, *Tales of Los Alamos,* 24–26; Jette, *Inside Box 1663*, 55.

8. Hoddeson et al., *Critical Assembly*, 107; Chambers, "Technically Sweet Los Alamos," 134, 136.

9. Brode, "Tales of Los Alamos," in Badash, et al., *Reminiscences*, 149.

10. Chambers, "Technically Sweet Los Alamos," 104–6; "Father of Los Alamos School System Returns to Scene of Early Efforts," *LASL Community News*, July 30, 1959, 6; Jette, *Inside Box 1663*, 50.

11. Brode, *Tales of Los Alamos*, 55–56.

12. Brode, "Tales of Los Alamos," in Badash, et al., *Reminiscences*, 149.

13. Chambers, "Technically Sweet Los Alamos," 98; "Father of Los Alamos School System Returns," *LASL Community News*, July 30, 1960, 6; Brode, *Tales of Los Alamos*, 55–56; Kathleen Manley, "Women of Los Alamos during World War II: Some of Their Views," *New Mexico Historical Review* (*NMHR*) 65 (April 1990): 254–55; Truslow, *Nonscientific Aspects*, 85.

14. Chambers, "Technically Sweet Los Alamos," 100; Manley, "Women of Los Alamos," *NMHR*: 257; Mason, *Children of Los Alamos*, 45, 47; Truslow and Thayer, *Manhattan District History*, 85; "Mental Hygiene Survey," 4, JRO.

15. Brode, *Tales of Los Alamos*, 111–12; Terell Tucker, interviewed by author, April 22, 1991, at Albuquerque, and Joan Mark Neary, interviewed by author, April 19, 1991, at Santa Fe, OHP; Jette, *Inside Box 1663*, 29.

16. Brode, *Tales of Los Alamos*, 58–59; Brode, "Tales of Los Alamos," in Badash, et al., *Reminiscences*, 151; Chambers, "Technically Sweet Los Alamos," 102.

17. Brode, *Tales of Los Alamos*, 59–60; Mason, *Children of Los Alamos*, 60.

18. Wilson and Serber, *Standing By*, 18.

19. "Mental Hygiene Survey," 2–3, JRO.

20. Campbell, *Women at War with America*, 32; Roensch, *Life within Limits*, 15, 21, Mason, *Children of Los Alamos*, 72; "Mental Hygiene Survey," 2, JRO.

21. Jette, *Inside Box 1663*, passim; Kistiakowsky, "Reminiscences of Wartime Los Alamos," in Badash et al., *Reminiscences*, 61.

22. Brode, *Tales of Los Alamos*, 73; Wilson and Serber, *Standing By*, 112.

23. Brode, "Tales of Los Alamos," *LASL Community News*, July 28, 1960, 5.

24. Ibid., 6. This story is altered in Brode's subsequent book, *Tales of Los Alamos*. The book was edited from the "Tales of Los Alamos" and published in 1997 by the Los Alamos Historical Society.

25. Felix Díaz Almaraz, Jr., "The Little Theater in the Atomic Age: Amateur Dramatics in Los Alamos, N.M., 1943–1946," *Journal of the West*, 7, no. 2 (April 1978): 73–80; Jette, *Inside Box 1663*, 82.

26. Brode, *Tales of Los Alamos*, 76; Brode, "Tales of Los Alamos," *LASL Community News*, July 28, 1960, 6; Jette, *Inside Box 1663*, 82.

27. Jette, *Inside Box 1663*, 70; Brode, *Tales of Los Alamos*, 89.

28. Wilson and Serber, *Standing By*, 115.

29. McMillan, "Inside the Outer Fence," in Badash et al., *Reminiscences*, 43.

30. Jette, *Inside Box 1663*, 22.

31. "Fortieth Anniversary of the United Church," 1987, 1, located in the United Church of Los Alamos Archives; "Mental Hygiene Survey," 4, JRO.

32. *Los Alamos Post Bulletin*, November 21, 1945, LAHMA; Marjorie Bell Chambers, "A Unique Church to Meet the Challenge of a Unique Community," 3, from the "Churches" vertical file, Mesa Public Library, Los Alamos.

33. Abraham Shinedling, *History of the Los Alamos Jewish Center*, 1; Fisher, *Los Alamos Experience*, 198–99.

34. Fermi, *Atoms in the Family*, 232.

35. Brode, *Tales of Los Alamos*, 15; Peggy Corbett, "Supply and Demand: It Looked Easy," *New Mexican*, July 21, 1960; Jette, *Inside Box 1663*, 92–93.

36. Jette, *Inside Box 1663*, 51.

37. Ibid., 52.

38. Wilson and Serber, *Standing By*, 9.

39. Carlos Vásquez, interviewed by author, July 23, 1991, at Albuquerque, N. Mex., OHP; Chambers, "Technically Sweet Los Alamos," 82.

40. Mason, *Children of Los Alamos*, 50–51.

41. Peggy Corbett, "Supply and Demand," *Santa Fe New Mexican*, July 21, 1960; Corbett, "Housing Office," *Santa Fe New Mexican*, July 24, 1960, 6; Wilson and Serber, *Standing By*, 80–83, reprints the "Rules for Household Help" that governed the maid service at Site Y.

42. Corbett, "Supply and Demand," *Santa Fe New Mexican*, July 21, 1960; Corbett, "Housing Office" *New Mexican*, July 24, 1960, 6; Wilson and Serber, *Standing By*, 68–69.

43. Brode, *Tales of Los Alamos*, 52.

44. "Trinity, July 16, 1945: A Time to Remember," *LASL Community News*, July 16, 1959, 6.

45. Szasz, *Day the Sun Rose Twice*, 27, 40–41; Chambers, "Technically Sweet Los Alamos," 142.

46. Hawkins, *Project Y*, 243–45; Szasz, *Day the Sun Rose Twice*, 39.

47. Szasz, *Day the Sun Rose Twice*, 121–26.

48. Ibid., 79–81; Hewlett and Anderson, *New World,* 380–82.

49. Szasz, *Day the Sun Rose Twice,* 79.

50. Fisher, *Los Alamos Experience,* 112.

51. Szasz, *Day the Sun Rose Twice,* 31.

52. Ibid., 82.

53. Szasz, *Day the Sun Rose Twice,* 83–87; Theresa Strottman, "How Witnesses to the Trinity Test of the First Atomic Bomb Remember the Event," presented at the Oral History Association conference, October 10, 1994, Albuquerque, N.Mex.

54. Howes and Herzenberg, *Their Day in the Sun,* 56.

55. Szasz, *Day the Sun Rose Twice,* 89.

56. Weart, *Nuclear Fear,* 101.

57. Frisch, *What Little I Remember,* 164.

58. Peierls, interview.

59. Szasz, *Day the Sun Rose Twice,* 89.

60. Ibid.

61. Ibid.

62. Ibid.

63. Kunetka, *City of Fire,* 170.

64. Szasz, *Day the Sun Rose Twice,* 91.

65. Elsie McMillan, "Outside the Inner Fence," in Badash et al., *Reminiscences,* 44; Dorothy McKibben, "The Woman Who Kept a Secret," videotape, KNME, Albuquerque, air date April 13, 1982, CSWR; Jette, *Inside Box 1663,* 102.

66. Jette, *Inside Box 1663,* 103; Kathleene Parker, "A Special Place, A Secret Place," *New Mexican,* December 28, 1992, A-1; Mason, *Children of Los Alamos,* 90.

67. Szasz, *Day the Sun Rose Twice,* 91.

68. Church, *The House at Otowi Bridge,* 91–92.

69. Fisher, *Los Alamos Experience,* 113.

70. Ibid.

71. Rhodes, *Making of the Atomic Bomb,* 627.

72. Letter from William Parsons to George Milton, December 3, 1946, Correspondence, 1943–46, box 1, WSP.

73. Receipt for Hiroshima bomb, August 6, 1945, Correspondence, 1948 file, box 1, WSP.

74. "A Time of 'Pride Tempered with Concern'," *LASL Community News* August 11, 1960, 10; Russ, *Project Alberta,* 62–64; Hiroshima bomb receipt, WSP.

75. "Statement by the President of the United States," Atomic Bomb—press releases (folder 1), Subject File, NSC-Atomic, President's Secretary's Files, HSTL; "Deadliest Weapons in History Made in Santa Fe Vicinity," *Santa Fe New Mexican,* August 6, 1945, 1.

76. "Deadliest Weapons . . ." and "Now They Can Be Told Aloud, Those Stories of 'the Hill'," *New Mexican,* August 6, 1945, 1.

77. "Now They Can Be Told Aloud . . . ," *New Mexican,* August 6, 1945, 1.

78. Ibid.

79. "Press Failure," *New Mexican*, August 7, 1945, 1.

80. Reid, interview.

81. "A Time of 'Pride Tempered with Concern'," *LASL Community News*, August 11, 1960, 10.

82. "Jap Shipping Center Second City to Meet Disaster from New American Super-Weapon," *Albuquerque Journal*, August 9, 1945, 1; United States Strategic Bombing Survey, *Effects of the Atomic Bombs on Hiroshima and Nagasaki*, 15.

83. Laura Fermi, "Los Alamos Revisited," printed material, 1951 file, box 3; WSP.

84. Fisher, *Los Alamos Experience*, 122.

85. Smith and Weiner, *Robert Oppenheimer*, 297.

86. Paul Boyer, *By the Bomb's Early Light*, 7.

87. Kim Manley, interviewed by author, February 25, 1991, at Los Alamos, OHP, Fermi, *Atoms in the Family*, 240; "'Atomizers' from 'Hill' Enjoy Minor V-E Day," *Santa Fe New Mexican*, August 8, 1945, 1.

88. Fisher, *Los Alamos Experience*, 117.

89. Brode, *Tales of Los Alamos*, 114–17; Wilson and Serber, *Standing By*, 127–30.

90. Marie Kinzel, "The Town of Beginning Again," *Survey Graphic* (October 1946): 357.

91. "First Test of Atomic Bomb Made at Alamogordo," "Men Behind Atom Bomb," "Bomb May Avert Future Wars, Says One of Its Makers," and "Town Built at Los Alamos for Laboratory for Experiments," all in *Albuquerque Journal*, August 7, 1945, 1–2; "Deadliest Weapons in World's History Made in Santa Fe Vicinity," *Santa Fe New Mexican*, August 6, 1945, 1, "'Atomizers' from 'Hill' Enjoy Minor V-E Day," *New Mexican*, August 7, 1945, 1.

92. Truman's speech to Congress, transmitted by teletype to Bradbury from Oppenheimer, in Bradbury, Norris file, box 22; JRO.

CHAPTER 3

1. "Denies Atomic Bomb Will Cause Death 70 Years after Striking," *Santa Fe New Mexican*, August 8, 1945, 1.

2. Ibid.

3. "Nips List 480,000 as Atomic Bomb Victims," *New Mexican*, August 22, 1945, 1.

4. Stafford Warren, interview by Adelaide Tusler, 1966–67, at Los Angeles, 300/204, OHP-UCLA; Hacker, *Dragon's Tail*, 110–11.

5. "Memorandum of telephone conversation between General Groves and Lt. Col. Rea, Oak Ridge Hospital, 9:00 A.M., 25 August 1945," as reprinted in Stoff, Fanton, and Williams, *Manhattan Project*, 258.

6. Ibid., 259.

7. Ibid., 259–60.

8. Ibid., 262.

9. Hacker, *Dragon's Tail*, 80.

10. "Groves Scoffs After-Effects Reports," *Santa Fe New Mexican*, August 31, 1945, 2.

11. Hacker, *Dragon's Tail*, 73; "Bomb Worker Dies of Burns," *New Mexican*, September 21, 1945, 1; "Los Alamos Man Dies," *Albuquerque Journal*, September 21, 1945, 9.

12. Hacker, *Dragon's Tail*, 110.

13. United States Strategic Bombing Survey, *Effects of the Atomic Bombs on Hiroshima and Nagasaki* (aka *Bombing Survey*), 24–25; Hiroshima International Council for the Medical Care of the Radiation-Exposed, *Effects of A-Bomb Radiation on the Human Body*, 3–4.

14. *Bombing Survey*, 25.

15. Nagaoka, *Hiroshima under Atomic Bomb Attack*, 1.

16. Takaki, *Hiroshima*, 45.

17. Rhodes, *Making of the Atomic Bomb*, 723.

18. Rhodes, *Atomic Bomb*, 718.

19. Nagaoka, *Hiroshima under Atomic Bomb Attack*, 7.

20. Palevsky, *Atomic Fragments*, 78.

21. Hershey, *Hiroshima*, 29.

22. Nagaoka, *Hiroshima under Atomic Bomb Attack*, 4.

23. Ibid., 10; *Bombing Survey*, 33; Kunetka, *City of Fire*, 187.

24. Powaski, *March to Armageddon*, 27. For a recent study on the long-term health effects of radiation exposure, see Hiroshima International Council, *Effects of A-Bomb Radiation on the Human Body*, 1995. A variety of health effects are studied in this report about the atomic bomb survivors in Hiroshima and Nagasaki.

25. *Bombing Survey*, 18–19.

26. Ibid.

27. Ibid.; Hershey, *Hiroshima*, 74.

28. *Bombing Survey*, 18–19.

29. Palevsky, *Atomic Fragments*, 79.

30. Walker, *Permissible Doses*, 6.

31. Ibid.

32. Powaski, *March to Armageddon*, 27.

33. "President Truman's Message to Congress on the Atomic Bomb, October 3, 1945," *International Conciliation*, 416 (December 1945): 775; box 21, Charter Heslep Collection, #1626, AHC.

34. Brode, *Atomic Scientists' Journal* 3 (November 1953): 89.

35. *Los Alamos Post Bulletin*, September 14, 1945, 1.

36. *Bulletin*, November 5, 1945, 1; Marjorie Bell Chambers, "Technically Sweet Los Alamos," 176–77.

37. "Justice's Summons," Bevers Collection, M5695/87.1021, folder 9, LAHMA.

38. Szasz, *British Scientists and the Manhattan Project*, 43–44; Ralph Carlisle Smith, interview by Robert Krohn, December 12, 1981 (T-81-0009), LANLA; Brode, "Tales of Los Alamos," *LASL Community News*, August 11, 1960, 8.

39. "Thermometer Skids to New Lows in State," *Santa Fe New Mexican*, December 15, 1945, 1; Chambers, "Technically Sweet Los Alamos," 176–77; William McNulty, "Dogs Live Like Riley on the Hill," *New Mexican*, December 22, 1945, 1; *Los Alamos Post Bulletin*, November 5, 1945, 1.

40. "Hillites Lap It Up From Many Sources," *LASL Community News*, September 24, 1959, 4; Fermi, *Atoms in the Family*, 246; Kunetka, *City of Fire*, 190–210; Brode, "Tales of Los Alamos," *LASL Community News*, September 22, 1960, 6.

41. Untitled address, Box 182, "Los Alamos Correspondence, 1942–46," JRO.

42. Letter from John Manley to Oppenheimer, January 17, 1951, box 49, "Manley, John, to and from Oppenheimer," JRO.

43. "Groves Presents E Award to Los Alamos," *Albuquerque Journal* October 17, 1945, 2; "The First Twenty Years at Los Alamos: January 1943–January 1963," *LASL Community News*, January 1, 1963, 32; Hoddeson et al., *Critical Assembly*, 402.

44. Memo from Oppenheimer to All Division and Group Leaders, October 15, 1945, Bradbury, Norris file, box 22, JRO.

45. Truslow and Smith, *Project Y*, 361.

46. Ibid., 369.

47. Groves, *Now It Can Be Told*, 377.

48. Al Rosenfeld, "Mister Los Alamos," *LASL Community News*, October 20, 1960, 8–9; "Bradbury New L.A. Chief," *Albuquerque Journal*, October 18, 1945, 9; Badash et al., *Reminiscences*, 177.

49. Groves, *Now It Can Be Told*, 382.

50. Letter from Bradbury to Oppenheimer; Bradbury, Norris file; box 22; JRO.

51. "Project's Program Big Topic," *Los Alamos Times*, August 23, 1946, 4.

52. Rosenfeld, "Mister Los Alamos," 9; Chambers, "Technically Sweet Los Alamos," 167.

53. Letter from Bradbury to Blandy, January 7, 1946; Correspondence 1943–46 file, box 1, WSP.

54. Chambers, "Technically Sweet Los Alamos," 190–93; *Los Alamos Times*, April 19, 1946, 2.

55. Rosenfeld, "Mister Los Alamos," 9.

56. Untitled compilation of questionnaire responses and "Some Comments of the Results of the Questionnaire," Box 182, "Los Alamos—Correspondence, 1942–46," JRO.

57. Ibid.

58. Chambers, "Technically Sweet Los Alamos," 194–98.

59. "Western Area . . . Plug for a Dike," *LASL Community News*, June 18, 1959, 6; *Los Alamos Times*, August 2, 1946, 2; Jackson, *Crabgrass Frontier*, 234.

60. Jackson, *Crabgrass Frontier*, 13, 174, 233.

61. Ibid., 234–37.

62. Chambers, "Technically Sweet Los Alamos," 197; "Western Area . . . Plug for a Dike," *LASL Community News*, June 1, 1959; Boyd C. Pratt, "A Brief History

of the Architecture of Los Alamos County," (RL) 5464/86.939, 1985, 10, Bevers Collection M5695/87.1021 at LAHMA.

63. Chambers, "Technically Sweet Los Alamos," 197; "240 More Housing Units Authorized," *Los Alamos Times*, October 18, 1946, 1.

64. Chambers, "Technically Sweet Los Alamos," 200; "Community Center Plans Approved," *Los Alamos Times*, September 6,1946, 1; Elizabeth Giorgi, "Early Los Alamos Businesses," 8, History of Towns and Places, History File # 126, NMSARC.

65. Boyer, *By the Bomb's Early Light*, 122.

66. "Early Los Alamos Businesses," 5–8, NMSARC; "Drug Store to Open Here," *Los Alamos Times*, November 27, 1946, 1; "Shoe Repair Shop Opens in T-133," *Los Alamos Times*, December 13, 1946, 2.

67. Hill Streets Named as Contest Closes," *Los Alamos Times*, December 6. 1946, 2; "Streets Gain Identity as Name Signs Appear," Ibid., December 13, 1946, 1.

68. Robert McKee, *Zia Company*, 5.

69. Ibid., 2, 8; Mason, *Children of Los Alamos*, 24, Chambers, "Technically Sweet Los Alamos," 269.

70. McKee, *Zia Company*, 8.

71. Ibid., 8–10.

72. "Will A-Bomb Nip Battleship?" *New Mexican*, September 17, 1945, 1.

73. "Underwater Test for A-Bomb," *Albuquerque Journal*, October 27, 1945, 1; Thompson and Jones, *Reinventing the Pentagon*, 29; "Will Test A-Bombs on Warships," *New Mexican*, December 11, 1945, 1.

74. Office of the Historian, Joint Task Force One, *Operation Crossroads*, 8–9; Truslow and Smith, *Project Y*, 273–74.

75. For a thorough history of this movement, see Wittner, *One World or None*.

76. Newhouse, *War and Peace in the Nuclear Age*, 55.

77. Smith, *A Peril and a Hope*, 115; *Los Alamos Post Bulletin*, November 2, 1945, 1.

78. Brode, "Tales of Los Alamos," *LASL Community News*, September 8, 1960, 6.

79. *Albuquerque Journal*, August 15, 1945, 3; Brode, "Tales of Los Alamos," *LASL Community News*, September 8, 1960, 6; *Los Alamos Post Bulletin*, October 12, 1945, 1; Howes and Herzenberg, *Their Day in the Sun*, 187.

80. "Give Atom to World, Urge LA Scientists," *Albuquerque Journal*, October 14, 1945, 1.

81. Smith and Weiner, *Robert Oppenheimer*, 319.

82. Ibid., 321–22.

83. "Policy of the ALAS," *Los Alamos Newsletter*, no. 5, November 20, 1945, 1. Newsletter found at NMSARC, Adjutant General–Armed Services and Other Government Activities file, "Conversion of Boys' Ranch to U.S. Government Facilities."

84. Boyer, *By the Bomb's Early Light*, 59.

85. "Serber Describes Japan," *Los Alamos Newsletter*, no. 5, November 20, 1945, 1; Serber also took photographs of the ruins of Hiroshima and Nagasaki that can be seen in Fermi and Samra, *Picturing the Bomb*, 186–93.

86. "Serber Describes Japan," 1.

87. William McNulty, "Bomb Makers Urge Control of Their Weapon," *Santa Fe New Mexican*, November 27, 1945, 1.

88. Smith, *A Peril and a Hope*, 300; "Bomb Makers Urge Control," *New Mexican*, November 27, 1945, 7.

89. "Bomb Makers Urge Control," 7; Witter Bynner, "New A-Bomb Meet Fills Public Demand," *New Mexican*, December 5, 1945, 4.

90. Smith, *A Peril and a Hope*, 98, 124, 135, 138; Hewlett and Anderson, *New World*, 445, 447–48; Newhouse, *War and Peace in the Nuclear Age*, 55.

91. Letter from Bradbury to AEC, November 1946, Los Alamos Program file, Subject File, 1947–1949, Office Files of Robert Bacher, Records of the Commissioners, Records of the AEC, RG 326, NACP.

92. Newhouse, *War and Peace in the Nuclear Age*, 56; Hewlett and Anderson, *New World*, 516, 528, 530.

93. Sanger, *Working on the Bomb*, 238.

94. Boyer, *By the Bomb's Early Light*, 145.

95. Titus, *Bombs in the Backyard*, 21.

96. Quoted from *The Best Years of Our Lives*, 1946, directed by William Wyler, written by Robert E. Sherwood.

97. Hewlett and Anderson, *New World*, 580–82; *Operation Crossroads*, 8–10, 118, 72–73.

98. "Details of Slotin's Death, Accident Disclosed," *Los Alamos Times*, June 28, 1946, 1; Clifford T. Honicker, "The Hidden Files: America's Radiation Victims," *New York Times Magazine*, November 19, 1989, 39–40; Truslow and Smith, *Project Y*, 325–26; Hacker, *Dragon's Tail*, 73.

99. Truslow and Smith, *Project Y: The Los Alamos Story*, 326; "Condition of Slotin, Radiation Victim, Is 'Serious', 4 Released," *Los Alamos Times*, May 29, 1946, 1; "Louis Slotin, Radiation Victim, Mourned by Hill," *Los Alamos Times*, June 7, 1946, 1; "Details of Slotin Death" *Los Alamos Times*, June 28, 1946, 3.

100. "Louis Slotin, Radiation Victim, Mourned by Hill," *Los Alamos Times*, June 7, 1946, 1.

101. Hacker, *Dragon's Tail*, 73.

102. Warren, "Antipersonnel Effects," *Air Affairs*, March 1947, 350–51.

103. Hewlett and Anderson, *New World, 1936–1946*, 378; Richard White, "Hanford, the Columbia, and Energy," lecture presented at the "Atomic West, 1942–1992: Federal Power and Regional Development" conference, Seattle, Washington, September 26, 1992.

104. Truslow and Smith, *Project Y*, 275, 291–96.

105. Letter from Compton to Oppenheimer, January 15, 1947, "Crossroads–Joint Commission, Joint Chiefs of Staff Board, 1947, J. R. Oppenheimer," box 178, JRO.

106. *Operation Crossroads*, 154–71,184–88,196–99.

107. Hewlett and Anderson, *The New World*, 581.

108. *Public Reaction to the Atomic Bomb*, 28–29, box 22, Charter Heslep Collection, #1626, AHC. The results of the survey also were reviewed in Sylvia Eberhart, "How the American People Feel about the Atomic Bomb," *Bulletin of Atomic Scientists* 3:8 (June 1947): 146–49.

109. Palevsky, *Atomic Fragments*, 4–5.

110. Susan Tiano, interviewed by author, February 12, 1991, in Albuquerque, N. Mex., OHP.

CHAPTER 4

1. Executive Order from President Truman, December 31, 1946, Transfer of Manhattan Project to the AEC file, Subject File, 1947–49, box 4, Office Files of Robert F. Bacher, Records of the Commissioners, Records of AEC, RG 326, NACP.

2. "Site Transfers to Atomic Commission," *Los Alamos Times*, January 3, 1947, 1, 4.

3. "Message from General Groves: To All Members of the Manhattan Project," *Los Alamos Times*, January 3, 1947, 1.

4. "Maintenance Function Outlined," *Los Alamos Times*, January 10, 1947, 4; "Zia Assumes New Work," *Los Alamos Times*, February 7, 1947, 1.

5. AEC Announces New Manager for Los Alamos and Program Improvements for Town, AEC News Releases 1947, January to December, Office of Public Information, Box 1, Records of the AEC, RG 326, NACP.

6. USGPO, *Investigation into the U.S. Atomic Energy Project: Hearing before the Joint Committee on Atomic Energy of the 81st Congress, Part 15, June 24, 1949* , 638.

7. Memo from Bayer to Wilson, "Los Alamos Community Development under AEC Management," 680.6, "Los Alamos," Records of the AEC, RG 326, NACP; "Who Are the People?" *Annual Report,* Mesa Public Library, July 1, 1952 to June 30, 1953; Pratt, "A Brief History of the Architecture of Los Alamos County"; "AEC Announces Award of Lab, Housing Contracts," *Los Alamos Skyliner*, June 23, 1949, 2; LASL, *Housing Manual for Laboratory Employees and Supervisors*, 16–20.

8. Information Report Covering the Period April 1, 1947 to May 25, 1947, Miscellaneous—Bacher file, Subject File 1947–49, box 2, Office Files of Robert F. Bacher, Records of the Commissioners, Records of the AEC, RG 326, NACP.

9. Feinberg, *What Makes Shopping Centers Tick*, 3–6; "Community Center Plans Approved," *Los Alamos Times*, September 6, 1946, 1; "Community Center Marks First Birthday," *Santa Fe New Mexican*, October 26, 1949, 5.

10. "Community Center Marks First Birthday," *New Mexican*, October 26, 1949, 5; Hosokawa, "Life with the Bomb: Part III: Civic Center—2000 A.D.," *Denver Post Rocky Mountain Empire Magazine*, June 26, 1949, 4.

11. *Albuquerque Journal,* July 3, 1949, 11; Joe Alex Morris, "Cities of America—Los Alamos," *Saturday Evening Post* (December 11, 1948): 164; letter from AEC acting chairman Summer Pike to Senator Bourke Hickenlooper, January 1, 1948, Chairman's reading files, December 1948–July 1950, Office Files of D. E. Lilienthal, Records of Office of Chairman, Records of AEC, RG 326, NACP; "New Building Will Replace Old Army-Type Facility," *New Mexican,* October 16, 1949, 4; "Best in Modern Architecture Will Make Los Alamos High Pace-setter for Nation," *Los Alamos Skyliner,* June 23, 1949, 1; Sheldon Moyer, "Life at Los Alamos," *Big* 5 (1949), 6, 8; Hanson W. Baldwin, "Fast Reactor, Electrostatic Accelerator among Newest of Hill Laboratory's Equipment," *Los Alamos Skyliner,* March 24, 1949, 6; "McKee Low for Hill Hospital Contract," *New Mexican,* April 23, 1950.

12. "Memorandum for Mr. Clark Clifford," Atomic Energy—Manhattan Project—Status of Funds 1948 file, box 1, Clifford Papers, HSTL.

13. Morris, "Cities of America—Los Alamos": 25, 164, 166; USGPO, *1950 Census of Population,* showed the median family income for neighboring Rio Arriba County was $1,333; letter from Darol Froman to Robert Bacher, January 23, 1947, "Los Alamos Laboratory," Subject file 1947–1949, box 2, Office Files of Robert Bacher, Records of Commissioners, Records of the AEC, RG 326, NACP.

14. Hewlett and Anderson, *New World,* 344–45, 356.

15. Information about Clementine quoted from a plaque installed at the site of the Water Boiler Reactor by the American Nuclear Society (ANS). The plaque commemorated the reactor as a Nuclear Historic Landmark approved by the ANS board of directors; AEC, *Los Alamos Scientific Laboratory, Los Alamos, New Mexico,* 5.

16. "Lady Reactor Operators Enjoy Making Neutrons," *LASL Community News,* December 1, 1960, 3.

17. "Hill Woman Scientist Named to AEC's Key Advisory Group," *New Mexican,* February 5, 1956.

18. "Bradbury Asserts A-Bomb Strength May Be Weakness," *Los Alamos Herald,* February 16, 1951, 6.

19. Lecture given by Dr. Joseph C. Martz, group leader, Weapon Component Technology, Nuclear Materials Technology Division, Los Alamos, June 15, 1995.

20. Bill Hosokawa, "Life with the Bomb: Part 1," *Denver Post Rocky Mountain Empire Magazine,* June 12, 1949, 3.

21. Palevsky, *Atomic Fragments,* vi.

22. Ronald Sawyer, "Los Alamos: The Town Few Can See–But the Whole World Watches," *Christian Science Monitor,* November 18, 1949," 9.

23. Feynman, *"What Do You Care What Other People Think?",* 243.

24. Powaski, *March to Armageddon,* 51–52; White, *Operation Sandstone,* 3; Fradkin, *Fallout,* 84; Hewlett and Duncan, *Atomic Shield,* 161–64.

25. Fradkin, *Fallout,* 84–85.

26. Office of the Historian, Joint Task Force One, *Operation Crossroads,* passim; *Operation Sandstone,* passim. An insightful account of the American public's

reaction to the first five years of the Atomic Age is detailed in Boyer's *By Bomb's Early Light*.

27. Asher and Domrzalski, "Atoll Blast Badly Blisters Hands of Lab Workers," *Albuquerque Tribune*, April 26, 1994, A6.

28. "Four Burned in A-Bomb Test-Run," *New Mexican*, September 23, 1949, 1.

29. Ed Asher, "Radiation Burned Two in Canyon Testing," *Albuquerque Tribune*, March 28, 1994, A1; "Wind Shift Spread Radioactivity into Bayo Canyon 40 Years Ago," *New Mexican*, February 3, 1994, A2; Rex Graham, "Lab Tests Sent Fallout over Houses," *Albuquerque Journal (North Edition)*, February 3, 1994, B1.

30. Town Council Minutes, August 26, 1946, 3, EL 584 (e) 71.80, LAHMA.

31. Ed Asher, "Lab Let Children Play on Contaminated Ground," *Albuquerque Tribune*, March 28, 1994, A1.

32. Tiano, interview, and Jack Bell, interviewed by author, March 9, 1991, at Auburn, California, OHP.

33. Sawyer, "Los Alamos: The Town Few Can See," November 18, 1949.

34. AEC, "Handling Radioactive Wastes in the Atomic Energy Program," 18, Box 28, Charter Heslep Collection, 1626, AHC.

35. John Fleck, "LANL Workers Used in N-Tests," *Albuquerque Journal*, January 11, 1994, A1, A5.

36. Dennis Domrzalski, "Plutonium Injections Were Tests for Poison," *Albuquerque Tribune*, June 21, 1994, A1; "Radiation Studies Likely Victimized Disadvantaged," *Santa Fe New Mexican*, January 9, 1994, A3; "Pregnant Women Given Radioactive Pills in 40's," *Albuquerque Journal*, December 21, 1993, A5; Robert Burns, "Radiation Tests Touched 16,000, Government Says," *Albuquerque Journal*, August 18, 1995, A11; "1 Million Vets Exposed to Nuke Tests, Expert Says," *Albuquerque Tribune*, January 24, 1995, C10; Rosenberg, *Atomic Soldiers*, passim. For a comprehensive account of radioactive testing on humans, see Welsome, *Plutonium Files*.

37. McKee, *Zia Company*, 24.

38. Reid, interview.

39. Donald Marchi, interviewed by author, February 19, 1991, at Albuquerque, N. Mex.; Deborah Jackson, interviewed by author, March 2, 1991, at Albuquerque; and Jim Graebner, interviewed by author, May 7, 1991, at Albuquerque—all in OHP.

40. Sawyer, "Los Alamos: The Town Few Can See," 9; "Best Sailing Lures Kids to Radioactive Waste Deposit Area," *Los Alamos Skyliner*, April 21, 1949, 1.

41. Tiano, interview.

42. George Fitzpatrick, "Los Alamos . . . The World's Most Important Small Town," *New Mexico Magazine* 27 (August 1949): 23.

43. "Best in Modern Architecture Will Make Los Alamos High Pace-Setter for the Nation," *Los Alamos Skyliner*, June 23, 1949, 1.

44. "Local School Plans Told by Wegner," *Los Alamos Skyliner*, June 16, 1949, 9.

45. Ibid.

46. AEC, *Los Alamos: City of Your Future*, 13–14, RCS.

47. Morris, "Cities of America—Los Alamos": 164; Chambers, "Technically Sweet Los Alamos," 347–49; letter from David Lilienthal to Rep. Cleveland Bailey, February 9, 1950, Chairman's Reading File, Jananuary '50–June '50, Office Files of D. Lilienthal, Records of Office of Chairman, Records of AEC, RG 326, NACP.

48. Morris, "Cities of America—Los Alamos": 164; Chambers, "Technically Sweet Los Alamos," 347–49, 352.

49. Chambers, "Technically Sweet Los Alamos," 337, 352–53.

50. Ibid., 346.

51. Ibid.

52. Manley, interview.

53. Reid, interview.

54. Bill Hosokawa, "Quiz Kids—By the Dozen," *Denver Post*, June 19, 1949, 2.

55. Ibid.

56. Ibid.

57. Morris, "Cities of America—Los Alamos": 25.

58. A list of the some of the major magazines that featured stories about the residential part of Los Alamos includes *New Republic*, March 17, 1947; *New Yorker*, April 17, 1948; *Business Week*, December 18, 1948; *New York Times Magazine*, April 24, 1949; *Life*, June 27, 1949; *National Geographic*, December 1949; *Nation*, December 31, 1949; and *Time*, December 18, 1950.

59. Mason Sutherland, "Abode New Mexico," *National Geographic* 96 (December 1949): 807.

60. Daniel Lang, "Reporter in New Mexico," *New Yorker* (April 17, 1948): 72.

61. Jane Holt, "Santa Claran Sees 104th Winter," *Los Alamos Skyliner*, December 23, 1948, 1.

62. Morris, "Cities of America—Los Alamos": 166.

63. Lang, "Reporter in New Mexico": 76.

64. W. Thetford Leviness, "Atomic By-product: Around Los Alamos, N.M., the Local Population Enjoys New-found Prosperity," *New York Times*, June 17, 1950; "San Ildefonso Pueblo Watched Secret City Grow," *Albuquerque Journal*, November 29, 1970, E1.

65. Chambers, "Technically Sweet Los Alamos," 237, 258; *Laws of New Mexico 1949*, 322; "Newest County Names Officials," *Los Alamos Skyliner*, June 16, 1949, 1; "Recent Business Activity," *New Mexico Business* 2 (June 1949): 2; "School Funds Forthcoming for State," *Los Alamos Skyliner*, June 30, 1949, 1.

66. For a more detailed account of atomic espionage and the Soviet atomic programs, see Rhodes, *Dark Sun: The Making of the Hydrogen Bomb*.

67. Rhodes, *Dark Sun*, 356; letter to Truman from Secretary of Defense, August 5, 1949, Atomic Energy File, box 13, Naval Aide files, HSTL.

68. Newhouse, *War and Peace in the Nuclear Age*, 72; letter to Gen. Vandenberg, September 20, 1949, Atomic Bomb Long Range Detection Program file,

Subject file: National Security Council—Atomic, President's Secretary's files, HSTL; Rhodes, *Dark Sun*, 365–66.

69. Rhodes, *Dark Sun*, 242–43.

70. Tsukerman and Arzarkh, *Arzamas-16*, x.

71. Ibid., 55, 75.

72. Ibid., 75.

73. "Statement by the President," September 23, 1949, Atomic Energy—Newspaper Clippings and Releases file, box 1, Clifford Papers, HSTL.

74. Ibid.

75. "U.S. Detects Atomic Blast in Russia," *Life* (October 3, 1949): 17; "Soviet A-Bomb Rouses Stocks," *New Mexican*, September 23, 1949, 5.

76. "Local Residents Calm after News of A-Bomb," *New Mexican*, September 23, 1949, 1.

77. Tsukerman and Arzarkh, *Arzamas-16*, 77.

78. "More Funds for Bombs," *New Mexican*, October 4, 1949, 9.

79. "United States Launches Program for Giant Expansion of Plants," *New Mexican*, October 28, 1949, 3; "Russian Bomb Speeds Work on U.S. Unit," *New Mexican*, October 13, 1949, B6; "Sources Report Sandia Base Booming with Atomic Work," *New Mexican*, October 6, 1949, 11.

80. "Scientists Won't Talk," *New Mexican*, September 23, 1949, 1.

81. "Congressmen Visit Alamos," *New Mexican*, October 27, 1949, 1.

82. Ibid.; "Lawmaker Stresses A-Bomb Research Need," *New Mexican*, October 28, 1949, 1.

83. Hank Trewhitt, "What Happens When Bomb Goes Off Here?" *New Mexican*, November 3, 1949, 1.

84. Ibid.

85. Ibid.

86. "Civilian Defense Plan Shoved into High Gear for New Mexico," *New Mexican*, July 17, 1950, 1.

CHAPTER 5

1. "Recommendations [approving the Super] by Harry S. Truman," January 31, 1950, # 7 Super (File # 1) (6), Executive Secretary's Subject File Series, box 3, WHO, NSC Staff Papers, DDEL; Hewlett and Duncan, *Atomic Shield*, 392, 406.

2. Rhodes, *Dark Sun*, 404; Hewlett and Duncan, *Atomic Shield*, 376.

3. John Manley, "Working Memorandum," December 3, 1949, (File # 1) (3), Executive Secretary's Subject File Series, box 3, WHO, NSC Staff Papers, DDEL.

4. Letter from GAC to Chairman David Lilienthal, October 30, 1949, File # 1, Executive Secretary's Subject File Series, box 3, WHO, NSC Staff Papers, DDEL.

5. Palevsky, *Atomic Fragments*, 155.

6. "$100 Million Required to Make L.A. Permanent City," *Los Alamos News*, February 24, 1950, 1; "Los Alamos Operational Costs Rise to $160 Million Annually," *New Mexican*, March 30, 1950, 1, 5.

7. Letter from Sumner Pike to Senator McMahon, March 23, 1950, Classified File # 1, Chairman Reading File 12/46–7/50, Office Files of David E. Lilienthal, Records of the Office of the Chairman, Records of the AEC, RG 326, NACP.

8. Letter from David Lilienthal to Senator John McClellan, January 25, 1950, January 1950 file, Chairman's Reading File, 1/50–6/50, Office Files of D. E. Lilienthal, Records of the Office of the Chairman, Records of the AEC, RG 326, NACP; Paul M. Sears, "Los Alamos—Boom Town under Control," "Business Backgrounds" insert in *New Mexico Business* 6 (May 1953): 2; "Atomic Headquarters," *New Mexico Magazine* 31 (January 1953): 47; AEC, *Open House: July 16–17, 1955*, back cover.

9. Rhodes, *Dark Sun*, 207–8, 305, 416.

10. Ibid. 462–3; Hewlett and Duncan, *Atomic Shield*, 535–37.

11. Rhodes, *Making of the Atomic Bomb*, 711; Rhodes, *Dark Sun*, 482–512, contains a superb account of the construction and test of the first hydrogen bomb. Quotes are from 510 and 508.

12. Rhodes, *Dark Sun*, 463; Weiner, interview.

13. Neary, interview.

14. Lincoln Barnett, "J. Robert Oppenheimer," *Life* (October 10, 1949): 123.

15. Rhodes, *Dark Sun*, 487.

16. Reid, interview.

17. Sears, "Los Alamos—Boom Town under Control," 2; Tiano, interview.

18. Fred Othman, "Most Expensive Town in the World," *Atlanta Constitution*, April 1, 1950.

19. "Los Alamos Operational Costs Rise to $160 Million Annually," *New Mexican*, March 30, 1950, 1, 5.

20. Othman, "Most Expensive Town in the World."

21. Robert W. Seidel, "A Home for Big Science: The Atomic Energy Commission's Laboratory System," *Historical Studies in Physical and Biological Science* 16, no.1, (1986): 162.

22. Othman, "Most Expensive Town in the World."

23. Rhodes, *Dark Sun*, 561–62; the National Atomic Museum in Albuquerque, N. Mex., exhibits the vast array of nuclear weapons developed in the 1950s.

24. AEC News Release no. 335, January 11, 1951; AEC News Releases, 1951, nos. 334–407, Pt. 2, Office of Public Information, Records of the AEC, RG 326, NACP.

25. Gallagher, *American Ground Zero*, passim; Titus, *Bombs in the Backyard*, 57; "Costs of Full Scale Atomic Tests," # 1 Misc. (File # 1) (5), box 1, Executive Secretary's Subject Files, WHO, NSC, DDEL.

26. Othman, "Most Expensive Town in the World."

27. "Investigation of the Atomic Energy Commission at Los Alamos, New Mexico, 1/3/49," 2, Twenty-fourth Intermediate Report, 80th Congress, House of Representatives, Report No. 2478, GRRD-LC.

28. Ibid., 3; "Summary of Facts Concerning Western Housing Area Defects," June 1949, 3, Los Alamos file, AEC Secretary Correspondence, 634, Records of the AEC, RG 326, NACP.

29. USGPO, *Investigation into the United States Atomic Energy Project: Hearing before the Joint Committee on Atomic Energy of the 81st Congress: June 24, 1949*, 639.

30. Ibid., 640.

31. "Complaining Guards Get Axe," *Santa Fe New Mexican*, August 25, 1953, 1–2.

32. Ibid.

33. "Growth of Hill Medical Center Hasn't Always Been Smooth," *Santa Fe New Mexican*, June 19, 1960, 3; "Facilities Moved from AEC to Hill Medical Center," *Los Alamos News*, March 10, 1950; "Medical Research Lab to Examine Radiation," *Los Alamos Herald*, March 9, 1951, 1; John Manley, "The Los Alamos Laboratory," *Bulletin of Atomic Scientists*, 10–11.

34. "Alamos Bridge Wins Mention in Contest," *New Mexican*, December 14, 1952, 2-A; LASL, *Open House, July 16–17, 1955*, 3–4, "New Mexico Cities and Towns, Los Alamos file," NMSARC.

35. LASL, *Housing Manual for Laboratory Employees and Supervisors*, 20; Boyd C. Pratt, "A Brief History of the Architecture of Los Alamos County"; "Eastern Housing Area at Alamos Takes on Ghost Town Appearance," *New Mexican*, January 3, 1954, 12-A.

36. Pratt, "A Brief History," 10; "Construction Near for 129 Hill Homes," *New Mexican*, February 28, 1954, 6-A; Jack Bell, interview; "Day of Temporary Dormitories Ends after Sixteen Bustling Years," *LASL Community News*, February 11, 1960, 5.

37. "Expansion at Alamos to Revive White Rock," *Santa Fe New Mexican*, October 28, 1953, 2; Rothman, *On Rims And Ridges*, 243; "Growing Pains in White Rock as Enrollment Jumps from 84 to 300," *Los Alamos Herald*, March 2, 1951, 7.

38. "Growing Pains in White Rock," *Los Alamos Herald*, March 2, 1951, 7.

39. "Expansion at Alamos to Revive White Rock," *New Mexican*, 2.

40. Fermi, "Los Alamos Revisited." Another nickname for Los Alamos is "The Mesa." Technically, Los Alamos is on a plateau, not a mesa (which is a tablelike land formation with steep cliffs on all sides).

41. Ibid.

42. Ibid.

43. Lotchin, *Fortress California*, 345.

44. May, *Homeward Bound*, 23.

45. Ibid., 94.

46. Ibid., 11.

47. Jack Bell, interview.

48. Marchi, interview.

49. Mason, *Children of Los Alamos*, 122.

50. Shroyer, *Secret Mesa*, 197.

51. Reid and Tiano, interviews.

52. Richard Gerstell, "How You Can Survive an A-Bomb Blast," *Saturday Evening Post* (January 1950).

53. Ibid.

54. Ibid.

55. Ibid.

56. Ibid.

57. Guy Oakes, *Imaginary War*, 33.

58. Paul P. Kennedy, "How Much Civil Defense? Most of It Is on Paper," *New York Times*, July 16, 1950, E7.

59. "Los Alamos Civil Defense: A Ten-Year History 1952–1962," 1–3. This pamphlet had not been processed when I read it at the archives of the Los Alamos Historical Museum.

60. Oakes, *Imaginary War*, 85–86.

61. USGPO, *Annual Report for 1951 of the Federal Civil Defense Administration*, vii, Publication History Files; Records of the Defense Civil Preparedness Agency, RG 397, NACP.

62. Rhodes, *Dark Sun*, 253.

63. The 81st Congress approved the Federal Civil Defense Act of 1950 with S. 959-5-A; "Civil Defense Heads Meet at Los Alamos," *Santa Fe New Mexican*, January 10, 1951, 1.

64. "Evacuation Center Is Valley's System: Lack of Cash Doesn't Halt Preparations," *New Mexican*, January 12, 1951, 7.

65. "City Seems 'Wide Open' for Sneak Plane Attack," *Los Alamos Herald*, February 23, 1951, 1.

66. Joe M. Clark, "'Lying Flat' Best Defense from 'Bomb'," *Santa Fe New Mexican*, January 4, 1951, 3A.

67. Clark, "Top Radiation Doses Unlikely in Most Raids," *New Mexican*, January 11, 1951, 7A.

68. Clark, "Preventing Radiation Easier Than Removing It after It's There," *New Mexican*, January 9, 1951, 10.

69. Oakes, *Imaginary War*, 52.

70. "Plan Protection for School Children in Event of Air Raid or Disaster," *Los Alamos Herald*, March 2, 1951, 1.

71. Letter from Oakley to James Wadsworth, February 27, 1951, "N" file, box 4, Records Relating to Civil Defense, 1949–'53, Records of the Office Civil and Defense Mobilization, RG 304, NACP.

72. *Annual Statistical Report, Fiscal Year 1956*, 25; Publication History Files, 1950–1962, Box 2; Records of the Defense Civil Preparedness Agency, RG 397, NACP.

73. "Local Civil Defense Organization Steps Up Activity, Gets Budget Hike," *Los Alamos Herald*, March 30, 1951, 1.

74. Ibid.

75. "Hill to Test Evacuation," *Santa Fe New Mexican*, November 2, 1952, 6.

76. Herken, *Brotherhood of the Bomb*, 257.

77. "An Evacuation Study for the Milwaukee Metropolitan Area for the Federal Civil Defense Administration, November 1954," box 7, Publication History File, DCPA, RG 397, NACP.

78. "Mock Atom Raids Cause Evacuations of U.S. Millions," *Albuquerque Journal*, June 15, 1954, 1.

79. *Homemaker's Manual of Atomic Defense*, 10, 14, box 29, Chester Heslep Collection, American Heritage Center, University of Wyoming.

80. Newhouse, *War and Peace in the Nuclear Age*, 81. This insight into the difference between an atomic blast and a thermonuclear one in relation to effective civil defense came from Barton Hacker in a conversation we had during the Atomic West conference in Seattle, Washington, September 25, 1992.

81. Oakes, *Imaginary War*, 79.

82. Charter Heslep, "The Story of the First Live Televising of an Atomic Detonation," 1, 6, 11, 12, box 22, Heslep Collection, American Heritage Center, University of Wyoming.

83. Letter from Gordon Dean to Senator O'Mahoney, June 15, 1950, 2, Chairman's Reading File, January 1950–June 1950, Office Files of D. E. Lilienthal, Records of the Office of the Chairman, Records of the AEC, RG 326, NACP.

84. Ibid., 3.

85. Chambers, "Technically Sweet Los Alamos," 361–62; Hewlett, *Atomic Shield*, 459.

86. "AEC to Keep Los Alamos, Give Up Oak Ridge, Hanford to Residents," *Albuquerque Journal*, June 8, 1953, 1.

87. "Alamos to 'Open Up' within Year," *Santa Fe New Mexican*, April 18, 1954, 1.

88. Ibid.

89. Ibid.

90. "Hillsters Plan Mass Protest against Plan to Open Gates," *New Mexican*, April 25, 1954, 6A.

91. "Adversity into Triumph," *New Mexican*, April 25, 1954.

92. "Hill Residents Vote against 'Open City,'" *New Mexican*, April 27, 1954, 2.

93. Ibid.

94. "AEC Polls Los Alamos People on Opening Gates," *New Mexican*, August 31, 1954, 1.

95. Leif Erickson, "Hill Gate Poll 'Personnel', Says Leehey," *New Mexican*, September 8, 1954, 1.

96. Vásquez, interview.

97. Tiano, interview.

98. Ibid.

99. Suzanne Ray, interviewed by author, May 2, 1991, at Albuquerque, N.M., OHP.

100. Jack Bell, interview.

101. J. Robert Oppenheimer, "Atomic Weapons and American Policy," *Foreign Affairs* 31, no. 4 (July 1953): 529; Robert Erwin, "Oppenheimer Investigated," *Wilson Quarterly* 18 (Autumn 1994): 42.

102. Erwin,"Oppenheimer Investigated," 42; Oppenheimer, "Atomic Weapons and American Policy," 529.

103. Halberstam, *The Fifties*, 333–34.

104. Herken, *Brotherhood of the Bomb*, 264.

105. Ibid., 279.

106. Ibid., 292.

107. Rhodes, *Dark Sun*, 553.

108. Ibid., 536, 538.

109. Albert Einstein,"On Charges against Oppenheimer," *Bulletin of Atomic Scientists* 10 (May 1954): 190.

110. Rhodes, *Dark Sun*, 554–55.

111. Ibid., 556.

112. Erwin, "Oppenheimer Investigated," 43; Herken, *Brotherhood of the Bomb*, 297.

113. Al Glanzberg, "Hill Blasts Panel Opinion against Oppy," *Santa Fe New Mexican*, June 2, 1954, 1.

114. Ibid.

115. "AEC Board Splits against Oppenheimer: Upholds Bar From Secrets," *New Mexican*, June 2, 1954, 2.

116. Al Glanzberg, "A-Scientists Blast Teller's Testimony: Security Plan Is Condemned," *New Mexican*, June 17, 1954, 1; "Total of 474 Los Alamos Scientists Sign Protest in Oppenheimer Case," *New Mexican*, June 13, 1954, 14.

117. Glanzberg, "A-Scientists Blast Teller's Testimony," 1.

118. Ibid., 2.

119. "Impact of Oppy Case on Alamos Procurement," *New Mexican*, September 26, 1954, 5A.

120. Ibid.

121. "Hill Fears Scientists Might Be Driven Away," *New Mexican*, July 1, 1954.

122. Ibid.; "Los Alamos Scientists," *Bulletin of Atomic Scientists* 10, no. 7 (September 1954): 283.

123. Mason, *Children of Los Alamos*, 142.

124. "Ike Citation 'Clears Air,' Says Scientist," *Santa Fe New Mexican*, July 15, 1954, 1; "Citation," Whitman File, box 4, "AEC 1953–54 (4)," DDEL.

125. Letter from Eisenhower to Strauss, June 16, 1954, Whitman File, box 4 "AEC 1953–54 (4)," DDEL.

126. Hill Scientists Rap Strauss Statement," *New Mexican*, September 13, 1954, 1.

127. Ibid.

CHAPTER 6

1. Gene Lindberg, "Topsy, Jezebel, and Godiva," *Sunday Denver Post*, July 31, 1955, 6.

2. Mary Caveglia, "Thousands of People Visit 'Hill' Project," *Albuquerque Journal*, July 18, 1955, 1; Edwin Diamond, "Controlled Chain Reaction Is Shown Newsmen at Los Alamos Open House," *Albuquerque Journal*, July 16, 1955, 2.

3. Bob Brown, "Los Alamos Points to New Power Reactor as Example of Peacetime Use of Atom," *Albuquerque Journal*, July 17, 1955, 2.

4. Ibid.

5. Ibid.; Caveglia, "Thousands of People Visit," 1.

6. Caveglia, "Thousands of People Visit," 8.

7. Ray, interview.

8. Caveglia, "Thousands of People Visit," 8.

9. Dale Lane, "'Old' Alamos Building Starts Life All Over," *Santa Fe New Mexican*, October 22, 1959, DCF-LAHMA. Since the *New Mexican* in the 1950s published a sometimes different edition of the newspaper for the region of northern New Mexico, microfilms of the *New Mexican* for these dates do not necessary include these articles. Citations in this chapter that include "DCF-LAHMA" indicate that these articles can be found in the Frank Di Luzio Clipping File at the Los Alamos Historical Museum Archives under a chronological order. "Sanctuary Near Completion," *Los Alamos Herald*, February 16, 1951, 8; "Fortieth Anniversary History of the United Church at Los Alamos," 5, received by the author from Eric B. Fowler, Los Alamos; Marjorie Bell Chambers, "A Unique Church to Meet the Challenge of a Unique Community," 8, in "Churches" Vertical File, Mesa Public Library, Los Alamos.

10. Al Zerwekh, telephone interview with author, at Los Alamos, N.Mex., February 3, 1991.

11. Hudson, *Religion in America*, 382.

12. Ahlstrom, *Religious History of the American People*, 953–54.

13. Ibid., 951.

14. Hudson, *Religion in America*, 385.

15. "Deux ex Laboratorio," *Time* 58 (August 13, 1951): 64.

16. "Los Alamos at Long Last Is Going to Have a Cemetery," *Albuquerque Journal*, February 5, 1955, 1.

17. Paul Sears, "Los Alamos—Boom Town under Control," *New Mexico Business* 6 (May 1953): 4.

18. Los Alamos Public Schools, *Los Alamos Operating Procedures, 1953–54*, 1, 16, 26; pamphlet deposited at the NMSARC.

19. "40 Percent of Hill Teachers May Quit," *Santa Fe New Mexican*, April 8, 1954, DCF-LAHMA.

20. Ibid.

21. "Board Gives Allbee Its Firm Backing," *New Mexican*, April 21, 1954, 2.

22. Ibid.

23. "As-Is," *New Mexican*, April 21, 1954, 4.

24. Ibid.

25. "Classes to be Larger during Next Season," *New Mexican*, April 21, 1954, DCF-LAHMA.

26. "Allbee Quits Alamos Post,'" *New Mexican*, March 3, 1955, DCF-LAHMA.

27. Ibid.

28. "Wyoming Educator Appointed Alamos School Superintendent," *New Mexican*, May 12, 1955, 2A.

29. "Hill Teacher Turnover Rate Decreases Sharply This Term," *New Mexican*, June 15, 1955, DCF-LAHMA.

30. "LA Pupils Get Fast Start at Sciences," *New Mexican*, November 21, 1955, DCF-LAHMA.

31. Ibid.

32. "Booming Science Interest Plain at Hill Junior High," *New Mexican*, November 28, 1955, 2.

33. "LAHS Ranks High in Nation," *Los Alamos Lookout*, February 1958, 2; Henry A. Campbell, "In Mathematics Teaching," *New Mexico School Review* 38 (September 1958): 22, 24; E. L. Martin and J. L. Reibsomer, "Student Enrollment in Sciences in New Mexico High Schools," *New Mexico School Review* 36 (September 1956): 22.

34. "Science Popular Course at Hill School," *Santa Fe New Mexican*, December 5, 1955, DCF-LAHMA.

35. Ibid.; Reid, interview.

36. Cremin, *American Education*, 549–50; Martin and Reibsomer, "Student Enrollments in Sciences," 22; Martin and Reibsomer, "Who Wants to Be a Scientist?" *New Mexico School Review* 37 (January 1957): 20.

37. "Door to Books Opens Fast for Hill Students," December 12, 1955, "New Methods Adding Fun to Arithmetic," December 19, 1955,"Hill Kindergarten Gives Kids First Taste of Life in School," January 16, 1956; "Hill Primary Teachers Shoot for Three Principal Targets," January 23, 1956; "Reading Importance Stressed at Alamos," January 30, 1956; "Driving One of Hill 'Musts,'" February 13, 1956; "History, Geography Stressed in Hill Social Study Classes," February 27, 1956; "Student Council System Helping Train Hill Youngsters in Art of Government," October 8, 1956. All of these articles appeared in the *Santa Fe New Mexican* and can be found in DCF-LAHMA.

38. "Special High School Conference," *New Mexico School Review* 38 (January 1958): 24; Chester C. Travelstead, "A Report from the Conference on the Secondary Schools of the Future," *New Mexico School Review* 38 (March 1958): 35.

39. O'Neill, *American High*, 252–55; Halberstam *The Fifties*, 667–79.

40. Nelson Martínez, interviewed by author, March 22, 1991, at Albuquerque, N. Mex., OHP.

41. Vásquez, interview.

42. Ibid.

43. Jack Bell, interview.

44. The information about the racial composition of the high school and the elected positions comes from *La Loma*, the Los Alamos High School Yearbook, 1957, and from Mason, *Children of Los Alamos*, 119.

45. Tucker, Ray, Marchi, and Manley, interviews.

46. Jack Bell, Kathy Bell, and Martínez, interviews.

47. "Three Become First Completely Educated in Los Alamos Schools," *Santa Fe New Mexican*, June 5, 1955, 6B.

48. "Careers of LA Graduates Are Studied," *New Mexican*, April 15, 1955, DCF-LAHMA; Marchi, interview.

49. Los Alamos Public Schools, *Los Alamos Operating Procedures*, 41.

50. "Hill Test Evacuation Includes School Kids," *Santa Fe New Mexican*, January 9, 1956, DCF-LAHMA; "School Test Evacuation Termed Success," *New Mexican* January 20, 1956, DCF-LAHMA.

51. "Hill Apathetic toward Surprise 'Evacuation,'" *New Mexican*, May 2, 1956, DCF-LAHMA; "Only Locked Gate Mars Los Alamos 'Red' Alert," *Albuquerque Journal*, May 2, 1956, 16.

52. "Only Locked Gate," *Albuquerque Journal*, May 2, 1956.

53. "Los Alamos Girds for Friday Alert," *Albuquerque Journal*, July 15, 1956, 21.

54. Ibid.

55. Ibid.; "Operation Alert 1956—Public Information," June 12, 1956, 4; NSC: Subject Subseries, Office of Special Assistant, National Security Advisor, DDEL.

56. "Los Alamos to Observe Civil Defense Week," *Albuquerque Journal*, September 9, 1956, 11; "Los Alamos Family Voluntarily Living on Seven-Day Emergency Ration," *Albuquerque Journal*, September 12, 1956, 25; "'Hill' Family Gets Back to Normal after Living on Civil Defense Rations," *Albuquerque Journal*, September 16, 1956, 18.

57. "Bomb Spreads Death over Espanola," *New Mexican*, July 18, 1957, 18; "A Statement by Dr. Edward Teller," *Many Roads to Glory*, 30, found in "Federal Civil Defense Administration, 1957–58," Mechem Special Reports file, NMSARC.

58. *Atomic Café*, director Kevin Rafferty, 1982. This documentary film includes clips from governmental films made in the 1950s on how to survive a nuclear attack.

59. Walker, *Permissible Doses*, 22; "Los Alamos Joining Civil Defense Test," *New Mexican*, May 4, 1958, 6.

60. Charles Johnson and Charles Jackson, *City Behind a Fence*, 104; "Hill Opening Is Result of Long Planning," *New Mexican*, February 17, 1957, 6A.

61. "Los Alamos Hailed Isolation Ruling," *New York Times*, May 1, 1955, 45.

62. "Congressional Subcommittee Meeting Disposal of Government Property," 106, M1989-76-1-1, folder 5, box 19, LAHMA.

63. Reid, interview.

64. "Los Alamos Generally Happy with Seclusion," *Denver Post*, May 4, 1956.

65. Limerick, *Legacy of Conquest*, 95.

66. Peggy Felt, "Home Ownership on Hill Near Reality: Slow but Steady Progress Is Reported," *Santa Fe New Mexican*, December 23, 1956, 9A; "AEC Ready to Let Public Take Over Barranca Mesa," *New Mexican*, February 9, 1958, 9.

67. "Surprise 'Open City' Order Leaves Hill Flabbergasted," *New Mexican*, February 17, 1957, 1.

68. Ibid.

69. Ibid.

70. Ibid.

71. "Hill Opening Is Result of Long Planning," *New Mexican*, February 17, 1957, 6A.

72. "Los Alamos Throws Gate Wide Open," *New Mexican*, February 18, 1957, 2; "Mechem First to Pass Gate," *New Mexican*, February 19, 1957, 2; "Mechem Enters Los Alamos to Inaugurate Open City Policy," *Albuquerque Journal*, February 19, 1957, 1.

73. Advertisement in the *Santa Fe New Mexican*, February 17, 1957, 7A.

74. Roger Corbett, interview by Elizabeth Giorgi for "Early Los Alamos Businesses," History of Towns and Places, History File 126, NMSARC.

75. Ibid.

76. Marchi, interview.

77. Peggy Corbett, "Los Alamos Marks a Full Year as Open City Today," *Santa Fe New Mexican*, February 18, 1958, 7.

78. Weiner, interview.

CHAPTER 7

1. Reid and Graebner, interviews.

2. Martínez, interview.

3. Vásquez, interview. The interviews from Vásquez's *Impact Los Alamos* project are deposited at the Center for Southwest Research, General Library, University of New Mexico.

4. Jack Bell and Wiener, interviews.

5. Reid, interview.

6. "Investigators Say Los Alamos Managers Tolerated Corruption, Obstructed Probe," *Las Cruces Sun News*, February 27, 2003, A10; Adam Rankin, "Testimony on LANL 'Outrageous,'" *Albuquerque Journal*, February 28, 2003, B3; "Fired Investigators Call DOE Report 'Vindication,'" *Santa Fe New Mexican*, January 31, 2003; Robert Gehrke, "Energy Department Calls Firing of Whistle Blowers 'Incomprehensible,'" *New Mexican*, January 31, 2003.

7. Jeff Tollefson, "Critics say LANL Conceals Security Problems," *New Mexican*, November 20, 2002, A1, A4.

8. Gehrke, "Energy Department Calls Firing of Whistle Blowers 'Incomprehensible,'" *New Mexican*, January 31, 2003.

9. Tom Sharpe, "What Really Happened with Wen Ho Lee," *New Mexican*, January, 14, 2000; "Wen Ho Lee Goes Free," *New Mexican*, September 14, 2000; Lee and Zia, *My Country Versus Me*; Stober and Hoffman, *A Convenient Spy*.

10. Palevsky, *Atomic Fragments*, 107.

11. John Fleck, "Nuke Budget Soars," *Albuquerque Journal*, February 9, 2003, A1-A2.

12. Kristen Davenport, "Nuclear-lab Heads Discuss Recent Years' Woes," *Santa Fe New Mexican*, August 25, 2002, A1, A2.

13. John Fleck, "Nuke Budget Soars," *Albuquerque Journal*, February 9, 2003, A1–A2.

14. Jeff Tollefson, "Trickle-down Economics," *Albuquerque Journal*, November 17, 2002, A1.

15. "Study: U.S. Nuke Program Costs $35 Billion a Year," *Albuquerque Journal*, July 2, 1998, A7.

16. *Environmental Solutions*, 2, LANL.

17. Ibid., A-5.

18. Keith Easthouse, "Did Reactor Leak for Years?" *Santa Fe New Mexican*, February 24, 1994, A1.

19. *Biotechnology*, 2, LANL.

20. *Advanced Materials*, 2, LANL.

21. Marchi, Reid, and Manley, interviews.

22. Tucker, interview.

23. Tiano, interview.

24. Marchi, interview.

BIBLIOGRAPHY

ARCHIVES

American Heritage Center. University of Wyoming. Laramie, Wyoming.
—Charter Heslep Collection
Center for Southwest Research. University of New Mexico. Albuquerque, New
Mexico.
—Oral History Program.
—Ralph Carlisle Smith Papers.
—Special Collections.
Dwight David Eisenhower Library. Abilene, Kansas.
Harry S. Truman Library. Independence, Missouri.
Library of Congress. Washington, D.C.
Reading Room Division.
Manuscript Division.
—William S. Parsons Papers.
—J. Robert Oppenheimer Papers.
—John von Neumann Papers.
Los Alamos Historical Museum Archives. Los Alamos, New Mexico.
—Bevers Collection.
—DiLuzio Clipping Files.
Los Alamos National Laboratory Archives. Los Alamos, New Mexico.
—Dorothy McKibbin Papers.
Mesa Public Library. Los Alamos, New Mexico.
—Vertical Files.
National Archives II. College Park, Maryland.
—Records of Office of Civil and Defense Mobilization, Record Groups 304
and 304-G.
—Records of the Atomic Energy Commission, Record Group 326.
—Records of the Defense Civil Preparedness Agency, Record Group 397.
National Atomic Museum Library. Albuquerque, New Mexico.
New Mexico State Archives and Records Center. Santa Fe, New Mexico.
—Government Activities File.
—History File.
—Lucien File Papers.

—Mechem Special Reports File.

—Towns and Cities File.

United Church of Los Alamos Archives. Los Alamos, New Mexico.

GOVERNMENT DOCUMENTS

Advanced Materials. Los Alamos: Los Alamos National Laboratories, 1993.

Annual Report for 1951 of the Federal Civil Defense Administration. Washington, D.C.: GPO, 1951.

Annual Statistical Reports, Fiscal Year 1956. Washington, D.C.: GPO, 1956.

Biotechnology. Los Alamos: Los Alamos National Laboratories, 1993.

Environmental Solutions. Los Alamos: Los Alamos National Laboratories, 1993.

Homemaker's Manual of Atomic Defense. Atomic Energy Commission, n.d.

The Housing Manual for Laboratory Employees and Supervisors. Los Alamos, Los Alamos Scientific Laboratory, 1956.

Investigation into the U. S. Atomic Energy Project: Hearing before the Joint Committee on Atomic Energy of the 81st Congress, Part 15, June 24, 1949. Washington, D.C.: GPO, 1949.

Laws of New Mexico 1949. Santa Fe: Secretary of State, 1949.

Los Alamos Operating Procedures, 1953–1954. Los Alamos: Los Alamos Public Schools, 1953.

Los Alamos Scientific Laboratory, Los Alamos, N.M. Washington, D.C.: Atomic Energy Commission, 1951.

"Maintenance Map of New Mexico, 1941." Santa Fe: Records Room, New Mexico Highway Department, 1941.

1950 Census of the Population. Washington, D.C.: GPO, 1953.

Office of the Historian, Joint Task Force One. *Operation Crossroads: The Official Pictorial Record*. New York: William H. Wise Co., 1946.

Open House, July 16–17, 1955. Los Alamos Scientific Laboratory, 1955.

U.S. Department of Energy. *Radiological Survey of the Site of a Former Radioactive Liquid Waste Treatment Plant (TA-45) and the Effluent Receiving Areas of Acid, Pueblo, and Los Alamos Canyons, Los Alamos, New Mexico*. DOE/EV0005/30, LA-8890-ENV., Los Alamos, May 1981.

"Who Are the People?" *Annual Report*. Los Alamos, Mesa Public Library, 1952.

UNPUBLISHED MATERIAL

Chambers, Marjorie Bell. "Technically Sweet Los Alamos: The Development of a Federally Sponsored Scientific Community." Ph.D. diss., University of New Mexico, 1974.

Elder, Jane Lenz. "The Promise and Failure of a Territorial Economy: Mid-Nineteenth-Century Santa Fe, New Mexico." Paper presented at the New Mexico Historical Society Conference, April 19, 1996, Las Vegas, N.Mex.

Fermi, Laura. "Los Alamos Revisited." William S. Parsons Papers, Manuscript Division, Library of Congress, Washington, D.C.

Heslep, Charter. "The Story of the First Live Televising of an Atomic Detonation." Heslep Collection, American Heritage Center, University of Wyoming.

Hughes, Scott Daniel. "The Persistence of Plutonium: Health, Waste, and Weapons, 1943–1954." Master's Thesis, University of New Mexico, 1992.

————. "The Unclosed Circle: Los Alamos and the Human and Environmental Legacy of the Atom, 1943–1963." Ph.D. diss., University of New Mexico, 2000.

Hunner, Jon. "Family Secrets: The Growth of Community at Los Alamos, New Mexico, 1943–1957." Ph.D. diss., University of New Mexico, 1996.

————. "Shooting the Dragon: Coming of Age in Los Alamos." Master's Thesis, University of New Mexico, 1992.

Junck, Robert. "Los Alamos—Life in the Shadow of the Bomb." Ralph Carlisle Smith Collection, Center for Southwest Research, General Library, University of New Mexico.

Limerick, Patricia Nelson. "The Atomic West." Paper read at Atomic West 1942–1992: Federal Power and Regional Development Conference, September 25, 1992, University of Washington, Seattle, Washington.

Meyer, Jr., H. N. "Manhattan Engineering Project." Found in files. Albuquerque: National Atomic Museum, n.d.

Montoya, Maria E. "Landscapes of War." Paper read at Western History Association Conference, October 13, 1995, Denver, Colorado.

Pratt, Boyd C. "A Brief History of the Architecture of Los Alamos County." Bevers Collection, Los Alamos Historical Museum Archives.

Strottman, Theresa. "How Witnesses to the Trinity Test of the First Atomic Bomb Remember the Event." Paper read at Oral History Association Conference, October 10, 1994, Albuquerque, New Mexico.

Taylor, Bryan C. "Remembering Los Alamos: Culture and the Nuclear Weapons Organization." Ph.D. diss., University of Utah, 1991.

White, Richard. "Hanford, the Columbia, and Energy." Paper read at Atomic West 1942–1992: Federal Power and Regional Development Conference, September 26, 1992, Seattle, Washington.

Books

Abbott, Carl. *New Urban America: Growth and Politics in Sunbelt Cities.* Chapel Hill: University of North Carolina Press, 1981.

Adler, Irving. *Inside the Nucleus.* New York: New American Library, 1963.

Ahlstrom, Sydney. *A Religious History of the American People.* New Haven: Yale University Press, 1972.

Allardice, Corbin, and Edward R. Trapness, *The Atomic Energy Commission.* New York: Praeger Publishers, 1974.

Aries, Philippe. *Centuries of Childhood: A Social History of Family Life.* New York: Vintage Books, 1962.

Badash, Lawrence, Joseph O. Hirshfelder, and Herbert P. Broida, eds. *Reminiscences of Los Alamos, 1943–1945*. Dordrecht, Holland: D. Reidel Publishing Co, 1980.

Bailey, Janet. *The Good Servant: Making Peace with the Bomb at Los Alamos*. New York: Simon and Shuster, 1995.

Ball, Howard. *Justice Downwind: America's Atomic Testing Program in the 1950s*. New York: Oxford University Press, 1986.

Bartimus, Tad, and Scott McCartney. *Trinity's Children: Living along America's Nuclear Highway*. New York: Harcourt Brace Jonvanovich, 1991.

Beck, Warren A., and Ynez D. Haase. *Historical Atlas of New Mexico*. Norman, University of Oklahoma Press, 1969.

Behind Tall Fences: Stories and Experiences about Los Alamos at Its Beginning. Los Alamos: Los Alamos Historical Society, 1996.

Bell, Iris. *Los Alamos WAACs/WACs: World War II 1943–1946*. Sarasota, Florida: Coastline Printing, 1993.

Bernard, Richard M., and Bradley R. Rice, eds. *Sunbelt Cities: Politics and Growth Since World War II*. Austin: University of Texas Press, 1983.

Boorse, Henry A., Lloyd Motz, and Jefferson Hane Weaver. *The Atomic Scientists: A Biographical History*. New York: Wiley and Sons, 1989.

Boyer, Paul. *By the Bomb's Early Light: American Thought and Culture at the Dawn of the Atomic Age*. New York: Pantheon, 1985.

Brode, Bernice. *Tales of Los Alamos: Life on the Mesa, 1943–1945*. Los Alamos: Los Alamos Historical Society, 1997.

Burns, Patrick, ed. *In the Shadow of Los Alamos: Selected Writings of Edith Warner*. Albuquerque: University of New Mexico Press, 2001.

Campbell, D'Ann. *Women at War with America: Private Lives in a Patriotic Era*. Cambridge: Harvard University Press, 1984.

Casey, James. *The History of the Family*. New York: Basil Blackwell, 1989.

Chambers, William H., ed. *The Cold War and Its Implications: Locally, Nationally, and Internationally*. Los Alamos: Los Alamos Historical Society, 1998.

Church, Fermor, and Peggy Pond Church. *When Los Alamos Was a Ranch School*. Los Alamos: Los Alamos Historical Society, 1974.

Church, Peggy Pond. *The House at Otowi Bridge: The Story of Edith Warner and Los Alamos*. Albuquerque: University of New Mexico Press, 1959.

Copeland, Anne P., and Kathleen M. White. *Studying Families*. Newbury Park: Sage Publications, 1991.

Cremin, Lawrence A. *American Education: The Metropolitan Experience, 1876–1980*. New York: Harper and Row, 1988.

De Buys, William. *Enchantment and Exploitation: The Life and Hard Times of a New Mexico Mountain Range*. Albuquerque: University of New Mexico Press, 1985.

Del Tredici, Robert. *At Work in the Field of the Bomb*. New York: HarperCollins, 1987.

Deutsch, Sarah. *No Separate Refuge: Culture, Class and Gender on an Anglo-Hispanic Frontier in the American Southwest, 1880–1940.* New York: Oxford University Press, 1987.

Diggins, John Patrick. *The Proud Decade: America in War and Peace, 1941–1960.* New York: Norton, 1989.

Elder, Glen H., Jr., John Modell, and Ross D. Parke, eds. *Children in Time and Place: Developmental and Historical Insights.* Cambridge: Cambridge University Press, 1993.

Etulain, Richard W., ed. *Contemporary New Mexico, 1945–1990.* Albuquerque: University of New Mexico Press, 1994.

Feinberg, Samuel. *What Makes Shopping Centers Tick.* New York: Fairchild Publications, 1960.

Fermi, Laura. *All about Atomic Energy.* London: W. H. Allen, 1962.

———. *Atoms in the Family: My Life with Enrico Fermi.* Chicago: University of Chicago Press, 1954.

Fermi, Rachel, and Esther Samra. *Picturing the Bomb: Photographs from the Secret World of the Manhattan Project.* New York: Harry N. Abrams, 1995.

Feynman, Richard. *Surely You're Joking, Mr. Feynman: Adventures of a Curious Character.* New York: W. W. Norton, 1985.

———. *"What Do You Care What Other People Think?"* New York: W.W. Norton, 1988.

Findlay, John M. *Magic Lands: Western Cityscapes and American Culture after 1940.* Berkeley: University of California Press, 1992.

Fisher, Phyllis. *Los Alamos Experience.* Tokyo: Japan Publications, 1985.

Fradkin, Philip L. *Fallout: An American Nuclear Tragedy.* Tucson: University of Arizona Press, 1989.

Franklin, Wayne, and Michael Steiner, eds. *Mapping American Culture.* Iowa City: University of Iowa Press, 1993.

Frisch, Otto. *What Little I Remember.* Cambridge: Cambridge University Press, 1979.

Furman, Necah Stewart. *Sandia National Laboratories.* Albuquerque: University of New Mexico Press, 1990.

Gallagher, Carole. *American Ground Zero: The Secret Nuclear War.* New York: Random House, 1993.

Gerber, Michele Stenehjem. *On the Home Front: The Cold War Legacy of the Hanford Nuclear Site.* Lincoln: University of Nebraska Press, 1992.

Gofman, John W. *Radiation and Human Health.* San Francisco: Sierra Club Books, 1981.

Groves, Leslie R. *Now It Can Be Told.* New York: Harper and Row, 1962.

Hacker, Barton C. *The Dragon's Tail: Radiation Safety in the Manhattan Project, 1942–1946.* Berkeley: University of California Press, 1987.

———. *Elements of Controversy: The Atomic Energy Commission and Radiation Safety in Nuclear Weapons Testing, 1947-1974.* Berkeley: University of California Press, 1994.

Halberstam, David. *The Fifties*. New York: Villard Books, 1993.

Hales, Peter Bacon. *Atomic Spaces: Living on the Manhattan Project*. Urbana: University of Illinois Press, 1997.

———. "Topographies of Power: The Forced Spaces of the Manhattan Project." In *Mapping American Culture*, edited by Wayne Franklin and Michael Steiner. Iowa City: University of Iowa Press, 1993.

Hareven, Tamara, ed. *Transitions: The Family and the Life Course in Historical Perspective*. New York: Academic Press, 1978.

Hawkins, David. *Project Y: The Los Alamos Story, Part I: Toward Trinity*. Los Angeles: Tomash Publishers, 1983.

Herken, Gregg. *Brotherhood of the Bomb: The Tangled Lives and Loyalties of Robert Oppenheimer, Ernest Lawrence, and Edward Teller*. New York: Henry Holt and Company, 2002.

Hersey, John. *Hiroshima*. New York: A. A. Knopf, 1985. Originally published by in 1946.

Hewlett, Richard G., and Oscar E. Anderson. *The New World 1939–1946*. University Park: Pennsylvania State University Press, 1962.

Hewlett, Richard G., and Francis Duncan. *Atomic Shield, 1947–1952*. University Park: Pennsylvania State University Press, 1969.

Hiroshima International Council for the Medical Care of the Radiation-Exposed, eds. *Effects of Atomic Bomb Radiation on the Human Body*. Tokyo: Bunkodo Company, Ltd., 1995.

Hoddeson, Lillian, Paul W. Henricksen, Roger A. Meade, and Catherine Westfall. *Critical Assembly: A Technical History of Los Alamos during the Oppenheimer Years, 1943–1945*. Cambridge: Cambridge University Press, 1993.

Howes, Ruth H., and Caroline L. Herzenberg. *Their Day in the Sun: Women of the Manhattan Project*. Philadelphia: Temple University Press, 1999.

Hudson, Winthrop S. *Religion in America*. New York: Charles Scribner's Sons, 1965.

Jackson, Kenneth J. *Crabgrass Frontier: The Suburbanization of the United States*. New York: Oxford University Press, 1985.

Jette, Eleanor. *Inside Box 1663*. Los Alamos: Los Alamos Historical Society, 1977.

Johnson, Charles W., and Charles O. Jackson. *City behind a Fence: Oak Ridge, Tennessee, 1942–1946*. Knoxville: University of Tennessee Press, 1981.

Johnson, Leland, and Daniel Schaffer. *Oak Ridge National Laboratory: The First Fifty Years*. Knoxville: University of Tennessee Press, 1994.

Kunetka, James W. *City of Fire: Los Alamos and the Atomic Age, 1943–1945*. Albuquerque: University of New Mexico Press, 1979.

Lamar, Howard Roberts. *The Far Southwest, 1846–1912: A Territorial History*. New York: Norton, 1970.

Lapp, Ralph E., and Howard L. Andrews. *Nuclear Radiation Physics*. Englewood Cliffs, N. J.: Prentice-Hall, 1963.

Lee, Wen Ho, and Helen Zia. *My Country Versus Me: The First-Hand Account by the Los Alamos Scientist Who Was Falsely Accused of Being a Spy*. New York: Hyperion, 2001.

Libby, Leona Marshall. *The Uranium People.* New York: Charles Scribner's Sons, 1979.

Limerick, Patricia Nelson. *The Legacy of Conquest: The Unbroken Past of the American West.* New York: Norton, 1987.

Lotchin, Roger W. *Fortress California, 1910–1961: From Warfare to Welfare.* New York: Oxford University Press, 1992.

Lowitt, Richard. *Politics in the Postwar American West.* Norman : University of Oklahoma Press, 1995.

Luckingham, Bradford. *The Urban Southwest: A Profile of Albuquerque, El Paso, Phoenix, and Tucson.* El Paso: Texas Western Press, 1982.

Malone, Michael P., and Richard W. Etulain. *The Twentieth-Century West.* Lincoln: University of Nebraska Press, 1989.

Many Roads to Glory: The Story of Trucks and National Security, "A Statement by Dr. Edward Teller." Washington, D.C.: American Trucking Association, n.d.

Markuson, Ann, Peter Hall, Scott Campbell, and Sabina Deitrick. *The Rise of the Gunbelt: The Military Remapping of Industrial America.* New York: Oxford University Press, 1991.

Mason, Katrina R. *Children of Los Alamos: An Oral History of the Town Where the Atomic Age Began.* New York: Twayne Publishers, 1995.

May, Elaine Tyler. *Homeward Bound: American Families in the Cold War Era.* New York: Basic Books, 1988.

Mazuzan, George T., and J. Samuel Walker. *Controlling the Atom: The Beginnings of Nuclear Regulation 1946–1962.* Berkeley: University of California Press, 1984.

McKee, Robert E. *The Zia Company in Los Alamos: A History.* El Paso: Carl Hertzog, 1950.

McPhee, John. *The Curve of Binding Energy.* New York: Ballantine Books, 1973.

Melzer, Richard. *Breakdown: How the Secret of the Atomic Bomb Was Stolen during World War II.* Santa Fe: Sunstone Press, 2000.

Morgan, Ted. *Literary Outlaw: The Life and Times of W. S. Burroughs.* New York: Avon Books, 1988.

Nagaoka, Shogo. *Hiroshima under Atomic Bomb Attack.* Hiroshima: Peace Memorial Museum, n.d.

Nagatani, Patrick. *Nuclear Enchantment.* Albuquerque: University of New Mexico Press, 1991.

Nash, Gerald D. *The American West in the Twentieth Century: A Short History of an Urban Oasis.* Albuquerque: University of New Mexico Press, 1977.

Newhouse, John. *War and Peace in the Nuclear Age.* New York: Alfred A. Knopf, 1989.

New Mexico Geological Society. *New Mexico Geological Guidebook of the San Juan Basin.* Santa Fe: New Mexico Geological Society, 1950.

Oakes, Guy. *The Imaginary War: Civil Defense and American Cold War Culture.* New York: Oxford University Press, 1994.

Oliphant, M. L., P. M. S. Blackett, and R. F. Harrold. *The Atomic Age.* London: George Allen and Unwin, Ltd., 1949.

O'Neill, William L. *American High: The Years of Confidence, 1945–1960.* New York: Free Press, 1986.

Ortiz, Alfonso, ed. *Handbook of North American Indians: Southwest*, Vol. 9. Washington, D.C.: Smithsonian Institute, 1979.

Palevsky, Mary. *Atomic Fragments: A Daughter's Questions.* Berkeley: University of California Press, 2000.

Pearce, T. M., ed. *New Mexico Place Names.* Albuquerque: University of New Mexico Press, 1965.

Pettitt, Roland A. *Exploring the Jemez Country.* Revised by Dorothy Hoard. Los Alamos: Los Alamos Historical Society, 1990.

Powaski, Ronald E. *March to Armageddon: The United States and the Nuclear Arms Race, 1939 to the Present.* New York: Oxford University Press, 1987.

Public Reaction to the Atomic Bomb and World Affairs. Ithaca, N.Y.: Cornell University, 1947.

Quinn, Susan. *Marie Curie: A Life.* New York: Simon and Schuster, 1995.

Rabi, I. I., Robert Serber, Victor F. Weisskopf, Abraham Pais, and Glen T. Seaborg. *Oppenheimer.* New York: Charles Scribner's Sons, 1969.

Rhodes, Richard. *Dark Sun: The Making of the Hydrogen Bomb.* New York: Simon and Schuster, 1995.

———. *The Making of the Atomic Bomb.* New York: Simon and Schuster, 1986.

Rigden, John S. *Rabi: Scientist and Citizen.* New York: Basic Books, 1987.

Roensch, Eleanor Stone. *Life within Limits.* Los Alamos: Los Alamos Historical Society, 1993.

Rosenberg, Howard. *Atomic Soldiers: American Victims of Nuclear Experiments.* Boston: Beacon Press, 1980.

Rosenthal, Debra. *At the Heart of the Bomb: The Dangerous Allure of Weapons Work.* New York: Addison-Wesley Publishing Company, 1990.

Rothman, Hal K. *On Rims and Ridges: Los Alamos Area Since1880.* Lincoln: University of Nebraska Press, 1992.

Russ, Harlow W. *Project Alberta: The Preparation of the Atomic Bombs for Use in World War II.* Los Alamos: Exceptional Books, 1984.

Sando, Joe. *The Pueblo Indians.* San Francisco: Indian History Press, 1976.

Sanger, S. L. *Working on the Bomb: An Oral History of WWII Hanford.* Portland, Oregon: Portland State University Continuing Education Press, 1995.

Serber, Robert, and Richard Rhodes. *The Los Alamos Primer: The First Lectures on How to Build an Atomic Bomb.* Berkeley: University of California Press, 1992.

Shinedling, Abraham. *History of the Los Alamos Jewish Center.* Albuquerque: Valliant Printing, 1958.

Shohno, Naomi. *The Legacy of Hiroshima: Its Past, Our Future.* Tokyo: Kosei Publishing Company, 1986.

Shroyer, Jo Ann. *Secret Mesa : Inside Los Alamos National Laboratory.* New York : John Wiley & Sons, 1998.

Smith, Alice Kimball. *A Peril and a Hope: The Scientists' Movement in America: 1945–1947.* Chicago: University of Chicago Press, 1965.

———— and Charles Weiner, eds. *Robert Oppenheimer: Letters and Recollections.* Cambridge: Harvard University Press, 1980.

Smyth, Henry D. *Atomic Energy for Military Purposes: A General Account of the Scientific Research and Technical Development That Went into the Making of the Atomic Bombs.* Princeton: Princeton University Press, 1946.

Stegner, Wallace. *The American West as Living Space.* Ann Arbor: University of Michigan Press, 1987.

Stilgoe, Joe, R. *Borderland: Origins of the American Suburbs, 1829–1939.* New Haven: Yale University Press, 1988.

Stober, Dan and Ian Hoffman. *A Convenient Spy: Wen Ho Lee and the Politics of Nuclear Espionage.* New York: Simon and Schuster, 2001.

Stoff, Michael B., Jonathan F. Fanton, and R. Hal Williams, eds. *The Manhattan Project: A Documentary Introduction to the Atomic Age.* Philadelphia: Temple University Press, 1991.

Stone, I. F. *The Haunted Fifties, 1953–1963.* Boston: Little, Brown and Company, 2nd edition, 1989.

Sundt, Eugene, and W. E. Naumann. *M. M. Sundt Construction Company.* New York: Newcomen Society, 1975.

Sykes, Christopher, ed. *No Ordinary Genius: The Illustrated Richard Feynman.* New York: W. W. Norton, 1994.

Szasz, Ferenc Morton. *British Scientists and the Manhattan Project: The Los Alamos Years.* New York: St. Martin's Press, 1992.

————. *The Day the Sun Rose Twice: The Story of the Trinity Site Nuclear Explosion, July 16, 1945.* Albuquerque: University of New Mexico Press, 1984.

Takaki, Ronald. *Hiroshima: Why America Dropped the Atomic Bomb.* Boston: Little, Brown and Company, 1995.

Thompson, Fred, and L. R. Jones. *Reinventing the Pentagon: How the New Public Management Can Bring Institutional Renewal.* San Francisco: Jossey-Bass Publishers, 1994.

Titus, Costandina A. *Bombs in the Backyard: Atomic Testing and American Politics.* Reno: University of Nevada Press, 1986.

Tobias, Henry J. *A History of Jews in New Mexico.* Albuquerque: University of New Mexico, 1990.

Truslow, Edith, and Ralph Carlisle Smith. *Project Y: The Los Alamos Story—Part II: Beyond Trinity.* Los Angeles: Tomash Publishers, 1983.

————, and Kasha Thayer. *Manhattan District History: Nonscientific Aspects of Los Alamos Project Y, 1942 through 1946.* Los Alamos: Los Alamos Historical Society, 1973.

Tsukerman, Veniamin, and Zinaida Arzarkh. *Arzamas-16: Soviet Scientists in the Nuclear Age: A Memoir.* Nottingham: Bramcote Press, 1994. Translated by Timothy Sergay, 1999.

Turner, Frederick Jackson. *History, Frontier, and Section: Three Essays by Frederick Jackson Turner.* Albuquerque: University of New Mexico Press, 1993.

United States Strategic Bombing Survey. *The Effects of the Atomic Bombs on Hiroshima and Nagasaki.* Santa Fe: William Gannon, 1973.

Wade, James E., and G. E. Cunningham. *Radiation Monitoring*. Washington, D.C.: U.S. Atomic Energy Commission, 1967.

Walker, J. Samuel. *Permissible Doses: A History of Radiation Protection in the Twentieth Century*. Berkeley: University of California Press, 2000.

Weart, Spencer R. *Nuclear Fear, A History of Images*. Cambridge: Harvard University Press, 1988.

Webb, Walter Prescott. *The Great Plains*. Boston: Ginn and Company, 1931.

Weber, David. *The Spanish Frontier in North America*. New Haven: Yale University Press, 1992.

Weigle, Marta. *Hispanic Villages of Northern New Mexico*. Santa Fe: Lightning Tree, 1975.

Welsome, Eileen. *The Plutonium Files: America's Secret Medical Experiments in the Cold War.* New York: Dell Publishing, 1999.

White, Clarence H., ed. *Operation Sandstone: The Story of Joint Task Force Seven*. Washington, D.C.: Infantry Journal Press, 1949.

White, Richard. *"It's Your Misfortune and None of My Own": A New History of the American West*. Norman: University of Oklahoma Press, 1991.

Wilson, Jane S., and Charlotte Serber, eds. *Standing By and Making Do: Women of Wartime Los Alamos*. Los Alamos: Los Alamos Historical Society, 1988.

Wittner, Lawrence S. *One World or None: A History of the World Nuclear Disarmament Movement through 1953*. Stanford, California: Stanford University Press, 1993.

Writers' Program of the Works Progress Administration. *New Mexico: A Guide to the Colorful State*. New York: Hastings House, 1940.

Newspapers and Periodicals

Air Affairs: An International Quarterly Journal
Albuquerque Journal
Albuquerque Tribune
Atlanta Constitution
Atomic Scientists' Journal
Big
Bulletin of Atomic Scientists
Business Week
California Monthly
Christian Science Monitor
Denver Post
Foreign Affairs
International Conciliation
Journal of the West
Life
Los Alamos Herald
Los Alamos Lookout

Los Alamos Monitor
Los Alamos News
Los Alamos Newsbulletin
Los Alamos Newsletter
Los Alamos Post Bulletin
Los Alamos Scientific Laboratory Community News
Los Alamos Skyliner
Los Alamos Times
National Geographic
New Mexico Business
New Mexico Historical Review
New Mexico Magazine
New Mexico School Review
New York Times
New Yorker
Pacific Historical Review
Santa Fe New Mexican
Saturday Evening Post
Las Cruces Sun News
Scientific Monthly
Survey Graphic
Time
Wilson Quarterly

ORAL HISTORIES AVAILABLE IN DEPOSITORIES

Montoya, Joe G. Oral History Program, Center for Southwest Research, University of New Mexico.
Peierls, Genia. T-88-014, Los Alamos National Laboratory Archives.
Peierls, Rudolph. T-88-014, Los Alamos National Laboratory Archives.
Salazar, Nick L. Oral History Program, Center for Southwest Research, University of New Mexico.
Smith, Ralph Carlisle. T-81-0009, Los Alamos National Laboratory Archives.
Titterton, Peggy. T-89-90, Los Alamos National Laboratory Archives.
Warren, Stafford. 300/204. Oral History Program, University of California, Los Angeles.
Zuckert, Eugene M. Harry S Truman Library, Independence, Missouri.

ORAL HISTORIES CONDUCTED BY THE AUTHOR

All interviews listed below were carried out under the auspices of the Oral History Program, Center for Southwest Research, University of New Mexico (OHP-CSWR).

Bell, Jack. Auburn, Calif., March 9, 1991.

Bell, Kathy. Auburn, Calif., March 9, 1991.

Graebner, Jim. Albuquerque, N. Mex. May 7, 1991. He arrived in Los Alamos after 1957.

Jackson, Deborah. Albuquerque, March 2, 1991. She arrived in Los Alamos after 1957.

Manley, Kim. Los Alamos, N. Mex. February 23, 1991.

Marchi, Donald. Albuquerque, February 19, 1991.

Martínez, Nelson. Albuquerque, March 22, 1991.

Neary, Joan Mark. Santa Fe, N. Mex. April 19, 1991.

Ray, Suzanne. Albuquerque, May 2, 1991.

Reid, Ellen Wilder Bradbury. Santa Fe, January 27, 1991.

Tiano, Susan. Albuquerque, February 12, 1991.

Tucker, Terell. Albuquerque, April 22, 1991.

Vásquez, Carlos. Albuquerque, July 23, 1991.

Weiner, Claire Ulam. Santa Fe, March 17, 1991.

INDEX

Acid Canyon, 140–42, 143, 226, 233
Ackerman, J. O., 92
Advanced materials research, 233
Advisory Committee on Uranium, 18
Alamagordo Air Base, N.Mex., 65
Albuquerque Journal, 212
Alert America, 179
Alexander, Scott, 228–29
Allbee, Lewis, 202–204
Allen, Elizabeth Joan, 209
American Indians, 6, 13–14, 15, 30, 53, 63–65, 78, 150
Anchor Ranch, N.Mex., 29
Anderson, Clinton P., 216–17
Archuleta, Helen, 202
Arms race, 155–57, 158–60, 162, 165, 174, 204; Oppenheimer warns against, 94, 190
Army, U.S., 3; discord with civilians at Los Alamos, 23, 47–50, 55, 61, 112, 117; Military Police, 24, 27, 29, 75; morale, 55; Provisional Engineering Division, 29; scientists to enlist in, 23; Special Engineering Division, 29, 30; in Wild West, 15; Women's Army Corps, 28–29, 34, 55, 133
Army Corps of Engineers, 17–18, 31
Army-Navy "E" Award, 94
Arzamus-16, Soviet Union, 153

Ashbridge, Whitney, 16, 49–50
Aspen Elementary School, 202
Association of Los Alamos Scientists, 112–15, 226
Atomic Bomb Investigation Group of Hiroshima and Nagasaki, 82–83, 85, 114; eyewitness accounts of Japan bombings, 86–88
Atomic bomb program: Atomic Bomb Investigation Group of Hiroshima and Nagasaki, 85–86; casualties, 82, 88–91; destruction of Hiroshima and Nagasaki, 74–75, 88–90; early research, 17–18, 22; explosive power of bombs, 74; eyewitness accounts of Hiroshima and Nagasaki, 86–88; Fat Man, 40; fission, 40; justification for continued research, 136–37, 224; *Los Alamos Primer*, 38; petition against use on Japan, 73; plutonium, 40; post-war control of, 112, 114, 116; public fear of, 123; publicity after Hiroshima, 7; radiation hazards, 88–91, 142; recruitment of scientists, 25; remove control from Groves, 116; research program established, 38; "technologically sweet," 41; Trinity test, 65–71; Truman approves use against Japan, 73; uranium,